EU Trade Strategies

90 0589323 4

University of Plymouth Library

Subject to status this item may be renewed
via your Voyager account

http://voyager.plymouth.ac.uk

Exeter tel: (01392) 475049
Exmouth tel: (01395) 255331
Plymouth tel: (01752) 232323

EU Trade Strategies

Between Regionalism and Globalism

Edited by

Vinod K. Aggarwal

and

Edward A. Fogarty
University of California, Berkeley
USA

First published 2004 by
PALGRAVE MACMILLAN
Houndmills, Basingstoke, Hampshire RG21 6XS and
175 Fifth Avenue, New York, N. Y. 10010
Companies and representatives throughout the world

PALGRAVE MACMILLAN is the global academic imprint of the Palgrave Macmillan division of St. Martin's Press, LLC and of Palgrave Macmillan Ltd. Macmillan® is a registered trademark in the United States, United Kingdom and other countries. Palgrave is a registered trademark in the European Union and other countries.

ISBN 1–4039–1510–5 hardback
ISBN 1–4039–3258–1 paperback

This book is printed on paper suitable for recycling and made from fully managed and sustained forest sources.

A catalogue record for this book is available from the British Library.

Library of Congress Cataloging-in-Publication Data
    EU trade strategies: between regionalism and globalism / edited by Vinod K. Aggarwal and Edward A. Fogarty.
        p. cm.
    Includes bibliographical references and index.
    ISBN 1–4039–1510–5 (cloth) – ISBN 1–4039–3258–1 (paper)
    1. European Union countries–Commercial policy. 2. Trade blocs–European Union countries. 3. Regionalism–European Union countries. 4. Globalization–Economic aspects–European Union countries. 5. European Union countries–Foreign economic relations.
I. Aggarwal, Vinod K. II. Fogarty, Edward A. 1973–

HF1531.E78 2004
382'.3'094–dc22   2003057007

10   9   8   7   6   5   4   3   2   1
13   12   11   10   09   08   07   06   05   04

Printed and bound in Great Britain by
Antony Rowe Ltd, Chippenham and Eastbourne

Contents

List of Tables

List of Figures

Preface

All is not well in the World Trade Organization. Does a global economy require global institutions? If global institutions falter, one possible alternative is interregionalism: economic integration between two distinct regions. This book explores the logic of interregionalism by focusing on the European Union, which has pursued agreements with Latin America, East Asia, and the Southern Mediterranean, among others. Why has the EU pursued this strategy? In this book, we explore EU interregionalism in search of insights into this emerging face of the international political economy.

This project has been generously supported by the Institute of European Studies at the University of California, Berkeley. Not only did the Institute's funding allow us to hold conferences in California and Brussels over the course of a three-year period – and to produce this book – but IES's original funding guidelines provided a valuable winnowing tool for honing our conceptualization of interregionalism and its relevance in the international political economy. We owe particular thanks to Gerald Feldman, director of the Institute, and to associate director Beverly Crawford, who provided moral and intellectual support throughout.

This project also gave us an opportunity to engage with a network of top-notch European scholars who have worked on similar issues of interregionalism and the European Union. Under the leadership of Professor Mario Teló, these scholars shared their wisdom and perspective with our own group of scholars, and were gracious hosts of a conference in Brussels in October 2002 in which our two groups came together. But our primary intellectual debt is to our own authors – Beverly Crawford, Cédric Dupont, Hilde Engelen, Jörg Faust, Julie Gilson, and John Ravenhill – each a world-class expert in her/his respective field. The value of their contributions to our conceptual framework – in addition to their own first-rate chapters – cannot be understated.

And then there are of course the unsung heroes. In particular, we owe a debt of gratitude to the young minds at the Berkeley APEC Study Center who provided research and logistical support to this project along the way, including Joel Burgos, Mary Eddy, Eric Hausner, John Owens, Jennifer Rho, Henluen Wang, Derek Wong, Olivia Wu, and Daniel Xu. Special thanks go to Justin Kolbeck, Matthew Odette, and Devon Rackle, each of whom made sustained substantive contributions to the project. And the BASC-affiliated graduate students Ralph Espach, Min-Gyo Koo, Elaine Kwei, and Zachary Zwald provided valuable feedback along the way.

Finally, we want to acknowledge the excellent work of the Palgrave team in bringing this project to fruition, including Amanda Watkins, Kerry Coutts, and Shirley Tan. Without their skill and patience, this book simply would not have happened.

Vinod K. Aggarwal
Edward A. Fogarty
University of California, Berkeley
December 2003

Contributors

Vinod K. Aggarwal is Professor in the Department of Political Science, Affiliated Professor in the Haas School of Business, and Director of the Berkeley APEC Study Center (BASC) at the University of California, Berkeley.

Beverly Crawford teaches political economy and is Associate Director of the Institute of European Studies at the University of California, Berkeley.

Cédric Dupont is an Associate Professor of Political Science at the Graduate Institute of International Studies (Geneva, Switzerland).

Hilde D. Engelen is a doctoral candidate at the Graduate Institute of International Studies (Geneva, Switzerland).

Jörg Faust is a Senior Researcher at the German Institute of Development (DIE) (Bonn, Germany).

Edward A. Fogarty is a doctoral candidate in Political Science at the University of California, Berkeley.

Julie Gilson is a Senior Lecturer in the Department of Political Science and International Studies, University of Birmingham (United Kingdom).

John Ravenhill is Chair of Politics at the University of Edinburgh (United Kingdom).

List of Abbreviations

ACP: African, Caribbean, Pacific
AEBF: Asia–Europe Business Forum
AEETC: Asia–Europe Environmental Technology Centre
AEPF: Asia–Europe People's Forum
AFTA: ASEAN Free Trade Area
APEC: Asia Pacific Economic Cooperation
APII: Asia Pacific Information Infrastructure
APT: ASEAN Plus Three
ASEAN: Association of Southeast Asian Nations
ASEF: Asia–Europe Foundation
ASEM: Asia–Europe Meetings
BTA: Basic Telecom Agreement
CAEC: Council for Asia–Europe Cooperation
CAEU: Central Asian Economic Union
CAP: Common Agricultural Policy
CARIBCAN: Canadian Tariff Treatment for Commonwealth Caribbean
. Countries
CARICOM: The Caribbean Community
CBERA: Caribbean Basic Economic Recovery Act
CCP: Common Commercial Policy
CEECs: Central and Eastern European Countries
CEES: Common European Economic Space
CEFTA: Central European Free Trade Agreement
CEPT: Common Effective Preferential Tariff
CERT: Canada–Europe Roundtable
CFSP: Common Foreign and Security Policy
CIS: Commonwealth of Independent States
CMEA: Council of Mutual Economic Assistance
COPA: The European Farmers Federation
COREPER: Council's Committee of Permanent Representatives
CSCE: Conference on Security and Cooperation in Europe
CSCM: Conference on Security and Cooperation in the Mediterranean
DDA: Doha Development Agenda
DG: Directorates–General
EA: European Agreement
EAC: East African Cooperation
EBRD: European Bank for Reconstruction and Development
EC: European Commission
ECJ: European Court of Justice

ECOSOC: The EU's Economic and Social Committee
ECSC: European Coal and Steel Community
ECTI: EU–Canada Trade Initiative
EDF: European Development Fund
EEA: European Economic Area
EEC: Treaty of Rome
EFTA: European Free Trade Association
EIB: European Investment Bank
EMIFCA: EU–MERCOSUR Interregional Framework for Cooperation
   Agreement
EMP: Euro–Med Partnership
EP: European Parliament
EU: European Union
FDI: Foreign Direct Investment
FSA: Financial Services Agreement
FTA: Free Trade Area
FTAA: Free Trade Area of the Americas
GATS: General Agreement on Trade in Services
GATT: General Agreement on Trade and Tariffs
GCC: Gulf Cooperation Council
GDP: Gross Domestic Product
GMP: Global Mediterranean Policy
GSP: Generalized System of Preferences
IAI: Initiative on ASEAN Integration
IEG: Investment Experts Group
IMF: International Monetary Fund
IPAP: Investment Promotion Action Plan
IPRs: Intellectual Property Rights
IRELA: Institute of European Latin American Relations
IT: Information Technology
ITA: Information Technology Agreement
KOREN: High-speed Research Network in Korea
LDC: Less Developed Country
LDE: Less Developed Economy
M&As: Merger and Acquisitions
MEBF: MERCOSUR–Europe Business Forum
MEDA: Measures d'Accompagnement
MENA: Middle East-North African Countries
MERCOSUR: Common Market of the South
MFN: Most Favored Nation
MNMC: Mediterranean non-EU Member Countries
MRA: Mutual Recognition Agreement
NAFTA: North American Free Trade Agreement
NATO: North Atlantic Treaty Organization

NGO: Non-Governmental Organization
NIEO: New International Economic Order
NIS: Newly Independent States
NTA: New Transatlantic Agenda
NTB: Non-Tariff Barrier
NTM: New Transatlantic Marketplace
OPEC: Organization of Petroleum Exporting Countries
OSCE: Organization on Cooperation and Security in Europe
PCAs: Partnership and Cooperation Agreements
PHARE: Economic Reconstruction Aid for Poland and Hungary
QMV: Qualified Majority Voting
R&D: Research and Development
REPA: Regional Economic Partnership Agreement
RTA: Reciprocal Trade Agreement
SADC: South African Development Community
SEA: Single European Act
SMEs: Small and Medium-Sized Enterprises
SOMTI: Senior Officials' Meeting on Trade and Investment
SPARTECA: South Pacific Regional Trade and Economic Cooperation
    Agreement
TABD: Transatlantic Business Dialogue
TACIS: Technical Assistance to the Commonwealth of Independent States
TAFTA: Transatlantic Free Trade Area
TAP: Transatlantic Partnership
TCA: Trade and Cooperation Agreements
TEN: Trans-European Network
TEP: Transatlantic Economic Partnership
TFAP: Trade Facilitation Action Plan
TPA: Trade Promotion Authority
TRIPs: Trade-Related Intellectual Property Rights
UDEAC: Central African Customs and Economic Union
UEMOA: West African Economic and Monetary Union
UN: United Nations
UNCTAD: United Nations Commission on Trade and Development
VER: Voluntary Export Restraint
VIE: Virtual Information Exchange
WCO: World Customs Organization
WEU: Western European Union
WTO: World Trade Organization

1
Between Regionalism and Globalism: European Union Interregional Trade Strategies

Vinod K. Aggarwal and Edward A. Fogarty

1   Introduction

The collapse of multilateral trade talks under the auspices of the World Trade Organization (WTO) in Seattle in November 1999 challenged international policymakers' attempts to strengthen the institutional basis of the global economy. Yet these policymakers' failure in Seattle did not attenuate the expansion of global market forces, nor the strong incentives for governments to seek to institutionalize their transnational commercial relations at the broadest possible level. Although the November 2001 Doha trade talks succeeded in launching a new round of multilateral discussions, there is little question that the trading system looks increasingly fragile and the deadlines for a new round unrealistic – particularly after the failure of the talks at Cancun in September 2003. Moreover, leading governments, and especially the United States, have consistently proven receptive to calls for protection from hard-pressed domestic sectors.

With global institutions facing an uncertain future, could various types of "interregionalism" – the pursuit of formalized intergovernmental relations with respect to commercial relationships across distinct regions – emerge as a next-best strategy for states and firms to pursue trade liberalization? And will "pure interregionalism" – the formation of ties between two distinct free trade areas or customs unions – become the predominant form of trade organization in the global economy as the world increasingly divides up into regional groupings?

The recent interregional overtures of the European Union (EU) – easily the world's most coherent and institutionalized regional bloc – suggest that Europeans may indeed see this as a viable alternative.[1] The EU has initiated formal interregional talks with East Asian countries, developed an interregional accord with MERCOSUR, and is pursuing similar discussions with countries and groups in North America, the Southern Mediterranean, Eastern Europe, and the developing world. If this interregionalism is not an obvious response to market dynamics, the question remains: what factors are driving this phenomenon?[2] Does the European Union's new approach suggest that interregionalism is an emerging synthesis in the dialectic of market-driven globalism and politically-driven regionalism?

This chapter provides the analytical framework for this volume to examine and characterize many of the world's emerging interregional relationships. Focusing primarily on the motivations of the EU, we explore several potential explanations for the development of interregional agreements, including the interplay among sectoral interests, interagency rivalries, the dynamics of systemic level factors such as power balancing and nested institutions, and the vagaries of political and cultural identities. Our intent is to provide both analytical and policy-relevant work on the relatively new trend toward the formation of interregional agreements to examine if interregionalism represents more than a mere sideshow in the evolving face of international economic relations.

Section 2 begins with a conceptualization of interregionalism, in terms of both its differences from other types of trading arrangements and its own varieties. Section 3 then turns to some hypotheses that might account for variation both among types of trade arrangements and among different types of interregional arrangements. In Section 4 we examine the notion of counterpart coherence, that is, the extent to which the regions that the EU is engaged with have developed an institutional identity. Section 5 then previews the empirical analysis of the chapters that follow. An appendix describes the complex trade policymaking processes in the EU.

2   Conceptualizing interregionalism

First, what is interregionalism and how does it compare with other forms of trading arrangements? To answer these questions, it is useful to first conceptualize trade relations more generally before turning to a specific characterization of this phenomenon.

Classifying trade arrangements

Over the last fifty years, states have utilized a host of measures to promote or control trade and monetary flows. Commercial arrangements have varied along a number of dimensions, including the number of actors (unilateral, bilateral, minilateral, or multilateral), the scope of issue coverage (narrow or broad), and the geographic dispersion of participating countries (concentrated or dispersed). Other relevant characteristics include the timing of arrangements, their relative openness, their degree of institutionalization, and the scope of products covered therein.

Table 1.1 provides illustrative examples of trade arrangements along the dimensions of actor scope, geographical dispersion, and product scope.[3] In

Table 1.1 Classifying trade arrangements

Actor Scope / Product Scope	Unilateral	Bilateral		Minilateral		Multilateral
		Geographically concentrated	Geographically dispersed	Geographically concentrated	Geographically dispersed	
Few products (sectoralism)	Removal of Corn Laws (1848)	Germany–Finland treaty (1932) US–Canada Auto Pact (1965)	UK–Argentina (1930s) VERs (EC–Japan)	ECSC (1951)	Lancashire Pact (1958) in textiles	ITA (1997) BTA (1998) FSA (1999)
	(1)	(2)	(3)	(4)	(5)	(6)
Many products	UK unilateral liberalization (1850s) US Smoot-Hawley Act (1930)	US–Canada bilateral agreement (1988)	US–Singapore (2003)	EEC (1958) EFTA (1960) EEA (1994) NAFTA (1994)	APEC (1989) (*transregionalism*) EMIFCA (1995) (*pure interregionalism*) Lomé (1975) (*hybrid interregionalism*)	GATT/WTO (1947/1994)
	(7)	(8)	(9)	(10)	(11)	(12)

Note: Dates refer to effective date of agreements. European agreements whereby "Europe" is considered as "one country" are listed in parentheses.
Source: Based on Aggarwal (2001) and Aggarwal and Dupont (2002).

brief, the top row (cells 1–6) refers to different forms of *sectoralism*. Cell 1 includes such measures as the British Corn Laws, which were a forerunner to the unilateral and then bilateral removal of tariffs in the late 1800s. Cell 2 contains geographically concentrated agreements in specific products, such as the 1932 German-Finnish treaty that gave Finland preferential treatment in butter imports (and which went against the prevailing most favored nation norm).[4] Cell 3 refers to bilateral agreements that are geographically dispersed, such as a treaty between the United Kingdom and Argentina in the 1930s calling for the purchase of specific products.[5] In cells 4 and 5, we have product-specific sectoral agreements. An example of a geographically concentrated agreement that focuses on few products (cell 4) is the 1951 European Coal and Steel Community (ECSC), which, while an agreement to liberalize trade, violated Article 24 of the GATT.[6] Cell 5 provides an example of dispersed sectoral minilateralism, as in the case of the Lancashire Agreement that "managed" trade in cotton textile and apparel products in the 1950s between the United Kingdom and Commonwealth members India, Pakistan, and Hong Kong. Cell 6 provides an example of multilateral sector-specific accords such as the Information Technology Agreement (ITA), negotiated in 1996, and the Basic Telecom Agreement (BTA) and Financial Services Agreement (FSA) a year later.[7]

The second row focuses on multiproduct efforts. Cell 7 refers to unilateral liberalization or restriction, and includes such actions as the British phase of liberalization in the 1850s or the protectionist 1930 Smoot-Hawley tariff in the United States. In cell 8 are geographically concentrated accords such as bilateral agreements between the United States and Canada. Cell 9 features cases of geographically dispersed bilateral agreements, for instance the free trade agreements between the United States and Israel. Cell 10 includes geographically-concentrated minilateral agreements such as the European Economic Community (EEC), European Free Trade Association (EFTA), the European Economic Area (EEA), and the North American Free Trade Agreement (NAFTA).[8] These geographically-concentrated minilateral accords have traditionally been referred to as "regionalism." As should be clear from the table, however, cells 2, 4, and 8 also represent forms of "regionalism," although theoretically they may have quite different political-economic implications. Cell 12 refers to global trading arrangements, namely multilateral, multiproduct arrangements such as the GATT and its successor organization, the WTO.

Characterizing interregionalism

Cell 11 encompasses varieties of interregional arrangements. Examples of interregionalism involving the EU include the Lomé Agreement, the EU-MERCOSUR Interregional Framework for Cooperation Agreement (EMIFCA), and Asia-Europe Meetings (ASEM), all of which span regions, but which do not necessarily link the EU with a coherent counterpart regional grouping. The United States has also pursued cross-regional arrangements, in the Asia-Pacific Economic Cooperation (APEC) forum and the Free Trade Area of the Americas (FTAA).

We define an agreement as "pure interregional" if it formally links two free trade areas or customs unions, as in the case of EU-MERCOSUR. If one customs union negotiates with a group of countries from another region, but the second group is not a customs union or free trade agreement, we refer to this as "hybrid interregionalism" (e.g., the Lomé Agreement). Finally, if an accord links countries across two regions where neither of the two negotiates as a grouping, then we refer to this as "transregionalism" (e.g., APEC). Transregionalism as a concept can encompass a broader set of actor relationships than simply those among states. Any connection across regions – including transnational networks of corporate production or of nongovernmental organizations – that involves cooperation among any type of actors across two or more regions can in theory also be referred to as a type of transregionalism. In this chapter and book, however, we use both the terms transregionalism and interregionalism to refer specifically to interstate commercial arrangements.

What our definition entails is that interregionalism – whatever its ultimate manifestation – is fundamentally cooperative in nature, intended to bring benefits to both parties through voluntary negotiation and mutual agreement regarding a certain set of rights and responsibilities in cross-regional commerce. How these benefits are distributed, and how they affect third parties, varies by case. As such, interregional arrangements can be treated as "international regimes" – albeit more limited in actor scope and with some specific characteristics that distinguish them from purely multilateral accords.

In this book, we focus on three dimensions of regime outcomes to classify interregional arrangements.[9] First, we can examine the *strength* of the arrangement: to what degree does the arrangement constrain actors' behavior? Strong regimes generally prescribe and proscribe actions within a clear and coherent set of rules. These rules, meanwhile, may display a range of institutionalization – i.e., they are manifested to some degree in formal organizations such as a secretariat, parliamentary assembly, dispute settlement bodies, working groups, and the like. In other words, the strength of the regime involves a certain mix of behavioral rules and mechanisms to monitor and enforce compliance among participants.[10]

A second characteristic of interest is the *nature* of the regime, which refers to the objectives promoted by the regime rules and procedures. In trade, the simplest distinction is between protectionist and liberally oriented accords. However, within the context of this book, we are primarily interested in two other, somewhat related aspects of the nature of the regime: its issue scope and its development emphasis. Issue scope in this context involves the range of economic (and political) issues included in the regime – does it cover only trade, or are there provisions for investment, aid, and/or social issues such as human rights, labor and environmental standards, and cultural exchanges? Similarly, does the regime feature specific provisions, such as preferential market access or import credits, for promoting economic development among some subset of regime participants?

A third characteristic of interregional regimes which is more specific to our approach in this book is that of the *EU's commercial treatment of the counterpart* region. Does the EU treat all countries in a counterpart region uniformly, or does it prefer different rules for different countries? And does the type of trade the EU pursues represent a pure interregional approach (i.e., the EU treats the counterpart as a unitary regional actor), does it prefer to deal with individual countries in a counterpart region on a bilateral basis, or does it pursue some mix of interregional and bilateral approaches?

This last question introduces a key theme of this book: under what conditions will we see pure interregionalism as opposed to more mixed forms of interregional regime? In the context of EU-centered cross-regional trade arrangements, we expect to see one of two types of inter-regional regimes: pure interregionalism or hybrid interregionalism. (By definition, the EU cannot be engaged in transregional accords.) (See Figure 1.1)

3 Hypotheses on the origin of EU interregional trade strategies

The question of which factors explain EU commercial relations with other regions is the central puzzle of this book.[11] Our primary objective is to

| | | Region B | |
		Unified	Plural
Region A	Unified	pure interregionalism	hybrid interregionalism
	Plural	hybrid interregionalism	transregionalism

Figure 1.1   Types of interregionalism

determine which factors affect EU policymakers' inclinations or disinclinations to adopt an interregional approach, beginning from a set of theoretically grounded hypotheses. Our contending hypotheses fall within two broad categories: those that explore factors below the unit (i.e., European Union) level, and those that look at the EU as an actor in the international system. These two groups of hypotheses derive from a variety of traditions in the international relations and comparative politics literatures, including those focusing on sectoral interests, bureaucratic politics, security competition and nested institutions, and transnational identity formation. These hypotheses are neither exhaustive nor mutually exclusive – some of them are quite closely interrelated – but as a starting point, we treat them as discrete. (For a short description of the defining processes of EU commercial policymaking, see the appendix to this chapter.)

Hypothesis 1: EU trade strategies, interregional or otherwise, are determined by the relative influence of specific interest groups within Europe.

In this "pluralist" view, European Union commercial policy is a forum for competition among various societal interests (i.e., firms, industry associations, environmental groups, etc.) as they seek to capture the EU policymaking apparatus to promote policies that reflect their particular preferences. Interest groups employ strategies that maximize the probability that their specific preferences will prevail, with lobbying being the most visible such activity. However, these actors face a tradeoff: acting alone reduces the likelihood of capture but increases the chance that "successful" lobbying will lead to policies reflecting their *specific* preferences; acting collectively increases the chances of capture but reduces the likelihood that resulting policies will reflect the preferences of any individual actor. Thus interest groups seek to construct minimum winning coalitions to capture the Union's broader trade policy agenda, with the interplay of economic actors in particular broadly representing a contest between those sectors and factors that support openness in trade policy and those that oppose it. The dynamics of the resources and strategies in these two broad camps will thus determine the shape of EU trade strategies, interregional or otherwise.[12]

Given these groups' strategic imperatives, a set of resources, and the particular EU policymaking structure, we can make predictions about which interest groups are most likely to influence EU trade policy. But to understand EU interregionalism, we need to know why influential interest groups would lobby for an interregional approach – as opposed to a multiproduct global or bilateral, or some type of single-product sectoral, approach. Here we can consider EU interest groups' preferences in terms of four subtypes: (1) internationally competitive actors that seek general, global liberalization; (2) export-oriented actors that rely substantially on EU subsidies or protection; (3) nonexport-oriented actors that rely substantially

on EU protection; and (4) societal groups that are generally opposed to economic internationalization (see Table 1.2).

This first group of internationally competitive actors – such as many European media groups, telecommunications firms, financial sector firms, some automakers, chemical companies, and increasingly Airbus – are not particularly threatened by import competition. They seek general liberalization at the broadest possible level to take advantage of their own competitive position and economies of scale to penetrate previously closed international markets. The best EU trade posture for such firms would be global liberalization through the WTO; and for competitive sectors it would be either the WTO or multilateral sectoral liberalization (such as the ITA). In both cases, an interregional approach would be seen as second best, though still good to the extent that it could succeed in improving European firms' access to desirable foreign markets. In a context in which liberalization through the WTO was blocked, however, these actors would likely be strong advocates of an interregional approach.

Export-oriented sectors that rely on EU protection – notably, agriculture – may also be positively disposed toward an interregional approach. The imperative for those in this category is to maintain their own protection (i.e., minimize import competition) while increasing access to other markets. As such, the best EU strategy for them is one that follows a political rather than a market logic, maximizing the asymmetries in the Union's bargaining power *vis-à-vis* other actors. Best here would be a straight bilateral approach that dealt with individual countries, in which the EU would dwarf any interlocutor bar the United States (and, to a lesser extent, Japan and China). Here again interregionalism would be a second-best strategy, since in most cases a counterpart region would be far smaller and less coherent than the EU – and thus these groups' protection would be less endangered by a trading partner's bargaining strength.

Table 1.2   EU trade agreement preference rankings by group

Group category	Type of trade agreement			
	Unilateral (EU only)	Bilateral	Interregional	Global (sectoral or multiproduct)
Global competitors	4	3	2	1
Protected exporters	3	1	2	4
Protected nonexporters (esp. unions)				
Factoral	1	2	3	4
Sectoral	4	3	2	1
Anti-global groups	1	2	3	4

Nonexport-oriented groups that rely on EU protection are likely to be ill-disposed toward interregionalism, and to liberalizing international agreements more generally. While small, nonexport-oriented firms are unlikely to have much influence at the EU level (though they may exercise influence at the national level), other economic actors in this category – in particular, unions – have much greater sway. Unions' posture depends in large part on the degree to which they act as a single, coherent economic actor (i.e., the degree to which they view trade strategies along factoral as opposed to sectoral lines). If there is broad agreement across sectors that trade liberalization poses a threat to workers' well-being, whether through factory relocation, worker compensation, or import competition, unions will likely advocate strongly against global and, to a lesser extent, interregional agreements – unless these agreements contain strong safeguard and worker-rights clauses that protect European workers from displacement by their cheaper foreign counterparts. If unions split along sectoral lines, however, those in competitive sectors would be much better disposed toward global and interregional agreements (like competitive firms more generally) than those in uncompetitive sectors.[13]

Finally, societal groups such as environmentalists, human rights activists, and others that tend to oppose globalization will generally prefer to keep economic activity at a smaller scale, where it is more easily regulated. While some of these groups dislike capitalism in principle, most of them simply wish to curtail the human and environmental costs of international economic activity. As such, they might welcome international trade agreements to the extent that they enforce strong protections for individuals, groups, and the environment. However, they also understand that broader agreements can also be particularly difficult to embed such protections into, given both the greater relative strength of international firms and the diversity of national ideas regarding such protections. Therefore, these societal groups will support EU external trade agreements only to the extent to which they simultaneously retain EU safeguards and promote similar safeguards in other countries. This becomes possible as EU's relative bargaining strength increases, notably at the bilateral, but also potentially at the interregional, level.

More generally, all of these groups' preferences are likely to turn on the qualities of the trading counterpart in question when they consider bilateral or interregional arrangements. Some countries and regions present powerful threats to sensitive and politically powerful sectors in Europe. For example, India and other South Asian countries have globally competitive textiles sectors that have undercut inefficient European producers, a trend that will accelerate with the phasing out of the Multi-Fiber Agreement in 2005. On the other hand, other countries or regions present fewer threats to sensitive sectors in Europe. Sensitive, politically powerful sectors and actors must be appeased – or forsaken at a high political cost to EU policymakers – if bilateral or interregional arrangements are to be made with

countries or regions whose exports might directly compete with European goods.

In sum, an interest group hypothesis involves four elements: the institutional environment (which may or may not vary; see the next hypothesis); the resources of the interest group; the coherence of the interest group; and the preferences of the interest group. Preferences in particular can be expected to vary depending on the expected target market (country, region, etc.) of trade negotiations. Any interest-oriented explanation of EU trade policy and interregional posture would start with group preferences and consider how successful different groups are in translating those preferences – via resources, collective action, and institutions – into EU action.

Hypothesis 2: EU trade strategies, interregional or otherwise, are determined by EU bureaucracies' attempts to maximize their own influence in the European policymaking arena.

In the bureaucratic politics view, relevant European institutions contend to expand their control over EU commercial policy. To do so, these institutions – namely the Commission, the Parliament, the Council, and even the European Court of Justice – woo both private and public actors with an interest in trade policy. Meanwhile, the legacies of past relationships among the bureaucracies and private actors (i.e., policy networks) act as important constraints on future relationships. In this case, European trade policy will reflect one of two constellations of interests: (1) the combined interests of the "winning coalition" that any one institution puts together to become the dominant locus of European trade policy; or (2) the ongoing dynamics of contention among these institutions if none can obtain or sustain trade policy dominance. In the first sense, the substance of EU trade policy is determined by the interests co-opted by the most influential EU institutions. If the relevant institutions – particularly the Commission – can increase their own intra-EU influence by promoting trade negotiations and co-opting interest groups that favor interregional outcomes, this will become a focus of EU trade policy.[14] In the second sense, policy processes as defined in EU treaties are malleable and subject to interpretation, and EU institutions will by nature press for interpretations that expand their own remits. In this view, changes to the treaty base may arrive as exogenous shocks that formally reorder institutional responsibilities but do not alter the more general, ongoing dynamic of bureaucratic contention that shapes the processes that determine trade policy.

For a bureaucratic politics hypothesis to explain trade outcomes, then, we must know which institution stands to benefit in terms of intra-EU influence from different trade postures, and in particular whether an interregional outlook would benefit any one institution disproportionately.[15] As suggested by the discussion to this point, this question comes down to a

struggle between the Commission and the Council. The Commission, for its part, is the EU negotiator for any international trade agreement, and so will push for international trade negotiations whenever possible and appropriate. More specifically, however, the Commission sees its agenda expand as the scope of a proposed arrangement expands: the greater the number of sectors, countries, or policy areas (e.g., development, aid, etc.) involved, the greater the role for the Commission. However, broader trade arrangements/policy agendas do also raise the prospect of more intra-Commission wrangling between the various DGs regarding under whose purview certain subsets of trade negotiations will fall. Still, if task expansion is the primary goal, the Commission can be expected to prefer trade negotiations at the broadest possible level, and hence to be open to broad-scoped interregional negotiations when global processes falter. Interregional trade negotiations and arrangements potentially offer an array of bureaucratic opportunities for the Commission's DGs to establish institutionalized government-to-government contacts with their counterparts in other regions (i.e., external task expansion) and, perhaps more importantly, to tighten their control over their intra-EU policy briefs by managing any internal reforms necessitated by new trade accords (i.e., internal task expansion).

The Council (as well as the EP and ECJ) is unlikely to gain new powers through the manipulation of EU trade policy, and so simply seeks to prevent the Commission from gaining too much influence at its own expense.[16] Given that the Council is not likely to derive any institutional influence from any one type of trade arrangement over another, the Council's preferences as a whole on the merits of global vs. interregional vs. other trade strategies may simply derive from individual member preferences. EU member preferences, in turn, may be determined largely by powerful national interest groups' preferences. In other words, a bureaucratic politics hypothesis would not say too much about the Council's institutional preferences regarding different types of trade arrangements on the merits of those arrangements per se,[17] but rather simply suggest that the Council will brandish its oversight and approval powers to prevent the Commission from negotiating agreements in such a way that significantly extends the latter's overall policymaking authority within the EU.

However, the Council may have one reason to prefer interregional (or bilateral) agreements over global ones: they may give the Union's more geopolitically oriented member states an opportunity to push the EU into a greater prominence in international politics. Despite halting moves toward a Common Foreign and Security Policy (CFSP) centered in the Commission, the EU's chief foreign representative (currently Javier Solana) reports to the Council, suggesting that big countries such as Britain, France, and Germany remain unwilling to cede their foreign policy powers to the technocratic and still relatively inward-looking Commission. As such, they may see interregionalism as a means not only to pursue their

vision of the EU's international political goals (see next hypothesis), but also to repoliticize trade relations in a way that better suits the Council's "political" intergovernmentalism than the Commission's more technocratic supranationalism.

Hypothesis 3: EU trade strategies, interregional or otherwise, are determined by international systemic constraints and opportunities. These constraints are of two types. The first is reflected in a need to respond to external threats to Europe's economic security and to promote Europe's influence as an international actor (a form of balancing behavior). The second is driven by considerations of broader institutions within which trade agreements might be nested.

In these two related approaches the European Union is treated analytically as a unitary alliance of constituent states. The first highlights the EU motivation of promoting its collective political and economic influence and security within the international system – particularly as a way to counter American hegemony.[18] This view would suggest that the EU sees interregionalism as an initial piece of an emerging common foreign and security policy that seeks to extend European influence in various strategic regions through a "hub-and-spoke" model with the EU at the center of a series of economic relationships in which it maintains ties to other regions that may or may not have ties to one another. In most interregional relationships, the European Union would be the dominant side, and thus could largely dictate the terms of these institutionalized relationships. To a certain extent, this European strategy could be seen as classic balancing behavior and a response to the American pursuit of a similar strategy, particularly through APEC and FTAA. Bhagwati and Arvind see this hub-and-spoke approach as a new direction for Europe: "The extension of RTAs [reciprocal trade agreements] to non-candidate countries represents a radical departure for the EC. By doing so, it joins the United States in promoting 'hegemon-centered' trade agreements..."[19]

This hypothesis is based on a certain interpretation of the attributes of both the international system in general and the EU in particular. The international system in the post-Cold War era is defined by two primary characteristics: the increasing importance of international economic competition (and competitiveness), and the rise of regionalism as a middle position of political and institutional organization between the nation-state and globalism.[20] Because of the former dynamic, the struggle among economic actors to redefine the rules of international commerce in ways that privilege themselves has become high politics, with states giving much greater attention to the ways in which their domestically-based firms and industries are affected by the rules underpinning international markets. Because of the latter dynamic, regions are becoming important manifestations of the rise of "geoeconomics" and potentially economic and political actors in their own right.[21]

In this approach, the use of trade policy as a means to manage international power relationships is a reflection of the inability of EU member states to generate any real momentum for a more "political" CFSP. Since trade policy already aggregates the member states into a coherent unit, and the basis of European influence in the world is more economic than political, the EU can best punch its weight in international politics by granting and/or restricting access to the large and rich European market. Even if a coherent CFSP does arise, it does not necessarily augur an immediate rise in Europe's political influence (not to mention military power) around the world; as long as Europe remains a "civilian power," commercial policy will be its primary means of international political influence.

The promotion of interregional trade ties may be a specific strategy that draws on both Europe's economic and institutional strengths. It allows the EU to be the senior partner in any interregional arrangement (except perhaps with North America), given its greater economic weight and the far more advanced institutionalization of its regional member states. A hub-and-spoke interregional system could act as a guarantor of economic security in the face of the not-unimaginable dangers of the collapse of the WTO and the multilateral trading system and/or a protracted trade war with the United States – not unlike the British withdrawal within its empire during the Great Depression of the 1930s.[22] An interregional system would also fit well with the EU's preference for "political" trade – in which solutions to trade disputes are negotiated by the disputants – over "legalized" trade (i.e., in the WTO).[23] As noted above, the EU would almost always be the (much) stronger party in any such negotiations, and thus would tend to prevail in such disputes.

The second systemic hypothesis focuses on the constraints of nested systems and institutions.[24] From this perspective, and consistent with the above discussion on balancing, the trading system is nested within the broader economic system, which is in turn nested within the security system. Following the logic of higher-level systemic objectives, this view focuses on the impact that a bipolar or unipolar security system has on economic and trade objectives. A classic example of this impact is the U.S. willingness to make concessions to the Europeans on trade in the 1950s and interest in promoting Japanese accession to the GATT (despite European opposition) – both in an effort to resist the Soviet Union. By contrast, with the decline of the Soviet Union and the increasing transformation of the security system into one of unipolarity in the wake of the Cold War, the United States became less willing to make concession in the name of security. This point is nicely illustrated by former U.S. Secretary of State James Baker, who noted in 1995:

Finally, the end of the Cold War has had important ramifications for the West itself. Absent concern about Soviet aggression, the traditional

alliance among the United States, Western Europe and Japan is showing patent signs of strain... U.S.–Japanese relations, plagued by rancorous trade disputes, are more troubled than they have been in decades.[25]

Tied to nested security considerations is the nesting of international institutions. The WTO is the dominant overarching trade organization. Under its auspices, following Article 24 of the GATT, regional free trade agreements and customs unions are permitted under certain conditions (such as the coverage of significant trade among the members and criteria on trade diversion and creation). In general, consistent with the nested systems notion, the principles, norms, rules, and procedures of broader international arrangements will have an effect on the negotiation evolution of narrower arrangements, be they on a sectoral basis as with the Multi-Fiber Arrangement in textiles and apparel or a regional basis such as NAFTA or the EU. We would expect such nested constraints to be operative in the case of interregional agreements as well, which themselves should in principle be justified under Article 24 of the WTO/GATT. A clear case of this would appear to be the European concern involving its trade conflict in bananas with the United States as a result of its preferential treatment of Lomé countries.[26]

Hypothesis 4: EU trade strategies, interregional or otherwise, are determined by the ongoing need to forge a common European identity among the people of its constituent nations and by a belief in the utility of regions as a unit for organizing the global economy.

In this view, European elites – particularly within the Commission but also in member countries – promote trade strategies that might help generate notions of pan-European interests and identity among the peoples of Europe. Moreover, this belief extends to other regions of the world, based on the notion that regions provide a logical mode of organizing the world economy and promoting economic development within regions.

The underlying dynamics of European identity building involves two lacunae in relative sympathy for the EU – between elites and masses and between Europhilic countries and Euroskeptic countries – and the desire of Europhilic elites to foster the internalization of European identities among all EU citizens. Thus these elites support trade strategies in which Europe-wide interests and identities can be articulated and promoted. Examples include creating and promoting European-wide firms such as Airbus or civil-society groups, or alternatively highlighting ways in which European norms and practices differ from those found in other regions and countries of the world.

This "constructivist" hypothesis starts from the view that international trade occurs in a social context that both constitutes and is constituted by actors' identities and actions.[27] Economic interaction is not simply an

objective, material exchange, but also involves the affective understandings of individuals and societies of the meanings of economic activity through their interpretation of available symbols. Through this lens, interregionalism is seen within the context of the broader project of European integration, and more specifically the desire of European elites to foster a more robust European identity among the citizens of member states. Hence interregionalism would be an institutional expression of European unity that, in practice, may be internalized by EU citizens. For instance, the common currency, whatever its economic rationale, may be one such institutional mechanism to create an identity-related response among Europeans. Interregional trade agreements, while much less a part of Europeans' everyday lives, would be a more abstract way of prodding them to view themselves as part of a cohesive economic, political, and social unit that interacts with other like-units – in a similar way as the completion of the single market did internally.

The underlying cognitive mechanism in this view is that only through self-conscious interaction with comparable "others" does the conception of "self" take shape. Karl Deutsch's "transactional" approach hypothesized that an increase in the number and frequency of transactions within Europe would help foster a European identity. The analogical thinking in the realm of international commercial policy is that increasing and formalizing transactions between Europe as a whole and other recognizable regions would serve the same purpose. The shared values and norms that are represented in European trade policy would trickle down to European citizens, who would recognize and perhaps internalize these shared values and norms into their own sense of identity.[28]

The creation of a greater sense of "self" among European citizens may be a prerequisite for the EU to generate a coherent CFSP as well – i.e., meaning that the EU could exercise its institutional capacity to pursue a common trade policy to help generate a more robust European identity, which would then feed back into European leaders' ability to craft new institutions that further solidify the EU as a coherent international actor. Put differently, the generation of a stronger European identity is valued both in and of itself as well as a means to future policy goals.

An overt connection between Europe's internal identity and its "international identity" – i.e., how Europeans conceive of their global role, and how this perceived role feeds back into Europeans' conceptions of themselves – also underlies this constructivist hypothesis. Some have suggested that European leaders have sought to foster an overall European identity through comparison to other peer nations – notably the United States and Japan.[29] A recurrent theme in this identity formation process is the casting of Europe as a "civil power," which highlights the normative aspects of Europe's values and identity (i.e., democracy, the rule of law, economic justice, pooling of sovereignty, etc.) and implicitly or explicitly juxtaposes

them to other leading nations (especially the military, commercial, and technological "hyperpower" of the United States).[30] Indeed, the United States is a useful basis for comparison on many fronts. Globalism – or, more specifically, globalization – is often associated with the United States, and possibly favors an American view of how the world should be organized. Interregionalism could be Europe's riposte, projecting the EU's success in creating a region and seeking to externalize the forms that have worked in Europe through region-to-region trade relationships. While the U.S. trans-regional ventures to date (APEC, FTAA) have deemphasized regional blocs as distinct halves of an interregional whole, the EU has specifically dealt with their counterparts as a "regional" group, no matter how disparate geographically or politically.

4   Counterpart evolution

The source and evolution of EU preferences toward different types of trade arrangements are the primary lenses through which this book examines interregional outcomes. But to satisfactorily account for international regime outcomes it is of course essential to consider the characteristics of the counterpart regions with which the EU engages. The chapter authors will address in some detail three interrelated aspects of the counterpart region.

First, they explore the individual and collective preferences of the countries in the counterpart region. To some extent, this analysis is possible through an approach similar to that applied to Europe: which societal groups are the most keen on – or opposed to – commercial agreements? How are preferences shaped by national or region-wide institutional structures? Does an incipient sense of regional identity lend momentum to region-to-region agreements? However, because the EU is at a far higher level of internal institutionalization than any of the counterpart regions under consideration, this approach to *regional* preferences cannot be borrowed too directly to explain motivations in counterparts where individual states are relatively much more important than any regional collective. Therefore, we expect counterpart motivations to be fairly region-specific and to not fit easily within a generalized formula.

Second, authors will consider configurations of power (particularly economic) both within the counterpart region and between the EU and all or some subset of the counterpart region. To a large extent, this is the reciprocal to hypothesis three of EU preferences: in what way do power considerations within the counterpart affect the willingness of all members of the region to engage in interregional ties with the EU? What's more, how do possible power asymmetries between the counterpart and the EU affect the former's attitudes toward negotiations and possible agreements with the latter? Does collective regional action represent the means of getting

the best possible deal from the EU? The authors consider these questions of counterpart power with an eye to how these configurations affect the intensity of preferences for different types of commercial arrangements both for states in the counterpart and for the EU.

Third is the idea of *counterpart coherence*, or the degree to which the counterpart region manifests a clear and coherent zone of political-economic activity and the institutional underpinnings to represent that zone *vis-à-vis* the rest of the world. In particular, the coherence of the counterpart region can be approximated through four dimensions that represent the political, economic, and cultural/geographic elements of regions.

- Is the counterpart region self-defined (e.g., MERCOSUR), or was it defined by the EU (e.g., the Southern Mediterranean)?
- What portion of the counterpart countries' economic exchange is conducted within the region as opposed to with countries outside the region?
- Of the broadest possible definition of what constitutes the "potential" region (in rough geographical and/or cultural terms), what portion of the countries in this potential region are drawn together in a regional regime of some sort?
- How strongly institutionalized is any region-wide regime?

Counterpart coherence, measured along these lines, helps to determine the nature of interregionalism we see when countries from two distinct regions make commercial agreements (i.e., pure interregionalism, hybrid interregionalism, or transregionalism). An example of pure interregionalism is the EU-MERCOSUR Framework Agreement, in which each side negotiates and presumably, will adopt new policies *vis-à-vis* the other as a coherent regional bloc. By contrast, APEC is a transregional arrangement that does not involve formal links among regional groupings. This accord, created in 1989, links a variety of countries across the Asia-Pacific including Japan, the United States, and China, among others. Although many APEC members are part of relevant regional groupings (NAFTA, the Andean Pact, and the putative Association of Southeast Asian Nations [ASEAN] Free Trade Area), they participate in APEC as individual economies and not as subsumed under their regional groupings.[31]

Descriptively speaking, then, we expect interregional regime outcomes – including the absence of a regime – to be a function of some constellation of received EU preferences and counterpart characteristics. This approach is represented in Figure 1.2.

It is worth noting that this "model" is not intended to represent the process by which regime outcomes are reached but simply the basic relationship between inputs and outputs. As such, two additional points bear making. First, we are less interested in understanding the course of events

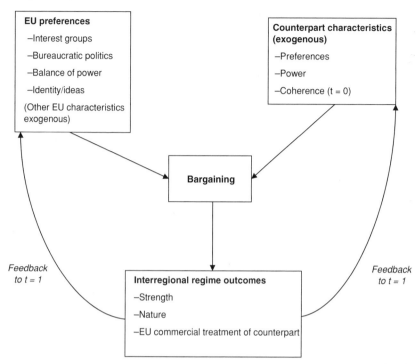

Figure 1.2   "Model" of interregional trade outcomes

in region-to-region interaction than in how certain values or configurations of the abovementioned variables are associated with particular regime outcomes. While the chapter authors will, for the purpose of illustration, present some details regarding the nature of interregional bargaining, we tend to discount the effect that particular aspects of the bargaining process have on regime outcomes. Second, as the figure suggests, we believe that the creation and existence of interregional regimes are likely to feed back into the political and economic characteristics of the participating regions. Commercial regimes can create vested interests within regions and countries, lead to differential growth rates that affect the international balance of power, and strengthen or weaken certain intraregional institutions.

Perhaps most interesting, however, may be the potential effect that a proliferation of interregional regimes has on the status of regionalism as a mode of supranational governance in the world political economy. Following along the logic of the constructivist hypothesis outlined above, the European Union's interregional overtures may promote increasing counterpart coherence over time. That is, European leaders' attempts to foster regional identities may also spread to counterpart regions, both creating effective trade partners and externalizing EU institutional forms.

Indeed, this institutional diffusion may be an overarching EU goal. Manners has referred to this as "meta-regionalism," in which the EU engages "in interregional diplomacy which implicitly and explicitly promotes *mimétisme* (regional replication) in places such as southeast Asia (ASEAN), southern Africa (SADC), and South America (MERCOSUR)."[32] In other words, the EU may see interregionalism as a means to promote counterpart coherence and institutional mimesis among potential and actual regional blocs, with its own model of regional integration being the exemplar.[33] This too could feed back into the European identity, promoting the view that the EU is at the vanguard of a movement toward a new form of political, economic, and social organization that renders old national identities obsolete (or at least less important).

5 Analytical expectations regarding hypotheses of interregional developments

Given these hypotheses regarding the most important determinants of EU (and counterpart) preferences *vis-à-vis* different commercial policies and relationships, there remains the question of how the sets of variables highlighted in each hypothesis relate to each of our three specific regime outcomes of interest. That is, as interregional trade regimes are negotiated, renegotiated, or left unnegotiated over time, which actors or contexts are most likely to have the greatest effect on the evolving strength and nature of the regime and the EU's treatment of its counterparts therein? While we begin from an understanding of a complex and multicausal world – and thus are skeptical about drawing straight lines from likely inputs to likely outputs – we set out with the following sets of expectations regarding the relationships between these inputs and outputs.

In considering the relative importance of these different factors, we use an ordinal ranking that scores them as 'most important,' 'very important,' 'important,' 'somewhat important,' and 'least important.' This, of course, does not mean that a variable identified as 'least important' is irrelevant; rather, it simply indicates that we expect it to have a less direct effect on the outcomes of interest than the other factors.

Regime strength

We define the strength of an interregional regime in terms of its formal institutionalization and the bindingness of its rules. Our expectations are as follows.

Systemic power and security considerations considerations should be most important. The relative importance of a particular interregional relationship (both for the EU and for the counterpart) in solidifying a strong and secure place in the international system – and for promoting domestic economic security and stability – can clearly be expected to affect each side's willingness to tie itself strongly to the other. This potentially reciprocal aspect of systemic considerations may be particularly reflected in the institutions of cooperation the two sides set up to manage relations. However, the bindingness of rules across relevant issues may be strongly shaped by the distribution of power within the interregional relationship. That is, when its relational power is asymmetrically great, the EU would be expected to seek to impose strong rules that force counterparts to open their markets, while denying or delaying the imposition of strong rules that would hurt its own domestic interests.

The interplay among interest groups should be very important for regime strength. Generally speaking, business groups will have very strong preferences regarding the bindingness of regime rules: they will be very positively disposed toward binding rules that improve their competitive position both in the European and counterpart markets, and negatively disposed toward binding rules that hurt their competitive positions. The intensity of their preferences – and thus the extent to which they will seek to sway policy-makers toward their viewpoints – will mirror the size of the impact of binding rules on their competitive positions. However, while all relevant private sector groups may support the creation of fora such as roundtables and working groups that include them in regime processes, their level of commitment to such fora may be mild if they believe domestic channels of influence to be more effective.

Nesting considerations are likely to be important in influencing the strength of regimes. States are likely to be concerned with compliance with higher-level institutions that affect broader trade and possibly security interests. Thus regime rules at the interregional level are likely to be brought in conformity with broader level trading arrangements such as the WTO, particularly if these interregional regimes undermine such broader arrangements or create conflicts with trading partners.

Inter-bureaucratic contention should be somewhat important. The institutional roles of the Commission and the Council may lead them to have divergent preferences regarding both rule bindingness and institutionalization. The Commission, which seeks to create and enforce binding rules within Europe, may be constitutionally better inclined toward such rules in an interregional arena, while the Council, to the extent that it is a forum for maintaining flexibility for national members, may be more skeptical. Similarly, a heavily institutionalized interregional regime may present more opportunities for the Commission to represent the EU as a whole, perhaps causing the Council to withhold support for proliferating official fora within the regime – or to push for institutionalization to focus on national and subnational private- and public-sector actors. However, it is not clear to us whether these divergent bureaucratic preferences regarding interregional regime strength would be strong enough to be decisive.

Identity considerations may be least important. In general, it is not immediately obvious why the strength of interregional rules and institutions should be a function of EU leaders' desire to foster a European identity; after all, the identification of and symbolic relation to the other should be more important than the nitty-gritty details of specific rules and institutions. However, if EU leaders believe that the relative strength of interregional rules and institutions is potentially constitutive of the two regions themselves, then they may seek a level of regime strength that best symbolizes the level of European commitment – and perhaps best promotes EU-style institutions in counterpart regions.

Regime nature

We define the nature of an interregional regime in terms of its issue scope and its development emphasis. Our expectations are as follows.

Identity considerations should be most important. As the EU continues to struggle to assert its identity within Europe and in the world, EU policy-makers are surely aware that the types of issues the EU emphasizes in its dealings with other "like" actors will reflect on the EU itself. Thus the EU may be expected to make strong efforts to show that it is much more than a mere regional FTA by emphasizing a broad range of issues in its region-to-region relationships, particularly those issues on which it sees itself having a "comparative advantage," such as human rights and social cohesion. Moreover, it may also seek to set itself up for a favorable comparison to the United States by including generous development terms where appropriate.

Nesting considerations should be very important. We expect significant efforts to be made to keep the nature of the interregional agreements consistent with the GATT/WTO. This does not, however, mean that the EU might not use the opportunity of developing interregional agreements to pursue "WTO-plus" arrangements that would allow it to both differentiate itself from the United States and meet its own objectives that cannot easily be pursued at the WTO level.[34]

Inter-bureaucratic contention should be important. Specifically with respect to the EU, we expect the Commission to pursue a broad issue scope, both to expand its overall role in the negotiation and maintenance of a given regime and to ensure that its various DGs are represented therein. This second reason also suggests that the Commission, and particularly its Development Directorate, will push for development provisions where appropriate. The extent to which the Council will resist, acquiesce, or support Commission initiatives in this area is somewhat less clear. The Council may weigh in on issue scope if one or several EU member states have particular sensitivities to the inclusion or exclusion of certain issues; it may weigh in on development emphasis if member states seek to manage relations with countries or regions of particular interest through an EU-led interregional forum.

Systemic power and security considerations should be somewhat important. The EU may seek both a broad issue scope and a development emphasis in any interregional regime with less-developed countries – particularly those

LDCs in relative proximity to Europe – if it is seen as a means to promote stability within the counterpart region and limit the flow of migrants to Europe. At a more systemic level, the EU's relatively greater willingness to include developmental and aid provisions in any such regime may allow it to be a more attractive partner than the United States to counterpart regions, though these counterparts' suspicion of environmental and labor provisions would suggest that the EU would have to leave these types of issues out to press this advantage.[35]

The interplay among interest groups should be least important for the nature of the regime. On the one hand, we expect all interest groups to have quite strong preferences with regard to issue scope, and to mobilize to impress those preferences on policymakers. For instance, while competitive firms will seek to focus the regime on trade and investment, European labor groups may seek the inclusion of strong labor and/or human rights clauses, green groups the inclusion of environmental rules, European farmers the exclusion of agricultural liberalization, and the like. However, we expect interest groups to have less of an interest (and thus likely effect) on the developmental emphasis of the regime, as this aspect of policy tends to derive from an agenda determined within the public sector – though poor-country-advocate NGOs may well have some influence here.

EU commercial treatment of counterparts

We define the EU's commercial treatment of the counterpart region in terms of its relative uniformity of treatment across countries in the counterpart and its inclination to deal with these countries as a single group or plurally. Our expectations are as follows.

Systemic power and security considerations should be most important. Different countries present the EU with different levels of political and economic challenges and opportunities, and the EU's commercial treatment of these different countries will reflect this balance of opportunities and threats. Some counterpart regions may have little differentiation among their constituent countries in this respect, providing little impetus for variable treatment or regional disaggregation. However, in other regions there may be one or a few countries that present either clear or unique challenges or opportunities, giving the EU a strong incentive to negotiate separate terms with the countries (if it chooses to negotiate with them at all).

Nesting should be very important. We expect this element to possibly conflict with the power-based objective of differential treatment, which may lead to conflict with the WTO requirements for most favored nation treatment. Thus, in this case, rather than a complementary cumulative effect, we might see conflicting objectives that may manifest itself in intra-EU bureaucratic contention.

The interplay among interest groups should be important for the type of EU commercial treatment. In particular, we expect interest group input to be quite strong with respect to the relative uniformity of treatment. Countries in a counterpart region may have different levels of comparative or competitive advantage across a number of politically salient sectors, leading EU interest groups seeking to maintain protection against competitors from particular countries to mobilize to ensure that the EU treats those competitors differently than less threatening counterparts. Alternatively, EU producers and investors may want special deals with countries that offer relatively greater commercial opportunities. Reflected in EU trade policy, these interest group pressures could be expected to affect both the uniformity of treatment and trade types, probably in the direction of a more plural approach.

Identity-related considerations should be somewhat important. Similar to the logic with regime nature, European policymakers may view EU commercial treatment of counterpart regions as a reflection on both the internal and external identity of a united Europe, with uniformity of treatment of countries – or perhaps respect for diversity therein – reflecting and retransmitting Europe's own experience. Nevertheless, we would expect these sorts of motivations to be an underlying, rather than dominant, factor. To the extent that the EU seeks to promote its own organizational forms abroad, however, we might also expect policymakers to favor interregional over plural-bilateral trade types.

Inter-bureaucratic contention may be least important. While the Commission seeks task expansion in general, it also prefers efficient modes of bargaining, and having to negotiate a separate set of terms with a number of different countries would not be the sort of task expansion the EC craves – especially if there is a large number of countries in the counterpart region. However, for both the Commission and the Council, other considerations may outweigh whatever (weak) inherent preferences they have regarding commercial treatment type such as the positions and activities of relevant interest groups (see above) and particularly the political-security relationships with countries in the counterpart region.

A preliminary "ranking" of the relevance of each of these hypotheses for our interregional regime outcomes of interest is summarized in Table 1.3.

Table 1.3   Ranking the expected explanatory power of hypotheses

Regime strength	Regime nature	Commercial treatment
1. systemic/balancing	1. constructivist	1. systemic/balancing
2. pluralist	2. nesting	2. nesting
3. nesting	3. bureaucratic politics	3. pluralist
4. bureaucratic politics	4. systemic/balancing	4. constructivist
5. constructivist	5. pluralist	5. bureaucratic politics

These rankings and the analysis that informs them suggest that, based on an initial assessment, none of the four hypotheses is likely to prove dominant across all relevant aspects of interregional regimes. However, our expectations are very preliminary. The indeterminacy of a purely deductive or logical approach to these questions only further highlights the importance of grounding this study in in-depth cases.

6   Preliminary snapshot of cases

Before moving on to the authors' analysis of the various cases of EU interregionalism, we want to establish the basis of comparison by providing a very brief snapshot of each. This snapshot portrays them only at their first stage of development, when the initial terms of the relationship were emerging. In the conclusion, we will contrast this initial snapshot to a later point in time, and will attempt to draw conclusions regarding both between-case and within-case variation in regime developments.

EU-Central and Eastern Europe (1990)

The relationship between the EU and the formerly communist states of Central and Eastern Europe (CEE) represents the case in which the dynamics of regionalism and interregionalism is most closely intertwined. The EU's answer to the question of how to reunite Europe after the parting of the Iron Curtain was initially interregional: since these poor, fragile new democracies could not immediately be brought within the Union, the existing EU members decided to encourage CEE countries to pursue their own subregional groupings as a means to promote stability and cooperation in the interim. Except for the Balkans – an area beginning to slip into chaos at the outset of the 1990s – the EU would see its relations with potential (though by no means certain) future members develop with three new blocs: the Visegrad group of Central Europe (including Poland, Czechoslovakia, and Hungary), the Baltic trio (Lithuania, Latvia, and Estonia), and the Commonwealth of Independent States (the former Soviet republics).

The encouragement of interregional relations with these subregional groupings represented a potentially practical solution to integrating these newly postcommunist countries into the zone of stability and prosperity that existed in Western Europe. It provided a short-term response to the inevitable difficulty of *formally* integrating these countries into Europe and a possible means for both coalescing and distinguishing among different classes of potential members, even as it established a set of vehicles for organizing EU assistance to and commerce with these countries.

EU-Southern Mediterranean (1995)

The European Union's "Mediterranean" policy began in the 1960s with loose concessionary trade agreements with the southern littoral countries, followed in the 1970s by an expansion of economic and financial co-operation. The EU's New Mediterranean Policy of 1990 introduced a financial partnership consisting of financial assistance from the EU to bolster economic and structural reforms along the southern Mediterranean.

The Barcelona Declaration of 1995 codified the aims of the EU and Med12 countries (Algeria, Morocco, Tunisia, Egypt, Israel, Jordan, Lebanon, the Palestinian autonomous territories, Syria, Turkey, Cyprus, and Malta), establishing 2010 as the goal for establishing a free-trade area. The aim of the declaration was to create an "area of shared prosperity" to meet three broad objectives: to accelerate sustainable socio-economic development, to improve living conditions, and to encourage regional cooperation and integration. The EU also promised a substantial increase in financial assistance to Med12 states.

EU-East Asia (1996)

Building on a generation of region-to-region ties between Europe and ASEAN, the EU and members of ASEAN plus Japan, China, and South Korea established the Asia-Europe Meeting (ASEM) in 1996. Intended to give institutional ballast to the relatively weak commercial and political relationship between Europe and East Asia, the EU and the ASEAN+3 created a process-oriented forum to strengthen interregional relations in general and, Europeans hoped, to expand trade and investment relationships through improved access for exporters and investors.

However, ASEM adopted a broad agenda, providing fora for policymakers and private actors to discuss a broad range of issues from business to development to cultural exchanges. While ASEM was explicitly born as a partnership of equals, the far lower regional institutionalization and political, economic, and sociocultural diversity among East Asian nations provided Europeans with the need – or perhaps the opportunity – to pursue a plural approach to relations with countries of East Asia within the ASEM forum.

EU-Africa, the Caribbean, and the Pacific (1975)

The Lomé Convention, first agreed to in 1975 by the EU and a large group of countries in Africa, the Caribbean, and the Pacific (ACP), was established to govern commercial relations between European countries and many of their former colonies. Created at the high-water mark of developing country unity in international trade and economic relations, the Lomé Convention strongly institutionalized European support for and preferential treatment of ACP countries industries and exports.

Specifically, Lomé codified EU–ACP relations across several areas – including trade, finance, and industry – with the goal of helping ACP countries to achieve self-sustaining economic development, and established a "permanent dialogue" through a joint council of ministers, committee of ambassadors, and assembly. Lomé provided for substantially equal treatment across the myriad ACP participants, though favored clients (or former colonies) received some special attention – although not necessarily or always within the specific Lomé framework.

EU-Southern Cone (South America) (1995)

Leaders from the EU and Brazil, Argentina, Uruguay, and Paraguay signed the EU-MERCOSUR Interregional Framework Cooperation Agreement (EMIFCA) in December 1995. Created to develop a pure-interregional regime, the EMIFCA process began with a few core ideas but with only hazy outlines of the rules that it sought to codify. While an interregional free trade area was a primary goal, the two sides would promote broader exchanges to reflect the deep historical and cultural links between them.

The forum was fairly weakly institutionalized, however, with unclear prospects for binding rules. The unique aspect of this relationship was the fact that it was born early simultaneously to the creation of the MERCOSUR customs union, which implied a pure interregional relationship in which the terms of any future agreement would reflect the economic unity of each of the two regions.

EU-North America (1990)

In 1990, policymakers on both sides of the Atlantic were pondering the future of their mutual relations after the end of the Cold War. While EU commercial ties to North America – and the United States and Canada specifically – were already strong and stable, in that year it signed separate agreements with the United States and Canada (which had themselves established a bilateral free trade area the previous year). These were political gestures more than concrete proposals, intended to reinforce the overall transatlantic partnership in the face of the disappearance of the common adversary – though in both cases they left the door open to future consideration of more institutionalized commercial relations. In the meantime, reconciliation of their distinct positions in the ongoing Uruguay Round negotiations was enough to fill the commercial diplomatic agenda.

Meanwhile, European commercial ties to Mexico had stagnated in the wake of the debt crisis, and little change outside the framework of multilateral talks seemed in the offing.

A summary of the relevant characteristics of each of these EU-centered interregional regimes appears in Table 1.4.

6   Conclusion

Having achieved a truly unified internal market and launched its single currency, the European Union must be viewed as a strong, coherent actor

Table 1.4 EU interregional relationships (initial)

Relationship (year)	Regime strength	Regime nature	EU commercial treatment
EU–Eastern Europe (1990)	Medium-strong	Comprehensive, developmental	Uniform, interregional + bilaterals
EU–Southern Mediterranean (1995)	Weak	Comprehensive, developmental	Nonuniform, bilaterals
EU–East Asia (1996)	Medium-weak	Comprehensive, quasi-developmental	Nonuniform, interregional + bilaterals
EU–ACP (1975)	Medium-strong	Comprehensive, developmental	Mostly uniform, interregional
EU–South America (1995)	Medium-weak	Medium-narrow, quasi-developmental	Uniform, interregional
EU–North America (1990)	US/Canada: medium Mexico: weak	US/Canada: narrow, nondevelopmental Mexico: comprehensive, developmental	Nonuniform, bilaterals

whose strategies are of central importance to international economic relations more generally. By exploring the EU's apparently growing appetite for interregionalism we seek to get at the core political and economic factors that will shape the evolving international economic system in the coming years. Power, interests, institutions, and ideas all matter a great deal in shaping EU trade policy. A similar but not identical set of factors among the counterpart region combines with these received EU preferences to create some sort of regime outcome. Our questions are: what matters most? What constellations of factors are associated with which outcomes? And what does the answer to these questions tell us about the future of interregionalism? As our authors demonstrate in the following chapters, the answers to the first two questions vary from case to case. We will address the latter, informed by the contributions of the authors, in the conclusion.

Appendix: EU trade policymaking processes

What follows is a brief discussion of the key political and institutional features of the EU trade policymaking and negotiating process, intended to identify the basic structure of actors, rules, and procedures that shape trade policy outcomes. The actual politics and processes are much more complex than what is outlined here; we simply introduce the basic components of a general policy process and environment that the other authors analyse with an eye to their respective interregional relationships.[36]

EU trade rules

The legal authority of EU institutions in trade policy is spelt out – with varying degrees of clarity – in the intergovernmental treaties signed by member states.[37] The Treaty of European Community, which was signed in Rome in 1957 and established the European Economic Community, mandated in its Article 133 (originally Article 113) the creation of a Common Commercial Policy (CCP) to complement a Common External Tariff. In the CCP, European countries shifted their authority to negotiate outside agreements to the European Commission – the supranational European bureaucracy – and bound themselves to seek changes or exceptions to these agreements only through EU-wide institutions (the Commission and the intergovernmental European Council of Ministers). Meanwhile, Article 133 permitted the negotiation of external trade agreements, but mandated that they must be consistent with the General Agreement on Trade and Tariffs (GATT, now the WTO) under Article 24. While Article 133 provides the legal authority for the EU's external trade negotiations, the specific type of trade agreement envisioned (i.e., preferential, reciprocal, etc.) affects the treaty provisions invoked. For example, in trade talks with developing countries, Articles 177 and 181, which deal with development issues, would also be a part of the legal basis of trade negotiations for what would likely be a preferential agreement. Meanwhile, Article 300 sets the rules on cooperation and association agreements, and Article 310 permits the Commission to negotiate reciprocal agreements with other countries or groups.[38] External trade negotiations have a special procedure under Article 133 that divides overall policy responsibilities for handling external trade negotiations between the Commission and the Council, and that relegates the European Parliament (EP), the Union's legislature, to an advisory role. Essentially, the following process is observed: first, the Commission initiates internal procedures for exploring an external trade agreement; second, the Council – more specifically, the Council's Committee of Permanent Representatives (COREPER) – defines the Commission's mandate regarding the possible shape of an agreement; third, the Commission's relevant Directorates-General (DGs) take the lead in negotiating an agreement on behalf of the EU while the Council monitors their progress through its Article 133 Committee;[39] fourth, the Commission concludes an agreement; and fifth, the Council approves (or rejects) the agreement.

Until the 1980s, voting in the Council on trade issues took place on a unanimous basis. As such, any member state that for whatever reason did not like an agreement could veto it and/or force changes. However, the adoption of the Single European Act in 1987 and the Maastricht Treaty in

1992 altered this procedure by instituting qualified majority voting (QMV) on trade in goods – though, significantly, not in services or intellectual property rights (IPRs) – thereby reducing the blocking power of recalcitrant parties.[40] However, this restriction of QMV to agreements based only on goods has hindered the EU's ability to negotiate pacts, whether in the WTO or in regional forums, that include these expanding sectors. "Mixed" trade agreements, which go into areas in which national governments retain competence, must be ratified by each member government.[41]

Still, the advent of QMV may have important repercussions for EU trade policy in general. An ever-shifting treaty base has slowly but steadily reduced the ability of individual member states to use their votes in the Council to impose particularistic agendas on the Commission in trade negotiation. Hanson has suggested that the completion of the internal market in the Single European Act and the ratification of the Maastricht Treaty have formally biased trade policy outcomes against protectionism by reducing the ability of individual member states – and the business interests that lobby them – to hold the process hostage to specific protectionist demands. Coalitions of EU member states can still put together a blocking majority in the Council, but the threshold is now higher and thus more difficult to achieve.[42] As such, the prevailing status of unanimity *vis-à-vis* QMV shapes trade policy by determining the extent to which interest groups and member governments have the scope to bend voting outcomes in the Council to their will – whether toward free trade or protectionism. Treaty changes that reduce the capacity of member states (or interest groups that capture them) to block the Commission's ability to make compromises in international trade negotiations will facilitate the EU's participation in broad trade negotiations at the global or interregional level.

The complexity of these formal rules and procedures, and their accessibility to interested parties of all types, push EU negotiators in several directions simultaneously. Nugent has noted four ways in which the institutional architecture of EU trade policy – and in particular the overlapping mandates of the Commission and the Council – muddies the waters in trade policy. First, there is institutional power jockeying between the Commission and the Council. Second, the differences in national interests among member states manifest themselves in the often hodge-podge mandate the Council gives the Commission. Third, the Commission roils with internal territorial skirmishes among the DGs and the Commissioners seeking to protect and expand their purviews. Fourth, the EP's striving for a greater role in trade policymaking adds an element of uncertainty to the existing interorganizational relationships among EU institutions.[43] Paemen has further lamented what he sees as the three "fundamental institutional flaws" that hamper the EU in external trade negotiations: (1) the "least common denominator" aspect of EU policy positions (a result of internal bargaining) limits EU bargaining leverage; (2) visible intra-EU bargaining before external negotiations provides foreign trade partners with significant amounts of information about otherwise secret EU bargaining positions; and (3) the Commission's relatively short leash prevents it from making on-the-spot decisions and interrupts the momentum of negotiations when its authority to make a deal is not clear.[44]

Formal EU trade policymaking procedures thus create myriad hurdles and inefficiencies, but also a set of opportunities for relevant institutional and private-sector actors to make their voices heard. Indeed, the relevant actors and institutions involved often vary by each individual item on the overall agenda, making it difficult to define a coherent set of procedures and processes whereby broad EU trade policy is made.

EU institutions

There is no shortage of Europe-wide institutions that have some say in trade-related issues. However, as noted above, three are legally endowed with the greatest responsibility for trade policy: the Commission, the Council, and the European Parliament. While the Commission has traditionally been the driver of European integration because it retains primacy in legislative initiative and executive implementation, it has seen its political influence wane in recent years after the departure of Jacques Delors in 1995. The previously impotent Parliament, which in 1999 brought the Jacques Santer-led Commission to heel for corruption and incompetence, has benefited somewhat from the Commission's malaise. But perhaps the most important locus of actual decisionmaking power remains in the Council, which represents the interests of individual countries in the Union. The relationship among these three institutions is complex: the Commission retains primary authority for representing the Union in external trade matters, but it must seek a mandate from the Council in its preferred agenda. While the Parliament is relatively less important here, it has seen a steady increase in its ability to hold up or even reject Commission initiatives since the implementation of the Maastricht Treaty beginning in 1992 and the fall of the Santer Commission.

EU institutions draw on the treaty base to enhance their own position in the trade policymaking process. According to Peterson, "the specific treaty article under which a proposal is bought forward [e.g., by the Commission] is a powerful determinant of the resources that different institutional actors wield in policy debates." But because each institution has treaty articles to draw upon in pressing its case, the resolution of procedural struggles may come down to how the various institutions use these articles, not the articles themselves.[45] Thus while the legal basis of trade policymaking is central to our understanding of process, EU institutions can try to manipulate "institutional uncertainty" to enlarge their own procedural influence. Control over process means control over outcomes.

Perhaps the key feature of interorganizational politics at the EU level involves the Commission's attempt to draw ever more of the trade policymaking process within its purview. According to Nugent, "The Commission has long pressed the other EU institutions to adopt an expansive approach toward what may be included in Article 133 agreements, arguing that this is necessary to reflect the fact that EU economic activity and trade has changed considerably since the EEC treaty was negotiated in the 1950s."[46] Others have suggested that the Commission's best tactic has been its support for negotiations on multiple fronts, which expands its extra-EU, and potentially intra-EU, competence.[47] For our purposes, however, perhaps the most significant way in which the Commission promotes its own influence is through the cultivation of interest groups, which, as participants in Commission-led policy processes, potentially support more Commission prerogative in the areas in which they are policy partners (see section below on interest groups). However, the Commission does not always or even usually act as a single, unified actor: there are territorial fights within the Commission among the various DGs, many of which have a small slice of control over trade policymaking and agenda setting, and which guard their briefs jealously. This bureaucratic infighting weakens the overall voice of the Commission in shaping – and hampers its ability to carry out – trade policy.

Other EU institutions have also sought to check the Commission's control over trade policy and negotiations. According to Meunier, the Council has managed to hold the Commission at bay in the realm of trade policymaking (unlike in some other areas). She argues that the Council remains central in this policy domain because of its role in aggregating national preferences, which are relatively strong in an important area such as trade. In this understanding, the Commission is simply the bargaining agent of the Council: "Unlike in most policy areas falling under Community competence, ...trade policy remains one of the last bastions of sole Council legislative power. [This will not change] as long as international trade negotiations are conducted under... Article 133."[48] The EP, for its part, like the Commission has an interest in seeing control over trade policy processes trickle up to the supranational realm, but would like to impose greater legislative oversight over the Commission's activities in this realm. However, oversight is probably the best the Parliament can hope for, as, in the EU as in governments around the world, trade policymaking is typically an executive prerogative. Meanwhile, the European Court of Justice (ECJ), while it has no formal role in trade policymaking, is the arbiter of disputes among EU institutions over legal authority in policy areas. As such, it becomes relevant to trade policy if and when one institution's attempt to assert its authority in a policy gray area is challenged by another.

EU interest groups

The clearest divisions among the social, economic, and political inputs into trade policymaking are along sectoral lines. Like any other large and diversified economy, Europe's economic sectors vary in their strategic salience, international competitiveness, and level of import competition; and like any other economy, these different sectors have varying amounts of political clout in Brussels as a result of their position along these dimensions.[49] Particular sectors are notable for their voice in EU policymaking – both in external trade and internal market issues – including steel, autos, textiles, fisheries, energy, and perhaps most prominently, agriculture. For instance, the importance of the steel industry and its sensitivity to import pressures after the 1970s has led to the adoption of a range of trade measures to protect this industry from external competition, measures helped in no small part by the growing participation of steel firms in the process of developing sectoral policies (notably in the Commission).[50]

Many firms and other actors within these and other sectors are intimately involved in EU policymaking through their participation in policy networks, which are relatively decentralized and informal relationships of varying durability among sectoral representatives, national governments, and supranational institutions (again, especially the Commission).[51] These sectoral actors play a large role in developing policies that link the internal and external market aspects of EU economic policy, with internal arrangements (such as the Common Agricultural Policy, or CAP) at times providing strong bases for shaping EU positions on international trade negotiations. The involvement of interest groups in EU policy processes suits the Commission quite well: these groups provide the Commission with resources of expertise in the process of policymaking and political support in policy implementation.[52]

Not all policy networks are equal, however. The ability of various interest groups to participate in EU policy networks depends largely on "structural" factors such as the effect of the sector's market dynamics on its political position and the accessibility of the various EU policymaking institutions. With respect to market environments, Hanson identifies three features of specific markets that potentially explain the varying effects of interest group activity on EU external trade policy outcomes: sectoral attrition, sectoral internationalization, and societal countermobilization.[53] Sectoral attrition denotes that trade liberalization occurs when uncompetitive industries get so weak that they lose their political influence, as authorities react to the falling political and/or electoral costs of ignoring failing industries' demands for protection. Sectoral internationalization, for its part, focuses on the degree of and change in specific sectors' relative dependence on international markets as a proportion of their revenues, with higher export dependence being associated with greater political support for trade liberalization.[54] Societal countermobilization suggests that liberalization begets liberalization: increasing openness increases the political power of groups benefiting from liberalization, and increases their incentives to mobilize against groups demanding protection.[55]

The relative penetrability of the relevant EU institutions, for its part, helps determine which ones interest groups target. The Council is in itself not directly accessible to interest lobbies. As such, interest groups attempt to influence the Council through one of three channels: national representatives of COREPER; members of Council working groups in particular issue areas; and national governments (the main channel).[56] While national governments of course remain a major – and often sympathetic – target for lobbying, the advent of qualified majority voting in most EU external trade matters has reduced somewhat the importance of national governments in this arena. Still, the norm of consensus remains strong in the EU, although this may well change in the next few years, particularly with EU expansion.

The European Parliament, while not a central institution in trade policy-making, may become an important lobbying target if it moves to pass legislation to regulate lobbying in general. So, groups that already have well established patterns of gaining access and influencing policy may find themselves hamstrung by new lobbying rules – unless, that is, if they are able to persuade the EP to protect their position. Groups lacking access, for their part, will of course seek new rules that will level the lobbying playing field. However, the Commission remains the most important lobbying target, given both its accessibility to lobbyists and industry representatives (especially *vis-à-vis* the Council) and its paramount trade negotiating authority. Interest groups that have access to the Commission can be involved at all relevant stages of the process of policymaking and trade negotiations. Moreover, as noted above, the Commission is intimately involved in intra-EU policy networks, interacting with interest groups in a symbiotic relationship based on lobbying and information-sharing. The Commission is thus at the center of the "intermestic" politics of EU external trade relations.

The resources interest groups bring to the table are of course central to their capacity – and strategy – to affect trade policy. Greenwood suggests that interest groups can draw on the following "bargaining chips" in their attempts to influence policies: (1) information and technical expertise; (2) economic muscle; (3) industry prestige/status; (4) ability to help enforce, or alternatively to challenge, implementation of EC policies; and (5) the internal noncompetitiveness of, and coherence of decisionmaking among, individual groups in an umbrella interest association.[57] Given the complexity and indeterminacy of policymaking authority in the EU, the most successful lobbying strategies tend to be those that are "multi-level" and "multi-arena" – i.e., that focus on both national and European levels, and on various institutions at those levels.[58] This state of affairs tends to further advantage those interests that already have ample resources, which they can spread effectively across levels and arenas.[59] These resources that interest groups can draw upon are thus a major determinant of the strategies they pursue to influence EU trade policy. In the actual content of these strategies, actors typically engage in issue-framing: interest groups that are able to convince the Commission that their input is predominantly "technical" – i.e., intended to make sectoral governance more effective and/or efficient – will tend to be more effective in gaining access than those that are overtly "political" in their approach.[60]

More generally, groups seek to get themselves "insider status" – i.e., to become part of the governance structure of trade policy.[61] Interests that can make themselves "indispensable" to the functioning of a policy network – i.e., that can plausibly claim to provide a "service" that is in the broader public interest – will be able to sustain their influence over time.[62] The establishment of stable policy networks – which include, in part, well-entrenched patterns of lobbying – tends to lead to vested interests and policy inertia.[63] Of course, this is familiar: interests that have been successful in capturing the state will do whatever they can to maintain their influence and the favorable policies that their influence has brought them, regardless of the optimality of those policies for Europe as a whole.

The EU as a whole must balance the needs of these networks and their particular intra-European arrangements – which represent an important facet of European integration – with the political demands of international trade politics. While the EU is a coherent and powerful actor in trade politics, it faces a litany of trade partners and rivals that seek to gain access to the European market, access that is complicated or even denied by the EU's internal market arrangements. Particularly intense of late have been interactions with the United States, which not only seeks to break down Europe's trade barriers but also competes with Europeans for influence in and access to emerging markets in East Asia, Latin America, and elsewhere. It is this tension between internal market arrangements – which represent the workings of networks of European interests and institutions, and which enhance European economic and political integration – and the exigencies of external trade politics that represent perhaps the major axis around which European external trade policy revolves.

Notes

1. For the sake of convenience, we use the name "European Union" when referring to this European grouping throughout its post-1958 history.
2. Grossman and Helpman 1996 have suggested that there *is* an inherent market logic to region-to-region trade agreements: they help overcome free-riding among industries that passively support free-trade policies. We begin from the premise that while such a market logic may exist, interregional agreements are often driven by political and security interests rather than pure market motivations.
3. This table was originally developed in Aggarwal 2001.

4. For a good discussion of bilateral agreements, see Snyder 1940.
5. Snyder 1940.
6. This article permits the creation of free trade agreements and customs unions – but only a *broad* product basis rather than only in a few sectors.
7. For a discussion and critique of these agreements, see Aggarwal 2001 and Aggarwal and Ravenhill 2001.
8. See Yarbrough and Yarbrough 1987 for a discussion of minilateralism.
9. On regime characteristics, see Aggarwal 1985, Krasner 1977, 1983, Keohane 1984, and Aggarwal 1998. For a review of the literature on regimes, see Haggard and Simmons 1987.
10. On compliance with international regimes, see Simmons and Oudraat 2001 and the extensive cites therein.
11. For a theoretical discussion of domestic and international links affecting the EU, see Verdier and Breen 2001.
12. This hypothesis is related to the idea of policy networks: given that the networks tend to be sectoral in scope, an analysis of the strength and stability of the networks (if they exist) in any one sector is the key determinant of the propensity of trade policy in that sector to change or remain stable. However, the literature on EU policy networks is typically more interested in examining policy processes than it is in articulating explanatory or predictive frameworks. As such we do not develop a specific policy networks hypothesis here, but rather accept the networks idea as one way to describe the nature of interaction between interest groups and governing institutions. Our explanatory hypothesis regarding interest intermediation corresponds to what factors cause these networks to be stable or unstable, and thus to lead to stasis or change in EU trade policies in given sectors.
13. See Rogowski 1989, Frieden 1991, Frieden and Rogowski 1996, and Hiscox 2001 for discussions of when economic actors split along sectoral and factoral lines.
14. The key difference between this aspect of the bureaucratic politics hypothesis and the interest intermediation hypothesis is the question of who co-opts whom. In the former, the institution co-opts the interest groups; in the latter, the interest groups co-opt the institution. The differences in trade policy outcomes predicted in each case, however, may be only moderate.
15. It is worth noting that the EU as a whole, as well as its constituent institutions and national governments, retain an official preference for multilateral trade negotiations under the auspices of the GATT/WTO.
16. To some extent the advance of qualified majority voting (QMV) has already decreased the role of the Council in trade policymaking by decreasing the scope for political "blackmail" by dissenting members in the Council. As such the political battles fought among interest groups and national delegations may be fought more within the Commission than within the Council.
17. From a more sociological institutionalist perspective, it is also possible to suggest that the organizational identities of these two institutions affect their views of the value of different types of commercial policy. Specifically, the Commission is often seen as bureaucracy whose core identity – and thus the policies it proposes – is strongly influenced by technocracy, universalism, and neoliberalism. As suggested, it is not clear that the Council has an institutional identity that may have as direct an effect on the policies it favors. While this institutional-identity approach is not at the heart of our bureaucratic politics hypothesis, we consider it to be a potentially important intervening factor. For more on this approach, see Powell and DiMaggio 1991; March and Olsen 1998; and Barnett and Finnemore 1999.

18. This hypothesis differs in its predictions from those put forth in the early 1990s that identified the specter of a regionalized system featuring both economic and political competition among distinct regions (see Weber and Zysman 1992). Whereas this earlier view focused on strategic trade and industrial policies, this new "realist" hypothesis argues that trade can be both mostly free *and* strategic. In this view, the EU will thus pursue interregionalism if it is deemed a useful strategy for increasing European influence and economic security, particularly *vis-à-vis* the United States.

19. Bhagwati and Arvind 1996, quoted in Sapir 1998: 729.

20. This depiction of the international system is not intended to capture the security issues driving the international "war against terrorism." By this time it seems clear that U.S. and EU leaders have abandoned the idea of using trade policy – particularly in the Doha Round of WTO negotiations – to ameliorate the potential economic causes of terrorism in poor countries. Rather, if anything, the transatlantic rift over the 2003 war in Iraq seems likely to reinforce EU incentives to pursue international commercial arrangements that exclude the United States.

21. See Ohmae 1995.

22. According to Telo, "Region building is seen by many actors as a willingness to react to uncertainties and to compete better with other regions and economic powers." Telo 2001: 6.

23. Sapir 1998: 730.

24. See Aggarwal (1985) on nested arrangements in textile trade and (1998) for a more general discussion of nested institutions in other contexts.

25. Baker 1995.

26. See Cadot and Webber 2002, as well as Ravenhill's chapter in this volume.

27. We label this hypothesis "constructivist" even though it imputes primarily instrumental goals to European policymakers. However, it involves the mechanisms of identity formation and the ways in which trade as a form of social interaction affects these identities, themes often found in the constructivist literature.

28. Deutsch 1957, 1966. Others, notably Nicolaïdis and Howse (2002), argue that an EU identity ought not be though of in terms of a "self" and "other," but rather that there be an understanding and tolerance of diversity in identification both within Europe and between Europeans and non-Europeans.

29. Manners 2000. Other authors have sought to understand this international identity in other policy arenas – security policy (Wæver 2000), Middle East policy (Soetendorp 1999), and competition policy (Damro 2001).

30. See Prodi 2000; Kagan 2002.

31. In APEC, membership is not based on regional groupings but on economies, since Hong Kong and Taiwan hold independent membership. On APEC, see Aggarwal and Morrison 1998 and Ravenhill 2002.

32. Manners 2001: 18. See also Lamy 2002; Nicolaïdis and Howse 2002.

33. On institutional mimesis, see Powell and DiMaggio 1983.

34. However, given the EU's likely dominant relational power within specific interregional relationships, the EU could conceivably insist on labor, environmental, or other potentially contentious provisions if it considered it important to do so.

35. The United States has used bilateral agreements for such a purpose, as with the introduction of service sector issues in the Canada-U.S. Free Trade Agreement in 1988 as a prelude to pressing for agreement in the sector in the Uruguay Round.

More recently, it has included labor and environmental provisions in its bilateral agreements, again as a device to possibly influence the course of multilateral negotiations in the WTO Doha Round.

36. For a more comprehensive treatment of EU trade policymaking processes, see Nugent 1999 and Cram et al. 1999.

37. Please note that this section was written before the completion of the European constitution in 2003–04, and thus does not include any alterations in the existing legal structure of trade policy that may have been included in the constitution.

38. Nugent 1999: 441.

39. Different DGs within the Commission have authority for different regions of the world. DGI oversees commercial relations with North America, East Asia, Australia, and New Zealand; DGIA oversees Eastern Europe and the former Soviet Union; DGIB oversees the southern Mediterranean, the Middle East, Latin America, and South and Southeast Asia; and DGVIII oversees relations with ACP countries.

40. The Council granted the Commission competence in services and IPRs in 1997, but Commission agreements involving these issues must be ratified unanimously.

41. Laursen 1999.

42. Hanson 1998.

43. Nugent 1999: 445.

44. Paemen 1996, quoted in Meunier 2000.

45. Peterson 1995: 6.

46. Nugent 1999: 441.

47. Sbragia 1992.

48. Meunier 2000: 20.

49. The modes of representation in these sectors vary. In lobbying and participating in policy processes in Brussels, some firms represent themselves while others are involved in industry-wide "peak" associations. Nationally-based firms in the most significant sectors have already established Europe-wide lobbying associations that maintain a presence in Brussels. Meanwhile, some associations – notably labor organizations and chambers of commerce – organize across sectors. See Greenwood 1997 and Dupont 2001 for a discussion of these forms of interest representation.

50. Nugent 1999: 357.

51. On policy networks see Peterson 1995, and Stone Sweet and Sandholtz 1997. For a skeptical view, see Kassim 1994.

52. On this point, see Greenwood 1997 and Mazey and Richardson 1999.

53. Hanson 1998. While Hanson focuses on liberalizing policy outcomes, each of these potential explanations can be applied to the counterfactual, with the absence of the relevant conditions accounting for the presence of protectionism.

54. See Milner 1988.

55. See Rogowski 1989; Frieden 1991; Keohane and Milner 1996; Frieden and Rogowski 1996; Hiscox 2001. Indeed, Grossman and Helpman 1996 argue that pro-free trade groups will lobby governments for domestic liberalization in service of reciprocal trade agreements to facilitate their governments' acquisition of market access abroad.

56. Mazey and Richardson 1999.

57. Greenwood 1997: 18–20.

58. See in particular, Dupont 2001.

59. Mazey and Richardson 1999.
60. Greenwood 1997: 14. The generally market-friendly outcomes of EU internal market and external trade policies in the 1980s and 1990s suggest that business groups seeking liberalization might have succeeded not just in getting their way on narrow aspects of liberalization in specific sectors, but in framing the issue as one of international competitiveness. See Mazey and Richardson 1999.
61. See Streeck and Schmitter 1991.
62. Greenwood 1997: 17.
63. Peterson 1995.

References

Aggarwal, Vinod K. (1985). *Liberal Protectionism*. Berkeley: University of California Press.

Aggarwal, Vinod K., ed. (1998). *Institutional Designs for a Complex World: Bargaining, Linkages, and Nesting*. Ithaca: Cornell University Press.

Aggarwal, Vinod K. (2001). "Economics: international trade." In P. J. Simmons and Chantal de Jonge Oudraat, eds., *Managing Global Issues: Lessons Learned*. Washington, DC: Carnegie Endowment for International Peace.

Aggarwal, Vinod K. and Charles Morrison, eds. (1998). *Asia-Pacific Crossroads: Regime Creation and the Future of APEC*. New York: St. Martin's Press.

Aggarwal, Vinod K. and John Ravenhill (2001). "How open sectoral agreements undermine the WTO." *Asia-Pacific Issues* 50 (February).

Aggarwal, Vinod K. and Cedric Dupont (2002). "A Leader in Institutional Design? Europe and the Governance of Trade and Monetary Relations." *Europe and Globalization*. New York: Palgrave Macmillan: 117.

Baker, James A. (1995). "Conflict and cooperation in the post-cold war era." Speech delivered at the First Annual Conference of the James A. Baker III Institute for Public Policy, Rice University (13 November).

Barnett, Michael and Martha Finnemore (1999). "The politics, power and pathologies of international organizations." *International Organization* 53, 4 (Autumn): 699–732.

Bhagwati, J. N. and P. Arvind (1996). "Preferential trading areas and multilateralism: strangers, friends, or foes?" In J. N. Bhagwati and A. Panagariya, eds., *Free Trade Areas or Free Trade? The Economics of Preferential Trade Agreements*. Washington, DC: AEI Press.

Cadot, Olivier and Douglas Webber (2002). "Banana splits: policy process, particularistic interests, political capture, and money in transatlantic trade politics." *Business and Politics* 4, 1: 5–39.

Cram, Laura, Desmond Dinan, and Neill Nugent, eds. (1999). *Developments in the European Union*. New York: St. Martin's Press.

Cram, Laura, Desmond Dinan, and Neill Nugent (1999). "Reconciling theory and practice." In Cram et al., eds., *Developments in the European Union*. New York: St. Martin's Press.

Damro, Chad (2001). "Building an international identity: the EU and extraterritorial competition policy." *Journal of European Public Policy* 8, 2 (April): 208–226.

Deutsch, Karl et al. (1957). *Political Community: North-Atlantic Area*. New York: Greenwood Press.

Deutsch, Karl (1966). *Nationalism and Social Communication: An Inquiry into the Foundations of Nationality*. Cambridge: MIT Press.

Dupont, Cedric (2001). "Euro-pressure: avenues and strategies for lobbying the European Union." In Vinod K. Aggarwal, ed., *Winning in Asia, European Style: Market and Nonmarket Strategies for Success*. New York: Palgrave.

Frieden, Jeffry (1991). "Invested interests: the politics of national economic policies in a world of global finance." *International Organization* 45, 4 (Autumn): 425–451.

Frieden, Jeffry and Ronald Rogowski (1996). "The impact of the international economy on national policies: an analytical overview." In Robert O. Keohane and Helen Milner, eds., *Internationalization and Domestic Politics*. Cambridge: Cambridge University Press.

Greenwood, Justin (1997). *Representing Interests in the European Union*. New York: St. Martin's Press.

Grossman, G. and E. Helpman (1996). "Electoral competition and special interest politics." *Review of Economic Studies* 63: 265–286.

Haggard, Stephan and Beth Simmons (1987). "Theories of international regimes." *International Organization* 41, 3 (Summer): 491–517.

Hanson, Brian T. (1998). "What happened to fortress Europe? External trade policy liberalization in the European Union." *International Organization* 52, 1 (Winter): 55–85.

Hiscox, Michael J. (2001). "Class versus industry cleavages: inter-industry factor mobility and the politics of trade." *International Organization* 55, 1 (Winter): 1–46.

Kagan, Robert (2002). "Power and weakness." *Policy Review* 113.

Kasim, Hussein (1994). "Policy networks, networks and European Union policy-making: a skeptical view." *West European Politics* 17, 4: 15–27.

Keohane, Robert (1984). *After Hegemony: Cooperation and Discord in the World Political Economy*. Princeton: Princeton University Press.

Krasner, Stephen (1977). *Defending the National Interest*. Princeton: Princeton University Press.

Krasner, Stephen, ed. (1983). *International Regimes*. Ithaca: Cornell University Press.

Lamy, Pascal (2002). "Stepping stones or stumbling blocks? The EU's approach towards the problem of multilateralism vs. regionalism in trade policy." *World Economy* 10 (November): 1399–1413.

Laursen, Finn (1999). "Trade and aid: the European Union in the global system." In Cram et al., eds., *Developments in the European Union*. New York: St. Martin's Press.

Manners, Ian (2001). "The 'difference engine': constructing and representing the international identity in the European Union." Web paper downloaded from CIAOnet.

March, James G. and Johan P. Olsen (1998). "The institutional dynamics of international political orders." *International Organization* 52, 4 (Autumn): 943–969.

Mazey, Sonia and Jeremy Richardson (1999). "Interests." In Cram et al., eds., *Developments in the European Union*. New York: St. Martin's Press.

Meunier, Sophie (2000). "What single voice? European institutions and EU–U.S. trade negotiations." *International Organization* 54, 1 (Winter): 103–135.

Milner, Helen (1988) *Resisting Protectionism: Global Industries and the Politics of International Trade*, Princeton, NJ: Princeton University Press.

Milner, Helen and Robert Keohane (1996). *Internationalization and Domestic Politics: An Introduction*, NY: Cambridge University Press.

Nicolaïdis, Kalypso and Robert Howse (2002). "This is my EUtopia...: narrative as power." *Journal of Common Market Studies* 40, 4: 767–792.

Nugent, Neill (1999). *The Government and Politics of the European Union*, 4th edn. London: The Macmillan Press.

Ohmae, K. (1995). *The End of the Nation State: The Rise of Regional Economies*. New York: Free Press.

Peterson, John (1995). "Policy networks and European Union policymaking: a reply to Kassim." *West European Politics* 18, 2 (April): 389–407.

Powell, Walter W. and Paul J. DiMaggio, eds. (1991). *The New Institutionalism in Organizational Analysis*. Chicago: University of Chicago Press.

Powell, Walter W. and Paul J. DiMaggio (1983). "The iron cage revisited: institutional isomorphism and collective rationality in organizational fields." *American Sociological Review* 48, 2: 147–160.

Prodi, Romano (2000). *Europe As I See It*. Cambridge: Polity.

Ravenhill, John (2002). *APEC and the Construction of Pacific Rim Regionalism*. Cambridge: Cambridge University Press.

Rogowski, Ronald (1989). *Commerce and Coalitions: How Trade Affects Domestic Political Alignments*. Princeton: Princeton University Press.

Sapir, Andre (1998). "The political economy of EC regionalism." *European Economic Review* 42: 717–732.

Sbragia, Alberta, ed. (1992) *Euro-politics: Institutions and Policymaking in the "New" European Community*. Washington D.C.: The Brookings Institution.

Simmons, P. J. and Chantal de Jonge Oudraat, eds. (2001). *Managing Global Issues: Lessons Learned*. Washington, D.C.: Carnegie Endowment for International Peace.

Snyder, R. C. (1940). "The most favored nation clause and recent trade practices." *Political Science Quarterly* 55, 1: 77–97.

Soetendorp, Ben (1999). *Foreign Policy in the European Union: Theory, History and Practice*. New York: Longman.

Stone Sweet, Alec and Wayne Sandholtz (1997). "European integration and supranational governance." *Journal of European Public Policy* 4, 3 (September): 297–317.

Streeck, Wolfgang and Philippe Schmitter (1991). "From national corporatism to transnational pluralism: organized interests in the Single European Market." *Politics and Society* 19, 2: 133–164.

Telo, Mario, ed. (2001). *European Union and New Regionalism*. London: Ashgate.

Verdier, Daniel and Richard Breen (2001). "Europeanization and globalization: politics against markets in the European Union." *Comparative Political Studies* 34, 3 (April): 227–262.

Weber, S. and J. Zysman (1992). "The risk that mercantilism will define the new security system." In Wayne Sandholtz et al., *The Highest Stakes: The Economic Foundations of the Next Security System*. New York: Oxford University Press, 167–196.

Wæver, Ole (2000). "Insecurity, security, and asecurity in the West European nonwar community." In Emmanuel Adler and Michael Barnett, eds., *Security Communities*. Cambridge: Cambridge University Press.

Yarbrough, B. and R. Yarbrough (1987). "Cooperation in the liberalization of international trade: after hegemony, what?" *International Organization* 41, 1 (Winter): 13–26.

2
Blueprint for an Interregional Future? The European Union and the Southern Cone

Jörg Faust

1 Introduction

The countries of Latin America and those of the European Union share a long tradition of intensive economic, political, and cultural relations. Driven by political crises in Central America and debt problems in the Latin American subcontinent, since the late 1970s political relations have been increasingly accompanied by an interregional political dialogue between the European Union and Latin American cooperation and concertation mechanisms.

The creation of MERCOSUR in 1991 favored the EU's preference for dealing with groups of countries rather than with individual countries on a purely bilateral basis. Paralleling increasing economic interaction between the EU and MERCOSUR, political actors from both regions started to build the necessary institutional framework for negotiating encompassing trade liberalization between the two integration schemes.[1] Within this context, a major step toward the beginning of official trade negotiations occurred in December 1995. On the same day that MERCOSUR officially converted itself from a free trade area to a customs union, the European Commission (EC), EU member states, and MERCOSUR members – Brazil, Argentina, Uruguay, and Paraguay – signed the EU–MERCOSUR Interregional Framework for Cooperation Agreement (EMIFCA). EMIFCA functions as a framework agreement for an interregional association agreement that is to ultimately include all aspects of trade liberalization as well as strengthened forms of political dialogue and cooperation.

Four years later, in 1999, the EC finally obtained authorization from member states to start official negotiations on tariff liberalization. Once this process was initiated, during their 2002 Madrid summit governments of both mechanisms again reasserted their commitment to successfully concluding such an agreement. Yet, both sides still confront major obstacles, especially with regard to liberalization in the agro-industrial sector.

Interregional relations between the European Union and MERCOSUR reflect a general trend of governments and firms to institutionalize their relations not only within but also across regions. Against this background, the following analysis focuses on the institutional development of EU–MERCOSUR relations and the driving forces behind this development from a European perspective. The EU and MERCOSUR are perhaps the two most ambitious regional integration mechanisms in the world, and thus an examination of their relationship – the best example among those in this volume of "pure interregionalism" – should provide unique insight into the forces shaping interregional commercial relations.[2] Rather than trying to explain the course of EU–MERCOSUR relations by one dominant hypothesis, I make an appeal for a multi-causal framework, highlighting three aspects of particular importance among those outlined by Aggarwal and Fogarty in the introduction to this volume.

First, one can observe that the interplay of economic interest groups has strongly influenced the course of interregional institutionalization between the EU and MERCOSUR. Even if a trade agreement creates an overall benefit for both mechanisms, economic gains and losses will be distributed unequally among economic actors. As such, potential winners and losers have attempted to influence the course of negotiations in order to serve their particular interests. From a European perspective, trade liberalization would be costly for the agro-industrial sector because of Brazil and Argentina's competitiveness in this highly protected market. By contrast, the steady upsurge of investment and exports from Europe to the Southern Cone of the Americas has increased the interest of more advanced and internationally competitive industrial sectors for deeper institutionalization of economic relations. This conflict among the interests of pro-free trade industries and the agricultural sector has shaped the course of interregional institutionalization.

Second, political actors have not acted as mere agents of private interest but also have followed their own political agendas. Therefore, the interplay among private interests is nested within a broader power game within the institutional framework of the EU, the European Commission and the European Council being the major players. In general, the EC has favored increasing trade liberalization more than the Council, because an interregional association agreement not only offers a vast array of bureaucratic opportunities for the EC but also gives it leverage for pushing its reform agenda with respect to the internal development of the European Union. Furthermore, protectionist interests in general have found a better reception within the Council, which is not only sceptical about enhancing the EC's responsibilities but also responds much more strongly to protectionist groups with electoral influence.

Third, the European Union's interregional trade strategy towards MERCOSUR has not been independent of the international context. Rather than treating private and political actors as the only relevant players, the EU as a collective actor is also firmly embedded in an international context that demands collective action toward collective challenges. Therefore, the EU's trade strategy toward MERCOSUR can also be interpreted as a response to growing American influence in the Cono Sur area. Contesting U.S. dominance in economic affairs, however, is not only about the size of market shares in MERCOSUR. By promoting its ideas of regionalism and interregional relations, the EU is also engaged in a competition about the institutional organization of economic cooperation within a globalizing world economy. Thus, the political interest of the European Union in building a deeply institutionalized relationship with MERCOSUR and helping MERCOSUR to augment its coherence is closely connected to the EU's normative ideas of how a new world order should be constructed.

In order to fully develop these arguments about the driving factors of the EU's trade strategy towards MERCOSUR, the analysis is organized as follows. To provide an empirical basis, in section two I describe the institutional development and the economic relations between the EU and MERCOSUR. Section three highlights some key elements of EMIFCA that are of primary interest in this book. Based on the given empirical information, section four explores the intra-EU bargaining process among private and public actors and connects these internal processes with the influences stemming from the international context. Section five outlines my conclusions regarding the primary causal factors in shaping the evolution of the EU–MERCOSUR interregional regime.

2 An overview of EU–MERCOSUR relations

The process of interregional institutionalization

With the creation of MERCOSUR in 1991, the new democracies of Cono Sur (with the exception of Chile) started an ambitious integration scheme. Member countries have been aiming not only to establish a free trade area but also to create a common market. During the first half of the 1990s, MERCOSUR was the most promising integration scheme of the developing world. Yet a less favorable political and economic environment for implementation of a free trade area and, ultimately, a customs union prevailed during the second half of the 1990s. The Tequila effect of 1995, the Asian Crisis, the devaluation in Brazil, and the acute recession in Argentina confronted the ambitious timetable with several internal and external challenges. However, despite these rising difficulties, most international observers have continued to perceive MERCOSUR as a viable means to strengthen economic development and political cooperation in the Southern Cone.[3] In general, such a perception also has been shared by the European political and administrative elite dealing with the external affairs of the European Union. Consequently, even if interregional relations with North America and the task of integrating some of the transition economies in Eastern Europe have remained on top of the EU's foreign economic policy agenda, the EU continues to favor and support the integration process in the Southern Cone. Notwithstanding the current difficulties of MERCOSUR, the development of institutional linkages with MERCOSUR has led to a unique form of interregional institutionalization.[4]

Only three days after signing the Asunción Treaty, foreign ministers of the MERCOSUR member-states visited the European Commission, resulting in the first signals of a future interregional cooperation agreement.[5] Already less than one year after the establishment of MERCOSUR, the European Commission signed an Inter-Institutional Agreement to provide technical and financial support for institution building in MERCOSUR. Even if this kind of cooperation agreement did not aim at trade liberalization, it did demonstrate the willingness of the EU to commit itself to concrete interregional institution building.

In 1994, the European Council decided to strengthen the institutional linkages with MERCOSUR and asked the Commission to provide an analysis of the feasibility of further interregional institutionalization. In December 1994, based on this analysis, the Council, the EC, and MERCOSUR governments agreed to negotiate an interregional framework agreement. Such a framework agreement was to define and structure the relevant policy fields of future interregional institutionalization. The main idea was to build the institutional platform for an interregional association agreement. After two rounds of negotiations in Brussels and Montevideo, the Commission presented a proposal to the European Council containing the framework agreement, EMIFCA. EMIFCA, signed in 1995 by the Council's members and the four presidents of MERCOSUR member states, underlined the EU's continued political commitment to fostering regional integration in the Southern Cone. Besides strengthening technical assistance and political dialogue, EMIFCA also formally stated the interest of both regional organizations in beginning serious talks on broad trade liberalization. EMIFCA's core function therefore has consisted of setting out the institutional framework for negotiating an interregional association, including liberalization of all trade in goods and services in conformity with WTO rules.

EMIFCA covered more than conventional trade in goods, focusing as well on investment, property rights, and liberalization in services, and including several aspects of purely political cooperation. Consequently, EMIFCA was classified a mixed agreement, requiring ratification by the European Parliament and by each member parliament. This ratification process lasted almost four years, so that EMIFCA acquired formal status as an interregional agreement only in July 1999. Parallel to the parliamentary process of ratification, the European Commission needed to obtain a negotiation

INCOTERMS
HELPS TO REDUCE NEGOTIATION PERIODS

mandate for officially starting negotiations on trade liberalization. Between 1995 and 1998, both blocs conducted several trade studies and concluded an agreement on statistical cooperation in 1997. Additionally, the EC began to informally negotiate possible courses of official trade negotiations with MERCOSUR members. In July 1998, the EC finally presented a proposal for a negotiation mandate to the Council, accompanied by an impact study analysing the possible consequences of trade liberalization with MER-COSUR. Finally, in September 1999, the European Council officially gave the negotiation mandate to the EC. The Council's decision was based on a political compromise reached by the EU ministers in Luxembourg in June of the same year, followed by a declaration by the heads of state of both integration mechanisms during the Rio Summit one week later.

However, the directive contained major deviations from the original proposal, which can be interpreted as signs of conflict among EU member states about the course of EU–MERCOSUR relations. First, the mandate allowed the EC to start negotiations on tariffs only from July 2001, meanwhile holding a dialogue about tariffs, services, and agriculture. Yet, the directive enabled the EC to start official negotiations on all trade issues connected with non-tariff barriers in 1999.[6] Second, the directive stipulated that trade negotiations may only be concluded after the end of the next WTO round. Linking the success of a trade agreement to progress at the WTO level has also been interpreted as a sign of heterogeneous interests within the Council. A third point regarded by some authors as a barrier for serious liberalization is that even the term "free trade area" was deleted from the final text of the directive.[7] However, as MERCOSUR and European member states are committed to WTO conformity, Article 24 of the GATT implies that a preferential agreement between both blocs should include all sectors and more than 90 percent of all products.[8]

Official trade negotiations between the two regions started in November 1999 in Madrid. At this initial stage, the Cooperation Council of EMIFCA tried to define the structure, methods, and timetable for further negotiations, and furthermore, created a Biregional Negotiation Committee. Additionally, a Subcommittee on Cooperation was established encompassing senior officials from the EC and the MERCOSUR members. While the abovementioned groups have been responsible for all issues involved in EMIFCA, the Biregional Negotiation Committee has been given the right to establish working groups responsible for working on the "technical" issues of economic liberalization.[9] With regard to the method of negotiation, the Cooperation Council of EMIFCA decided to commit itself to the principle of "single undertaking," meaning that negotiations on one topic may only be concluded when there is agreement in all policy fields involved in EMIFCA.[10]

After the negotiating mandate was finally approved and priority decisions were made about the structure, method, and timetable for further negotiations, several negotiation rounds took place between 2000 and 2002. While until July 2001 negotiations were restricted to the area of non-tariff barriers, the major issues during this period were concerned with setting up the specific technical groups, identifying non-tariff obstacles, and exchanging the technical data of trade and investment. As the progress of negotiations was slow, many observers remained doubtful that the EU would present a concrete proposal in July 2001. Much to the surprise of these sceptics, on the fifth round of negotiation in July 2001, the EC formally offered a concrete negotiation proposal for reducing trade barriers with regard to sectors of different sensitivity. Even though this proposal included almost 90 percent of all products and had several interesting aspects relating to the reduction of quantitative restrictions in the agricultural sector, MERCOSUR members qualified it as unacceptable because it did not offer a substantial removal of trade barriers in the agro-industrial sectors.[11] MERCOSUR's counter-proposal in October 2001, however, included less than 40 percent of all traded goods, thus being unacceptable to the EU because it failed to comply with WTO guidelines. Despite these differences, both sides were able to improve their proposals by the end of 2002, with the MERCOSUR offer being only slightly under the 90 percent margin.

Taken together, the course of EU–MERCOSUR institutionalization allows a division of the process into five stages. The first stage covers the period 1992–1994, with the agreement on technical assistance to foster the integration process in the Cono Sur area. The second stage covers 1994–1995, when the EU decided to commit itself to the establishment of EMIFCA. This step was a major shift in a qualitative sense, since EMIFCA implied the creation of an interregional association containing institutionalization in several important policy-fields including substantial trade liberalization. The third stage was the process of ratification and political bargaining around a negotiation directive for the EC. This process took almost four years, reflecting conflicts among actors involved in the European decisionmaking process. The fourth stage began in September 1999, when the EC obtained formal authorization for trade negotiations, and lasted until 2001. This period was characterized by formal activity but rather slow progress in substance regarding trade negotiations. A fifth stage began in 2001, when both sides began to present official proposals on tariff reductions. While the second proposals presented at the end of 2002 have undoubtedly improved, there is still no consensus on the most sensitive issues. In summary, there can be no doubt that the progress of trade negotiations has been very slow, with the sensitive agro-industrial issues still unresolved. However, there also can be no doubt that this process has been progressive in the sense that an evolution from non-trade cooperation to serious and formalized bargaining is observable.

shipping (cash-blood)

Economic relations between the EU and MERCOSUR

As the evolution of trade and investment flows between the two regions shapes the preferences of economic and political actors, it is necessary to highlight the dynamics of EU–MERCOSUR economic relations. With regard to trade flows, recent analysis has distinguished several points of interest.[12] The most striking aspect has been a substantial increase in trade in the 1990s followed by a period of only modest increase, due to the economic difficulties of the MERCOSUR economies (see Table 2.1). Between 1990 and 1998, the relative growth of interregional trade exceeded EU trade growth rates with all other regions and almost doubled the growth rate of global trade expansion. In the late 1990s, the EU was the most important trading partner for MERCOSUR. For the European Union, even if the relative importance of MERCOSUR as a trading partner has been very modest, it is remarkable that the relative importance of MERCOSUR almost doubled during the 1990s, exceeding its 1980 level, when neither Eastern Europe nor the Asia–Pacific were as attractive alternatives for expanding EU trade as they are today.

The evolution of total trade between both regions during the 1990s was highly favorable for the European Union. During most of the eighties, MERCOSUR countries had a surplus with the EU. But the 1990's saw rising MERCOSUR deficits – that is, until the macroeconomic problems in Argentina and Brazil caused a decline in the growth rates of EU exports, thereby substantially diminishing the EU's trade surplus with MERCOSUR.

The trade structure of EU–MERCOSUR commerce shows a rather typical pattern of North–South relations, in which low value-added products have characterized MERCOSUR exports. MERCOSUR has mainly exported raw materials and commodities from the agro-industrial sectors, accounting for more than 50 percent of total EU imports from MERCOSUR.[13] In contrast, EU exports to MERCOSUR have been more concentrated in technology intensive manufactured goods. Intra-industrial trade is still low.[14] With regard to the service sector, interregional trade has also been characterized by a surplus on the part of the EU, yet despite dynamic growth rates, EU

Table 2.1   Growth of trade flows: EU and MERCOSUR

	To/from MERCOSUR	To/from EU	To/from Extra Region	To/from World
MERCOSUR				
Exports	16.9	4.0	4.9	6.4
Imports	16.4	13.6	11.5	12.3
European Union				
Exports	13.0	5.8	7.0	6.1
Imports	3.4	5.4	7.0	5.9

Source: Giordano 2003: 13

service exports to MERCOSUR represent only a marginal amount of EU's worldwide exports in services.[15]

The existing trade structure is closely linked to protectionist measures of both blocs, which have revealed a clear divide with regard to each region's comparative advantages.[16] Besides facing strong tariff and quantitative barriers in the agro-industrial sector and semi-finished manufactured products, MERCOSUR economies have also been facing serious non-tariff barriers, such as phytosanitary standards and antidumping measures.[17] In contrast, even if MERCOSUR members have been liberalizing trade, protectionist measures are still concentrated in the manufacturing sector and consist mainly of tariff barriers.[18] The government of Brazil, by far the most important economy of MERCOSUR, appears to be especially interested in a rather slow liberalization process, since its large industrial sector would have to pay the highest cost of trade liberalization.

Against this background, increasing interregional market access through trade liberalization is expected to foster trade in those sectors in which the respective economies have comparative advantages. As Estevadeordal and Krivonos have observed, for the EU these advantages are located in sectors such as chemicals, plastic products, machinery, and transport equipment.[19] MERCOSUR economies would profit in the agricultural and fisheries sectors, foods, leather products, mining, and, in the case of Brazil, in rubber, iron, and steel manufacturing. Even if the dynamic effects of interregional trade liberalization might lead to a higher degree of competitiveness in some manufacturing sectors in MERCOSUR, agricultural exports will keep their predominant role and the composition of trade is unlikely to change dramatically.

As in the case of trade, European direct investment in MERCOSUR had been gaining momentum during the 1990s, when MERCOSUR was one of the most attractive areas for FDI in the developing world.[20] The increase in European FDI to MERCOSUR during the 1990s was mainly due to the economic reforms within MERCOSUR countries and the specific integration efforts of MERCOSUR itself.[21] During the first half of the 1990s, in comparison to Brazil, Argentina experienced a huge inflow of European FDI due to the neoliberal policies of the Menem government. The situation changed in the second half of the 1990s when FDI in Brazil became significantly stronger because of the government's successful attempts at implementing privatization and deregulation programs. As Nunnenkamp notes:

> it was mainly Brazil that suffered a seriously impaired attractiveness in the early 1990s. Brazil's share recovered precisely when it joined its neighbours in implementing economic policy reforms related to macroeconomic stabilization and structural adjustment.[22]

With regard to the composition and the source of European FDI, major changes took place during the 1990s. While traditionally European FDI was concentrated in the secondary sector, in the 1990s, flows of European FDI were largely concentrated in the services sector.[23] FDI in financial services, telecommunications, infrastructure, and energy was mainly linked to privatization programmes in the MERCOSUR countries and materialized in mergers and acquisitions. In this context, traditional European investor countries lost relative weight, while especially Spain, and to some extent Portugal, the Netherlands, and France grew more important.[24]

Besides domestic reforms, the integration scheme of MERCOSUR had an impact on European FDI. Because MERCOSUR has focused primarily on intraregional economic relations, the speed of trade liberalization within MERCOSUR has been faster than that of external tariff liberalization. The consequence of this discriminatory construction was that investors in MERCO-SUR during the 1990s mainly applied market-seeking strategies. This trend differs notably from investment activities in Mexico, where NAFTA allowed foreign investors to pursue efficiency-seeking strategies oriented towards the establishment of global production and distribution networks.[25] In contrast, production systems in MERCOSUR have largely been confined to the sub-region.[26] Thus, European FDI in MERCOSUR has been primarily oriented toward overcoming market barriers instead of making use of special MERCO-SUR advantages with regard to more globally oriented production networks. On the one hand, this development leads to the conclusion that European investors in MERCOSUR would only profit from trade liberalization in a limited way, since the connection with global production networks is relatively restricted. On the other hand, one might expect that with the extensive market experience many European companies have in the Cono Sur, they have probably foreseen the possibility of changing their strategies from market-seeking to efficiency-seeking in the case of interregional trade liberalization. Especially in some service sectors and in the automobile, chemical, and petrochemical industries (which have a relatively high degree of intra-industrial trade), European firms have shown clear signs of interest in interregional trade liberalization. As these companies perceive the limitations of the Cono Sur markets and are confronted with global or European restructuring of their own industries, they are interested in increasing their efficiency-seeking investments in MERCOSUR. Such a change, however, requires trade liberalization as a prerequisite to steer forthcoming FDI towards more globally oriented production networks.

3   Characterizing EU–MERCOSUR regime-building

EU–MERCOSUR relations are one of the few cases of "pure interregionalism." This characterization seems to be appropriate, even if MERCOSUR's customs union is still far from being fully implemented. Despite the return of trade conflicts within MERCOSUR beginning in the difficult years of the late 1990s, MERCOSUR governments have not reversed their aim of proceeding with the implementation of a customs union. The successful conclusion of an interregional free trade agreement could even foster the full implementation of a customs union, since such an agreement would require MERCOSUR members to implement a common tariff structure according to the timetable of interregional trade liberalization.

Besides being minilateral and geographically dispersed, the process of EU–MERCOSUR trade liberalization has to be classified as a liberally oriented attempt at creating an encompassing trade regime. In contrast to sector-specific liberalization, negotiations between the EU and MERCOSUR aim at trade liberalization on a broad product basis according to Article 24 of the GATT. With regard to the strength of EU–MERCOSUR institutionalization, the process has moved toward creating a strong and highly institutionalized international regime. While the organizational structure of EU–MERCOSUR relations does not include a secretariat, it still has to be considered relatively strong because of its well-defined working structure in all relevant policy-issues included in EMIFCA. Compared to other cases of interregionalism, the negotiation process is committed to create a set of strong and binding rules. With respect to trade liberalization, an interregional association agreement would not only constrain actors' behavior but also include mechanisms of dispute settlement.

The issue scope of EU–MERCOSUR regime-building is broad. Not only do negotiations focus on encompassing trade liberalization – including competition policy, government procurement, intellectual property rights, and liberalization in services – but an interregional association agreement would also comprise a broader political dialogue, with aid being of special importance. As it is an explicit strategy of the European Union to foster regional cooperation and integration among developing countries, there is also a quasi-developmental focus of the EU's posture towards MERCOSUR. In fact, the intraregional threats to MERCOSUR's coherence in the last years have been counterbalanced to some extent by its external agenda – especially the need to find a common position with regard to the EU, which made it clear that it was unwilling to negotiate on a bilateral basis with individual MERCOSUR countries. Consequently, with the exception of some minor issues in the area of non-tariff trade barriers, the EU's commercial treatment of MERCOSUR has been characterized by a high degree of uniformity, meaning that all MERCOSUR member countries receive similar treatment.

4   Private interests, intra-European politics, and the international context

The impact of free-trade-oriented and protectionist interests

The development of interregional economic relations between the EU and MERCOSUR offers strong evidence that the slow course of trade institutionalization between the two in part can be traced back to conflicts among economic interest groups.[27] From this perspective, interest groups have lobbied for an "insider status" in the decisionmaking process, thus becoming part of the governance structure and increasing their influence on the policy process.[28]

As attempts at advancing the global trading regime have borne little fruit in recent years, internationally competitive actors continue to struggle for interregional liberalization as a second-best strategy. They hope to take advantage of their own competitive position by penetrating previously closed international markets. By contrast, sectors that rely on the EU's protection, notably agriculture, have lobbied against an interregional agreement with MERCOSUR and its highly competitive agro-industrial branches. Instead, they prefer selected bilateral agreements with small countries such as Chile or countries with less sector competitiveness such as Mexico.[29] Bilateral agreements allow these protected sectors to maximize the asymmetries in the Union's bargaining power *vis-à-vis* smaller countries, thereby shielding their rents. The disagreements surrounding EU–MERCOSUR negotiations reflect a separation between economic interests in favor of trade liberalization with MERCOSUR and protectionist agro-industrial interest groups.[30]

Between 1991 and 1993, the issue of negotiating a trade agreement was not on the EU–MERCOSUR agenda. Consequently, lobbying was relatively limited. It started only in 1994, when the EU decided to commit itself to the establishment of EMIFCA. The European Farmers Federation (COPA) and national farmers associations pressured the Council and the EC not to commit themselves to the issue any longer. Lobbying against an agreement intensified after the signing of EMIFCA in 1995 and concentrated especially on the Commission's request for a negotiation mandate. The major argument of agricultural interest groups against such a mandate had been that an engagement in concrete negotiations would have overloaded the EU agenda with respect to the pending reform of the Common Agricultural Policy (CAP), the issue of expanding the EU to the east, and the fiscal discipline imposed by the monetary union.[31] This lobbying against a trade agreement with MERCOSUR has been persistent, and provides a credible explanation for the deliberateness of the EU's progress toward negotiating a free-trade agreement with MERCOSUR.

In contrast, more globally oriented European industries as well as the services sector would be beneficiaries of an agreement with MERCOSUR. Trade liberalization would provide those industries with better market access and enable them to reorient their investment strategies within MERCOSUR toward more globally integrated chains of production. Since the late 1990s, those pro-free trade actors have started to develop collective action capacities to push the EU toward interregional trade liberalization. The strongest evidence of such endeavours has been the creation of the MERCOSUR–Europe Business Forum (MEBF) in 1999. As a result of an initiative by the then-president of the Federation of German Industries, the MEBF, similar to the Transatlantic Business Dialogue, has aimed at pronouncing business interests involved in EU–MERCOSUR relations.[32] The motivation to create the MEBF was to join important, pro-free trade oriented business leaders instead of business federations with rather mixed motives regarding trade liberalization. As such, MEBF was strongly in favor of giving a negotiation mandate to the Commission. This demand was successfully channelled to the Council through MEBF's connections to the German government, which chaired the EU and had to organize the European part of the 1999 Rio summit.[33]

While the MEBF had a strong impact on the decision to give a negotiation mandate to the Commission and has made initiatives in the field of trade facilitation, its recent impact on the course of negotiations has been rather modest. With the beginning of concrete negotiations, different sector-specific positions within MEBF became more prominent and the forum's coherence diminished because of the short-term interests of MERCOSUR participants, which were facing domestic turbulence. While in the service and investment working groups the consensus on liberalization is still obvious, the market-access working group has been more divided. Therefore, on the one hand, the creation of a specific organization like MEBF has increased the capability of pro-free-trade oriented businesses to articulate their interests. On the other hand, after a mandate was given to the Commission and official negotiations started, collective action problems among pro-free-trade industries have increased. As negotiations about timetables for liberalization, exemptions clauses, and the like have become more concrete, specific concerns about possible trade deviation and restructuring of production processes have divided the heterogeneous group of pro-free-trade interests.

The Council, the Commission, and the international context

The focus on the interplay of economic interests highlights an important causal mechanism that explains the slow progress of trade negotiations.[34] However, a purely interest group-oriented approach ignores the influence of political actors and the institutional framework within the European Union. As such, leaving the constellation of political actors and the rules of EU policymaking unexplored would prove inadequate for explaining as complex a phenomenon as interregional commercial relationships.

The Commission has strong incentives to push further trade liberalization with MERCOSUR for two reasons. First, the EC could use interregional trade liberalization with MERCOSUR to expand its influence by pushing the EU into complex issue areas where bureaucratic expertise is needed. Secondly, trade liberalization with MERCOSUR would result in additional pressures on national governments and the Council to engage more profoundly in reforming the CAP. Thus, by advancing interregional trade liberalization, the Commission enhances its influence on urgently needed domestic reforms within the EU. In this context, allowing the involvement of pro-free-trade interest groups while excluding more protectionist ones from the decisionmaking process has been considered a strategy to provide the Commission with relevant information to pursue its own interest.[35]

However, the Council is generally more sceptical about Commission-endorsed trade liberalization, since it is interested in constraining the Commission's autonomy. National governments tend to attach more importance to protectionist interest groups and non-competitive industries for electoral reasons. However, it would be overstretching the argument to assume that the interplay between Commission and Council is merely defined by conflicting interests. Neither is the Council purely "protectionist," nor is the Commission a purely neoliberal free trade proponent. For instance, the Commission's free-trade approach may be hampered by intra-bureaucratic conflicts or by commissioners' devotion to their national career paths. The Council, well aware of domestic and external reform pressures confronting the Union, can also pursue liberalization measures if national governments successfully burden the EC with the responsibility of painful reforms.[36]

Furthermore, neither the Council nor the Commission are purely inward-oriented. Rather, their trade strategies also respond to international challenges. In a context of growing global economic interdependence, they have to consider the changing international environment, especially the development of the global trade regime and the international trade policies of the United States, their most important economic partner and competitor in international economic affairs. Thus, the Council and the Commission can join forces when it comes to adapting the EU's external relations to a changing international context. In such a case, the EU can be treated analytically as a unitary actor, which pursues the external goals of private and political interests. Supporting the objectives of Europe's international economic actors consists of expanding and protecting these actors' (privileged) reach to promising markets.

But while the EU's pursuit of closer ties with MERCOSUR is certainly consistent with its interest in improving its position in the international system, the EU has been notably respectful of the need to make EMIFCA consistent with existing – and future – global trade rules. Two examples demonstrate the influence of nesting considerations. First, the EU and MERCOSUR made a concerted effort over time to reach the threshold for the proposed free–trade area to cover substantially all products, with the 90 percent figure pushing the two sides to expand the terms of the arrangement – despite the obstacles (especially among wary European sectors) to reaching this breadth. Second, the EU tied final approval of the terms of trade liberalization within the interregional relationship to the

INCOTERMS
COULD AVOID
THAT

conclusion of the Doha Development Round, reinforcing the idea that WTO-consistency was an overarching consideration.

Furthermore, political actors of the European Union are interested in "exporting" their institutional environments to other parts of the world. As such, those interests are particularly linked to normative conceptions of liberal democracy, liberal economic governance, and regional cooperation as an institutional framework of international cooperation. Indeed, the EU and the United States pursue similar interests with regard to the promotion of liberal democracy and market economics. However, when it comes to fostering the interests of their internationally oriented firms and the export of specific modes of economic regulation and regional cooperation, they are competing providers on the "international market" of goods and institutions. Furthermore, the normative connotations connected to regional cooperation and integration tend to differentiate the EU's external policies from those of the United States. As such, the EU's interregional strategies tend to be more encompassing with regard to issue scope and give more importance to fostering regional cooperation in counterpart regions.

The Council's 1994 request to the Commission to study the feasibility of further interregional institutional-building with MERCOSUR contrasted with the typical perception of the Council as a primarily protection-oriented institution. In this act the Council was responding to international developments; protectionist lobbying had not yet started when the request was made. Accelerating American efforts to explore preferential agreements with other countries and regions – such as the successful conclusion of NAFTA, the free trade initiative within APEC, and the prospect of advancing the Initiative of the Americas – were threats to European economic and political interests. MERCOSUR, meanwhile, was perceived as the most promising integration scheme in the Southern hemisphere. With its European-style integration approach and advance of democratic and economic reforms, MERCOSUR was perceived as an attractive regional partner to counterbalance U.S. transregional activities.[37] Accordingly, the Council and the Commission worked together to achieve an agreement with MERCOSUR governments on negotiating an interregional framework agreement. The next step towards interregional trade liberalization also took place in a relatively short period, as EMIFCA was signed later in 1995. It was a unified EU that responded to an evolving international political-economic system, moving rapidly to establish the initial interregional framework.

However, the complex agenda of EMIFCA opened up space for interest groups to lobby against trade liberalization. Since EMIFCA had to be ratified by all member states, protectionist interests that had become aware of EMIFCA's content slowed down the ratification process. In general, the Commission's defense of EMIFCA during this period is in line with the argument stating that the EC is rather pro-free-trade oriented. Even though the EC had requested a negotiation mandate from the Council in 1998, this decision was not adopted unanimously. Four commissioners voted against such a request, demonstrating how, once the initial framework was adopted, intra-European struggles among institutions and interest groups prevented the EC from acting collectively as they had previously.[38]

The 1999 directive of the Council, which enabled the EC to restart official trade negotiations, can at first sight be interpreted as working against the assumption of the protectionist nature of this institution. However, the conflict in the making of this decision reveals the influence of protectionist interests.[39] Ministers hailing from the agricultural secretaries of France, Ireland, and the Netherlands opposed the directive.[40] In contrast, the governments of Germany, Italy, Portugal, and Spain strongly supported a mandate for the Commission.[41] The political compromise reached in Luxembourg included major changes from the original proposal into the mandate: allowing the EC to start negotiations on tariffs only in July 2001 and the conclusion of negotiations only after the end of the next WTO round. These amendments to the directive suggest that agricultural interests were particularly influential in slowing down the process via their influence on the Council.[42]

This argument is further sustained by the fact that international pressures on quickly crafting an interregional agreement had diminished at the end of the 1990s. The U.S. government had not succeeded in transforming APEC into a highly institutionalized trade regime, nor was it able to acquire the necessary Trade Promotion Authority from Congress to advance FTAA negotiations.[43] Additionally, a mandate was given before the WTO meeting in Seattle in 1999, which was expected to initiate a new WTO round. In this context, neither the EU nor MERCOSUR members were keen on committing themselves to an interregional agreement without knowing the outcome of the Seattle results, which were expected to have had far-reaching consequences for their overall trade strategies.[44]

In 2000–2002, the rift between Council and Commission became even more obvious. On the one hand, the EC surprisingly offered a concrete proposal to MERCOSUR in July 2001, thereby initiating a series of interregional negotiations rounds. At the same time, however, the Council ceased to push the agenda of EU–MERCOSUR, even as the European Parliament urged the Council to put more emphasis on the successful conclusion of an agreement. This passive attitude can best be explained by the existence of domestic issues diverting the Council's attention from EU–MERCOSUR relations and the absence of international factors pushing the interregional institutionalization process. With regard to the domestic issues, despite the European Agreements in Nice, major EU members' positions were still unclear on the future course of the CAP and the EU's expansion towards the east. In combination with elections in Spain,

[handwritten: about of world trade so if 1 falls other fall too]

France, and Germany during 2001 and 2002, the sensitive issues of trade liberalization in agriculture with MERCOSUR have almost disappeared from the Council's external agenda.

The Council's passive posture has been facilitated by the international context. First, the vanishing coherence of MERCOSUR, which has been buffeted by the Argentinean recession, has hurt the bloc's capacity to pursue negotiations with the EU. While the MERCOSUR is surely a self-defined region aiming for a high degree of intraregional institutionalization, its coherence has diminished since the beginning of Brazil's currency crisis in 1998 and it has faced its most serious crisis as monetary inconsistencies within the region were aggravated by the Argentinean recession and financial collapse. As intraregional trade as well as intraregional institution-building suffered severely from this crisis, it became uncertain during 2001–2002 whether MERCOSUR would survive its member countries' economic and political turmoil. Furthermore, the negative economic picture in the Southern Cone has made the Brazilian government in particular even more cautious with regard to further extraregional trade liberalization. Second, until August 2002 the U.S. government had been unable to obtain Trade Promotion Authority from Congress, which was a necessary precursor to beginning serious negotiations in the FTAA process. The absence of TPA diminished the external pressure on the European Council to respond to U.S. advances in the region.

More recent events continue the general pattern. First of all, the Bush Administration's acquisition of fast track authority has renewed pressure on the EU for a stronger commitment to interregional trade liberalization. Second, the disappointing course of the global trade regime has made it necessary to pursue "second-best-strategies" to expand the Union's international influence. Third, President Lula of Brazil has shown greater enthusiasm for partnership with his immediate neighbors than with the United States, which has been a boon for MERCOSUR's coherence and has called into question the existing timetables for the FTAA process. The renewed commitment to advancing EU–MERCOSUR trade negotiations in this changing environment is reflected by the improved proposal made by both parties in the late 2002 negotiation round.

4   Conclusion

The expanding institutionalization of the relationship between the European Union and MERCOSUR is one of the few cases of pure interregionalism. Within this context, the ongoing process of trade liberalization between both blocs has been the most important and at the same the time most controversial issue in a broad interregional agenda. The evidence demonstrates that there is no single variable with sufficient explanatory power to clarify the course of EU–MERCOSUR trade relations. Therefore, an adequate explanation of this case study of economic interregionalism has been to appeal for a multi-causal research strategy.

From a bottom-up perspective, societal pressures from economic interests have influenced the process of EU policymaking. As the trade structure between both regions follows a rather traditional path of North–South relations, the most obvious conflicting interests exist between free-trade-oriented industries and agricultural interests within the EU. Both have been trying to build up collective action capacities and to become indispensable parts of the policy process to influence political decisionmaking according to their interests. As the course of EU–MERCOSUR negotiations has demonstrated, agricultural interests are still strong, yet they could not prevent EU decisionmakers from committing themselves to formal negotiations with their MERCOSUR counterparts. Thus even if intra-industrial trade between both regions has been low, the course of interregional negotiations has slowly gravitated toward the interests of pro-free-trade business. Internationally oriented firms from industry and services have attempted to overcome collective action problems by creating an organization to promote their interests. The establishment of MEBF and its influence on the Council's decision to give a negotiation mandate to the Commission strongly suggests that pro-free-trade interests have become an integrative part of the EU–MERCOSUR policy-network, even if there coherence diminished after concrete negotiations started.

The specific institutions of the EU policymaking process and the interplay between the most important bodies of the EU's external trade policy have filtered these impacts of societal interests. Even if the Commission has not always been either unitary or consistent in the course of the policy process, it has been the body that has pushed interregional trade liberalization more thoroughly. This behavior is consistent with the argument that the EC has an interest in expanding the Union's interregional trade policies as a means of increasing its influence within the EU. However, the influence of protectionist interests, especially through the Council, has made it more difficult for the EC to use EU–MERCOSUR interregionalism to expand its influence on external affairs and on domestic reforms. On the one hand, even if the EC has the technocratic expertise in the complex field of trade negotiations, electoral cycles, the pending CAP reform, and EU expansion towards the east have all reduced the EC's ability to steer the EU–MERCOSUR negotiations according to its interest. On the other hand, the potential of protectionist interests to use the Council to block any advance in negotiations also has been limited. While the case of EU–MERCOSUR relations underlines the Council's status as representative of member states' interests, it is more reserved with respect to interregional trade liberalization, and the introduction of qualified majority voting has weakened the power of protectionist interests. Furthermore, the Commission as well as the Council share the goal of advancing regional cooperation and integration in Africa, Asia, and Latin America by fostering interregional agreements with a broad issue scope.

Finally, the ambivalent position of the Council becomes even clearer if one takes into account that the EU's interregional trade strategies also respond to international challenges. EU–MERCOSUR negotiations clearly reveal that cooperation between the Council and the EC has become a political project, particularly when mounting international pressures make it more attractive for the EU to pursue interregional trade liberalization. On a global level, the course of the WTO-led multilateral trade regime has clearly influenced the development of interregional institutionalization. As in MERCOSUR and the United States, pro-free-trade actors have perceived interregional trade negotiations to be second-best strategies in their pursuit of increasing international influence. Thus, EU–MERCOSUR relations have advanced when there seemed no significant possibility for substantial progress at the WTO level.

More importantly, the EU's strategy toward MERCOSUR has been closely connected to the FTAA process.[45] There is widespread concern among European firms and policymakers that an agreement between the United States and its Latin American counterparts would repeat the "Mexican experience" of losing market shares after the establishment of NAFTA. Any progress in the U.S. government's attempt to establish a Free Trade Area of the Americas thus should increase the European Council's keenness to advance trade liberalization with MERCOSUR. Therefore, as Felix Peña speculates, the influence of competition among EU and U.S. policymakers as well as the interests of transnational firms pursuing the expansion of their globally-oriented production networks will tie the FTAA process and EU–MERCOSUR negotiations even closer to each other.[46] The result could be a transatlantic economic triangle, if – in what currently seems to be the most intriguing question – MERCOSUR survives the current problems of its two biggest economies and regains its intraregional coherence.

Notes

1. For an introduction to EU–MERCOSUR relations see Bulmer-Thomas 2000, Müller-Brandeck-Bocquet 2000, Inter-American Development Bank 2002.
2. See the introduction to this volume for analytical discussions about the potential role of interregionalism in the international political economy and about pure interregionalism.
3. Müller-Brandeck-Bocquet 2000, p. 566.
4. Ayllón 2000.
5. Schulz 1997, p. 99.
6. Bulmer-Thomas 2000, p. 2.
7. Müller-Brandeck-Bocquet 2000, p. 569.
8. Bulmer-Thomas 2000, p. 1.
9. The Cooperation Council of EMIFCA consists of members of the European Council, the EC, the Council of MERCOSUR, and the MERCOSUR Group. The Biregional Negotiation Committee consists of Council members, members of the

EC's general directorates of Commerce and Foreign Relations, and the foreign ministers of MERCOSUR. Furthermore, three technical groups were created: 1) for trade in goods and tariffs, 2) for services and intellectual property rights, and 3) for competition and regulated markets (see Inter-American Development Bank 2002, p. 43). Regarding the timetable of negotiations, the different parties agreed that the Biregional Negotiation Committee and the Subcommittee on Cooperation should meet at least twice a year and that meetings should be prepared by the working groups, whose members were asked to create a network of political and societal interest groups.

10. Maukisch 2000, p. 71.
11. Benecke 2001.
12. See IRELA 1999b; Estevadeordal and Krivonos 2000; Rozo 2001, Inter-American Development Bank 2002; Giordano 2003.
13. The main imports within the agricultural and food sector in the late 1990s were coffee, soybeans, oil cake, fruit juices, non-manufactured tobacco, and meat (Estevadeordal and Krivonos 2000. p. 4). From 1998 onwards, MERCOSUR became the EU's most important extra-regional source of agricultural products, exceeding NAFTA's exports in this sector (Bouzas and Svarzman 2000: 8).
14. There is, however, a remarkable difference between the EU's trade with Argentina, Paraguay, and Uruguay on the one hand, and Brazil on the other hand, the latter revealing a much higher percentage of intra-industrial trade.
15. EU–MERCOSUR trade in communications, information technology, and financial services has been growing at a higher speed than overall trade in services, but the relative importance of these sectors for the EU is still very modest. However, the growing participation of European firms in the tertiary sector makes service liberalization an important issue in EU–MERCOSUR negotiations (IRELA 1999a: 15).
16. Bouzas and Svarzman 2000; Estevadeordal and Krivonos 2000.
17. Additionally, important export products from Brazil and Argentina have suffered from preferential agreements and reduced quantitative barriers that the EU has given to the ACP countries, Switzerland, several countries from Eastern Europe, Australia, and New Zealand (Bouzas and Svarzman 2000, p. 15; Giordano 2003).
18. IRELA 1999b; Bouzas and Svarzman 2000.
19. Estevadeordal and Krivonos 2000, p. 4.
20. In 1990–99, MERCOSUR accumulated an FDI inflow of US$104.45 billion compared with $78.42 billion in the case of ASEAN and $67.18 billion in Mexico. For an in-depth analysis of FDI flows to MERCOSUR during the nineties see Chudnovsky and López 2000.
21. Nunnenkamp 1997; IDB 2002.
22. Nunnenkamp 1999, p. 174.
23. IDB 2002, p. 25. In contrast, U.S. FDI in MERCOSUR was less dynamic. Instead, newly acquired U.S. assets have tended to go to the assembly of manufactures in Central America in order to allow American companies to compete more favourably in the U.S. domestic market against Asian imports.
24. As Nunnenkamp (2000: 12) assumes, "it was largely due to Spanish FDI that the sectoral composition of FDI in MERCOSUR countries shifted towards the service sector."
25. Mortimore 2000.
26. Nunnenkamp 2001, p. 19.
27. For a general argument on the influence of interest groups in the course of liberalization see Frieden 1991, Keohane and Milner 1996.

28. Streeck and Schmitter 1991; Kohler-Koch 1996.
29. The successfully concluded negotiations with Chile include liberalization in agriculture, yet Chile's agro-industrial sector differs in size and product scope from those of Argentina and Brazil making it easier to achieve an agreement. The EU–Mexico Free Trade Agreement excludes several agricultural sectors, in which European protection has remained crucial for producers (Schott 2001).
30. Sanchez Bajo 1999, p. 932.
31. IRELA 1998, p. 3.
32. MEBF is presided by two co-presidents, one from a European firm and one from a MERCOSUR firm. In 2001, the positions of two vice-presidents were created. Presidents and vice-presidents have originated from transnational companies with strong interest in interregional trade liberalization. The MEBF structure also contains technical working groups for market access, for services and for investment, the latter including the financial sector.
33. A more "intellectual" impact came from the Institute of European Latin American Relations (IRELA), financed by the European Union, whose studies were rather pro-free trade oriented and revealed to a certain extent the intra-European conflicts.
34. Sanchez Bajo 1999, p. 933.
35. Greenwood 1997.
36. For different perspectives on the interplay between Commission and Council in the EU's external trade policy, see among others Nugent 1999 and Meunier 2000.
37. The Committee on External Relations of the European Parliament in 1995 urged the Commission and the Council to speed up negotiations with MERCOSUR. "If the EU wishes to maintain its leading role in the trade policies of this region, and to prevent the entire South American continent from falling into the political and economic spheres of influence of the U.S., then the necessity of establishing a middle-term strategy towards the MERCOSUR is undeniable" (Committee on External Relations of the EP, 12.05. 1995, 10)
38. Four Commissioners voted against the initiative of the Commission to obtain a negotiation mandate from the Council on 22 July 1998, including the Commissioner for Agriculture, Franz Fischler, and the head of the Commission, Jaques Santer, who presented a study of the negative effects a trade agreement would have on the European agricultural sector. On the other hand, the Commission's Vice-President, Manuel Marín, strongly in favor of a negotiation mandate, presented another study, which revealed that only two percent of the products currently traded between both regions would be affected negatively, while the European automobile sector, chemical industries, IT, and services would gain from trade liberalization (IRELA 1998: 1).
39. Sanchez Bajo 1999, p. 932.
40. For instance, in September 1998, French foreign minister Hubert Védrine stated that his government was against negotiations before concluding the Agenda 2000, since the CAP reform and the structure of EU widening towards the East should be prior to any interregional commitment. Furthermore, the president of the Committee of Agricultural Organization of the European Union, Luc Guyau, considered that a free trade agreement with MERCOSUR would seriously affect the incomes of important agriculture sectors as well as creating structural problems in several regions of the European Union (IRELA 1998: 2).
41. Spain's center-right government, with close links to national farmers, did not obstruct EU–MERCOSUR negotiations, because of the increasing involvement of Spanish firms in Argentina and Brazil.

42. However, the decisionmaking rules of the Council made it more difficult for protectionist-oriented governments to veto trade liberalization. Until the 1980s, the
Council' decisions on trade required a unanimous basis. The adoption of the
Single European Act (1987) and the Maastricht Treaty (1992) introduced
qualified majority voting (QMV) on trade in goods – though, significantly, not
in services or intellectual property rights. Thus, even if the Council had granted
the EC competences to negotiate issues related to trade in services, mixed agreements still have to be ratified by each member country. As such, coalitions of
member states still could put together veto majority, but the threshold for such
blockade policies has become higher. See Laursen 1999.
43. For a critical perspective on the development of APEC see Ravenhill 2001, for an
analysis on the FTAA process see among others Feinberg 2002; Wise 2003.
44. Bulmer-Thomas 2000, p. 5; Peña 2001, p. 103.
45. Peña 2001, p. 103, Page 2001, p. 15.
46. Peña 2001, p. 99.

References

Aggarwal, Vinod (ed.) (1998). *Institutional Designs for a Complex World: Bargaining,
Linkages and Nesting.* Ithaca: Cornell University Press.
Ayllón Pino, Bruno (2000). "Perspectivas de una Asociación Interregional Unión
Europea-MERCOSUR: Una Visión desde Brasil." *Revista Electrónica de Estudios
Internacionales* 1: 2–48.
Barrios, Harald (1998). "MERCOSUR: Ein Versuch koordinierten Regierens als
Antwort auf externe Herausforderungen." *Ibero-Amerikanisches Archiv* 24, 1/2:
165–187.
Benecke, Dieter W. (2001). "MERCOSUR–EU-Verhandlungen: Überwindung des
Königskindersyndroms." *Weltreport der Konrad-Adenauer-Stiftung* (September):
15–17.
Bouzas, Roberto and Gustavo Svarzman (2000). "Estructura del comercio y de la pro-
teccion arancelaria en las relaciones entre el MERCOSUR y la Union Europea."
Boletín Informativo Techint, Buenos Aires (October).
Bulmer-Thomas, Victor (2000). "The European Union and MERCOSUR: Prospects for
a free Trade agreement." *Journal of Interamerican Studies and World Affairs* 42, 1:
1–22.
Chudnovsky, Daniel and Andrés López (2000). "El boom de inversión extranjera
en MERCOSUR en los anos 1990: características, determinantes e impactos."
Manuscript, Centro de Investigaciones para la Transformación (CENIT), Buenos
Aires (November).
Estevadeordal, Antoni and Ekaterina Krivonos (2000). "Negotiating market access
between the European Union and MERCOSUR: issues and prospects."
Occasional Paper No. 7 (December), Institute for the Integration of Latin
America and the Caribbean (INTAL) and the Integration and Regional Programs
Department (ITD) of the Inter-American Development Bank, Buenos Aires
(www.iadb.org/intal/pub).
European Commission (2001). "The EU & MERCOSUR." (http://europa.eu.int/
comm/external-relations/MERCOSUR/intro/index.htm).
Feinberg, Richard (2002). "Regionalism and domestic politics: U.S.–Latin American
trade policy in the Bush era." *Latin American Politics & Society* 44, 4: 127–151.
Frieden, Jeffrey (1991). "Invested interests: the politics of national economic policies
in a world of global finance." *International Organization* 45, 4: 425–451.

Giordano, Paolo (2003). "The external dimension of MERCOSUR: prospects for North–South integration with the European Union." Occasional Paper 19, Inter-American Development /Institute for the Integration of Latin America and the Caribbean IDB-INTAL, Buenos Aires.

Greenwood, Justin (1997). *Representing Interests in the European Union.* New York: St. Martins Press.

Inter-American Development Bank (2002). "Integration and trade in the Americas." Special Issue on Latin American and Caribbean Economic Relations with the European Union, Periodic Note, Washington (May).

IRELA (Institute of European-Latin American Relations) (1998). "Preparando la Asociación UE–MERCOSUR. Beneficios y Obstáculos." Informe de IRELA, Madrid (November 20).

IRELA (1999a). "Las Perspectivas de un Acuerdo de Libre Commercio UE–MERCOSUR y las opciones para la Política de EEUU." Informe de IRELA, Madrid.

IRELA (1999b). "Relaciones Económicas entre el MERCOSUR y la UE: Perpsectivas para la nueva Década." Informe IRELA, Madrid.

Keohane, Robert O. and Helen V. Milner (eds.) (1996). *Internationalization and Domestic Politics.* Cambridge: Cambridge University Press.

Kohler-Koch, Beate (1996). "Die Gestaltungsmacht organisierter Interessen." In Jachtenfuchs, Markus, and Beate Kohler-Koch (eds.). *Europäische Integration.* Opladen: Leske + Budrich, 193–222.

Laursen, Finn (1999). "Trade and aid: The European Union in the global system." In Cram, Laura, Desmond Dinan, and Neill Nugent (eds.). *Developments in the European Union.* New York: St. Martin's Press.

Maukisch, Marc André (2000). "Interregionale Kooperation am Beispiel der Beziehungen zwischen der Europäischen Union und dem MERCOSUR." Unpublished Master Thesis, Institute of Political Science, University of Mainz.

Meunier, Sophie (2000). "What single voice? European institutions and EU–U.S. trade negotiations." *International Organization* 54, 1 (Winter): 103–130.

Mortimore, Michael (2000). "Foreign investment in Latin America and the Caribbean: 1999 Report." ECLAC, Unit on Investment and Corporate Strategies. Santiago de Chile.

Müller-Brandeck-Bocquet, Gisela (2000). "Perspective for a new regionalism: relations between the EU and the MERCOSUR." *European Foreign Affairs Review* 5, 4: 561–579.

Nugent, Neill (1999). *The Government and Politics of the European Union,* 4th ed. London: The Macmillan Press.

Nunnenkamp, Peter (1997). "Direct investment in Latin America in the era of globalized Production." *Transnational Corporations* 6, 1: 51–81.

Nunnenkamp, Peter (2000). "Possible effects of European Union widening on Latin America." *European Journal of Development Research* 12, 1: 124–139

Nunnenkamp, Peter (2001). "European FDI strategies in MERCOSUR countries." Paper for the Experts Workshop "An Integrated Approach to the EU–MERCOSUR Association," INTAL, Buenos Aires (May 17–18).

Page, Sheila (2001). "Trade and foreign policy in the EU." Paper for the Experts Workshop "An Integrated Approach to the EU–MERCOSUR Association," INTAL, Buenos Aires (May 17–18).

Peña, Felix (2001). "La relación entre el MERCOSUR y la Unión Europea: una perspectiva del sentido estratégico de la negociación interregional." *Contribuciones* 3: 85–106.

Ravenhill, John (2001). *APEC and the Construction of Pacific Rim Regionalism.* Cambridge: Cambridge University Press.

Rozo, Carlos A. (2001). "Protectionism in the European Union: implications for Latin America." *Intereconomics, Review of European Economic Foreign Policy* 36, 3: 141–152.

Sanchez Bajo, Claudia (1999). "The European Union and MERCOSUR: a case of inter-regionalism." *Third World Quarterly* 20, 5: 927–941.

Schott, Jeffrey (2001). "Europa and the Americas: toward a TAFTA–South?" *The World Economy* 24, 6: 745–759.

Schulz, José B. (1997). "Die Außenwirtschaftsbeziehungen der Europäischen Union zu Lateinamerika: Analyse und Möglichkeiten zur Verbesserung unter besonderer Berücksichtigung des MERCOSUR." Passau.

Streeck, Wolfgang and Philippe Schmitter (1991). "From national corporatism to transnational pluralism: organised interests in the Single European Market." *Politics and Society* 19, 2: 133–164.

Wise, Carol (2003). "The FTAA: trade preferences as the art of what's possible." In Aggarwal, Vinod, Ralph Espach, and Joseph S. Tulchin (eds.), *The Strategic Dynamics of Latin American Trade.* Washington, D.C.: The Woodrow Wilson Center.

3
Weaving a New Silk Road: Europe Meets Asia

Julie Gilson

1 Introduction

This chapter examines the most recent of the EU's forays into interregional encounters: its engagement with East Asia through the Asia–Europe Meeting (ASEM). Established formally in 1996, this loosely institutionalized forum in many ways provides a vehicle for European approaches to the disparate states of East Asia. Although the ASEM process was initiated by members of the Association of Southeast Asian Nations (ASEAN), EU and EU member state representatives have utilized this forum as a means of coordinating and supplementing pre-existing bilateral attempts to improve trade relations with the economies of the region and to address specific concerns of common interest on political and other issues.

In these ways, the forum offers a form of hybrid interregionalism to offset increasingly complex bilateral relationships, and embraces a broad but often diluted scope of activities.[1] ASEM is by its very nature and origins broad in issue scope and a meeting of the geographically dispersed; there is no notion of neighborhood among its members. It straddles the boundaries between a post-colonial donor-recipient relationship and a putative attempt to embrace a partnership of "equals." Related to this, the gradual transformation from an EU-ASEAN arrangement to the new and broader concept of an ASEAN Plus Three (APT) region is played out within the ASEM process. Part of this shift derives from the learning process encountered by the Asian grouping within fora such as ASEM itself and for this reason the "counterpart coherence" is slowly developing new forms. EU approaches to this East Asian grouping have been reformulated since the mid-1990s and now encompass interregional and bilateral linkages within the portmanteau of Asia–Europe relations.

Despite its three-pillar structure of economic dialogue, political dialogue, and cultural agenda, ASEM functions primarily to further trade and investment negotiations. As the nature of the EU itself changes, however, the future profile of the European project hinges upon the close interconnections between economic issues and the Common Foreign and Security Policy (CFSP) mechanisms that increasingly affect or are affected by them. As noted in the introduction by Aggarwal and Fogarty, trade strategies themselves frequently reflect the ongoing process of creating a common European identity among the people of its constituent nations and a belief in the utility of regions as a unit for organizing the global economy. In the context of ASEM, this process is demonstrated further by the apparently trilateral interests prevalent among the economies of North America, East Asia, and Europe. ASEM serves to correct the "weak side of the triangle" and to enable the EU to consolidate its regional trade strategies.

The impact of this embryonic relationship has been small, on account of its lack of formal institutionalization, broad agenda, and waning interest of many of its constituent actors. The EU–Asia interregional relationship is still very hard to assess, but it is increasingly apparent that there is an emerging notion of economic Asia – in particular, a desire to collectivize responses in the face of differentiated resource allocation – and a growing dominance of the form of regionalism demonstrated by the EU.

2   Origins and evolution of the Asia–Europe Meeting

Originally proposed by Singaporean Prime Minister Goh Chok Tong, the formal inauguration of ASEM took place in Bangkok in March 1996 at a summit meeting of twenty-five heads of state or government from East Asia and Europe.[2] On the Asian side were representatives from seven countries of ASEAN alongside China, Japan, and South Korea.[3] The European side comprised all fifteen EU member states, along with the president of the European Commission. The first summit was welcomed as a "whole new game" by *The Economist* and praised for bringing together previously distant interlocutors. However, it was simultaneously dismissed as a gathering of the "politically wobbly, disunited, and paralyzed," and the substance of the initial encounter was found to be rather exiguous.[4] The second summit, it was expected by the optimistic observer, would elaborate ASEM's substantive goals. In fact, ASEM 2, held in London in April 1998, was overshadowed by the effects of the Asian financial crisis that had begun in June 1997, and as a result the agenda focused predominantly on this issue.

It was, then, left to ASEM 3 to chart the future course of Asia–Europe engagements, but it, too, was somewhat overtaken by events. In June 2000, four months before ASEM 3 took place in Seoul, an historic meeting was held between the leaders of North and South Korea. Not only did this provide an obvious point of departure for discussions at ASEM 3, but just prior to the summit South Korean President Kim Dae Jung was also awarded the Nobel peace prize. Although the Seoul Declaration for Peace on the Korean Peninsula was adopted as an adjunct to the Chair's

Statement, the Korea question dominated proceedings, particularly in the eyes of the media. Nevertheless, this summit, which was attended by more than three thousand people, reiterated in its final statement a joint Asia–Europe commitment to close the mutual [*sic*] gaps in knowledge and understanding within the three established ASEM pillars of economic, political, and cultural dialogue. ASEM 4, held in Copenhagen in September 2002, also drew breath from recent events, by taking as its starting point the events of 11 September 2001 and investigating prospects for "New Security Issues," as well as including a discussion of the August 2002 Johannesburg summit on the environment. However, this summit, too, failed to set a comprehensive agenda for a future ASEM structure and illustrated a number of the weaknesses inherent in the aspirations of this project.

ASEM has been dominated to date by the economic agenda. Copenhagen's discussions over the need to strengthen mutual support for the Doha Development Agenda (agreed at the fourth WTO ministerial meeting in Qatar in November 2001) and the issue of the significance of the euro are typical areas of interest and concern. A representative speech by EU commissioner for trade, Pascal Lamy, in Brussels on 15 February 2002 illustrates this point:

> We face a roller coaster of a ride for the next three short years, but we have to make a top priority of the DDA [Doha Development Agenda], and we will. And we want Asia as a key partner in this endeavor. I want to continue the close cooperation with my Asian colleagues – and not just on those issues where our interests coincide, such as market access or geographical indications in the TRIPs agreement, but also in areas where our perceptions still differ...[5]

In the same speech he notes the importance of "the further enhancement of our two-way trade and investment relations, and the development of a global partnership with our Asian partners." Based on the European concept paper outlining aims for ASEM 4 ("Unity in Diversity"), it is clear that the EU continues to push for "deliverables" from summit meetings, including the pursuit of a new WTO trade round, discussion of the euro, and the enhancement of the two flagship projects of the Trade Facilitation Action Plan (TFAP) and the Investment Promotion Action Plan (IPAP).[6]

TFAP was agreed upon at a Senior Officials' Meeting on Trade and Investment (SOMTI) in 1996 and endorsed by the Economic Ministers' Meeting, before being adopted at ASEM 2. It aims to reduce non-tariff barriers (NTBs) relating to a number of fields, including customs, standards and certification, and the mobility of business people, although it is not a forum for negotiation. TFAP is also expressly designed to complement negotiations elsewhere, especially within the WTO and World Customs

Organization (WCO). IPAP, proposed at ASEM 1, was also adopted at the second summit and was set up to generate greater investment flows between the two regions.[7] It contains two pillars: one for investment promotion and one for regulation, both of which are coordinated by an Investment Experts Group (IEG), endorsed at ASEM 2. The IEG has held a number of meetings to explore avenues for best practice in areas such as barriers to investment, attraction of foreign direct investment (FDI), transparency, nondiscrimination, investment incentives (tax/regime breaks), and investors' behavior, and also established a Virtual Information Exchange (VIE) on the Internet, created by the European Commission (subsequently renamed as ASEM Invest Online).[8] As will be suggested below, IPAP has not been successful in both of its principal remits.

Information technology (IT) initiatives have also been pursued, by bringing together the EU's existing Trans-European Network (TEN)-155 and Korea's KOREN (high-speed research network in Korea), in order to begin to create a Trans-Eurasia Information Network Project. This project is designed to increase cooperation, diversify research exchange, and make speedier telecommunication connections, in recognition of the key role played by IT in the expansion of trade potential. Like many other ASEM endeavors, this initiative resembles an Asia–Pacific Economic Cooperation forum (APEC) precedent, in this case the Asia Pacific Information Infrastructure (APII), which was proposed at the APEC Economic Leaders' meeting in Bogor in 1994.

In addition to these large projects, ASEM has made small and medium-sized enterprises (SMEs) the target of many of its objectives. These are especially important in driving technological cooperation and development. SMEs in Asia, most of which are export-oriented, constitute over 90 percent of all enterprises and cover 30–85 percent of employment in individual economies. Similarly, according to the European Commission, in 1996 SMEs represented 99.8 percent of all EU companies, 66 percent of employment and 65 percent of business turnover.[9] ASEM also encourages private-sector activities such as the Asia–Europe Business Forum (AEBF), designed to promote business partnerships through dialogue and exchanges. Working groups were established by AEBF IV, to deal specifically with particular sectors, including trade, investment, and financial services. In both regions, increased competition as a result of globalizing processes threatens the sustainability of SMEs, and this sector has thus become an important target of region-to-region negotiations. While these initiatives propose channels for the resolution and improvement of sectoral concerns, the loose framework of ASEM makes it difficult (if not impossible) to ensure accountability and to threaten sanctions for nonparticipation. Furthermore, as will be shown below, the nature of the regime and the scope of the actors make it difficult to sustain interest in these types of activities.

The ASEM process has also failed to eradicate a number of areas of protectionism such as within the agricultural sector of the EU. Indeed, where EU protection has begun to lessen, it is largely due to the effects of European intraregional changes in trade policy and technical barriers, through the reduction of voluntary export restraints (VERs) and commitments made as part of the Uruguay Round. Meanwhile, European anti-dumping measures continue to be aimed at the countries of Southeast and East Asia as a useful means, according to some observers, of counteracting threats from Asian competition.[10] The "strict and less-than-transparent application" of this form of protectionism has also been complemented by a range of obscure safeguard measures. At the same time, Europeans, particularly through the European Parliament, continue to emphasize the need to address the social issues damaging interregional trade. In Asia, too, a variety of "hidden barriers" continue to stymie European attempts to promote trade and investment.[11]

Throughout all four summits and among the plethora of lower level meetings held under its umbrella structure, ASEM's less-developed political dialogue has continued to embrace security and "soft" issues such as the international fight against the trafficking of people and drugs, and pollution and other environmental problems. Although this pillar is located within the realm of ministerial and bureaucratic interests, it also involves nongovernmental organizations (NGOs), which hold their own "people's forum" on the fringes of the summit meetings. Alongside these concerns, a socio-cultural pillar has also been put into place, culminating in Copenhagen's "retreat" to examine "Cultures and Civilizations." While this initiative may be interpreted as a means to further address mutual incomprehensibility, it could also be viewed as a refuge for unanimously agreeable discussion.

Its laudable aims and numerous activities notwithstanding, ASEM continues to suffer from an absence of clearly defined goals and lacks an externally visible (and credible) presence. This remains the case in spite of attempts by the *de facto* ASEM track-two process, the Council for Asia–Europe Cooperation (CAEC), to articulate a "rationale" for the meeting,[12] and despite a report by a wise-men "Vision Group" to propose concrete means for pushing forward the ASEM agenda. Nevertheless, these pillars, especially that of political dialogue, have offered important conduits for airing issues related to trade and investment, and European partners have also acknowledged their value. Before considering this and other issues, it is worth assessing the initial value of the ASEM process as a whole for the EU.

3   Characterizing ASEM interregionalism

When applying the criteria outlined in the introduction, ASEM lies at the relatively weak end of the spectrum. Its participants, particularly on the

Asian side, have deflected suggestions to introduce a greater degree of formality into the ASEM structure. As a result, ASEM has little effect on action taken by its constituent member states, offering rather an opt-in, opt-out solution for specific areas of mutual interest.

Strength of ASEM

As has been shown above, ASEM remains a weak arrangement, based upon its open, consensus-led formulation. While it has offered a useful means of consolidating minilateral agreement prior to global fora, it is not a negotiating forum and retains no form of sanction. Its strength, therefore, lies more in its ability to bring together representatives from a range of fields from two large continents. At the same time, the "vision" of ASEM, from the summit statements, to the CAEC process and the Vision Group report itself, has promoted a broad scope for ASEM but by so doing has failed to determine tangible and realizable goals possible within the structure of ASEM.

One reason for the apparent weakness of ASEM rests on the measurement of institutionalization. To date, ASEM, unlike APEC, does not have a secretariat, despite calls for one by the Vision Group and the request for at least a virtual secretariat to deal with the dissemination of ASEM-related affairs. The European Commission has been the only consistent coordinator and therefore functions as a *de facto* informal secretariat. Moreover, the European Commission president attends the biennial summit meetings, but the High Representative of the CFSP is not present and there is little interaction between the High Representative and the European Commission on issues pertaining to ASEM.

However, while much has been discussed about the relative lack of institutionalization of ASEM, in many ways a focus on this aspect of the regime obscures comprehension of how it functions. In fact, ASEM may be called a "semi-institutionalized" relationship, since it is bounded by regular and clearly demarcated heads of state and ministerial meetings as well as formal structures of the AEBF and ASEF.[13] Even the AEPF, held on the margins of ASEM, has formalized its own arrangements by creating a committee to sustain momentum. While this informality is frequently said to rest on an "ASEAN way" of conduct, the "learning" developed through this means reinforces pre-existing institutional parameters and creates for the EU a means of channeling its vested interests.[14] In the case of ASEM, it is arguable that this derivation of institutional credibility contributes in fact to the further strengthening of European agendas and procedures, which come to be presented as the "evolution" of collective practice.

As noted above, ASEM is premised upon a number of pre-existing institutional mechanisms such as the EU–ASEAN and EU–Japan dialogues. Despite its lack of formal institutional parameters, ASEM offers for each side of the partnership a nascent institutional formula for cooperation, regular channels of dialogues, means of reducing costs in both economic and security concerns, and an ideal venue for diffuse reciprocity. In this way, it provides an advantageous level for negotiation, in the face of stalled negotiations within broader, diluted fora such as the WTO and narrower, often conflict-ridden fora such as the EU–ASEAN dialogue. In Asia – since the financial crisis in particular – that viewpoint has been reinforced, as Asian representatives have perceived in the extant ruling bodies (the WTO, IMF, and the United States itself) a lack of a credible future-oriented alternative.[15]

Yet ASEM's formal institutional poverty has become self-reinforcing. Not only is it becoming increasingly difficult to muster presidential and prime ministerial enthusiasm to attend summit meetings every two years, but senior official meetings are frequently not peopled by representatives carrying adequate seniority, and are, instead, attended by heads of unit or directors. In addition, a number of working groups (for example, on public procurement and the mobility of business people) have now been phased out, due to lack of interest. The mandate for the IEG also expires in 2003 and it has yet to be decided whether and how it is to be replaced. Given the lack of secretariat, official preparatory meetings are also burdened by the organization of ministerial meetings and do not provide an opportunity for substantive discussion that could feed into the debating process.

The nature of ASEM

Open regionalism, or, more appropriately, "open continentalism"[16] put forward by ASEM, underlines its pledged adherence to the principles of free trade and to the tenets of a number of multilateral regimes. This association had already become deeply entrenched within the EU, particularly the Commission, which, as Rosamond notes, developed during the 1980s a discursive "space" in which to justify market liberalization, regulation, and deeper integration.[17]

The scope of issues covered by the ASEM structure is extremely broad on paper, but somewhat narrower in practice. On the one hand, while many of its structural premises and rhetorical aspirations emulate the mantras of existing regimes, particularly those of the WTO, the UN, and APEC, it accommodates a uniquely broad scope and embraces explicitly two regions within an ostensibly equal partnership. In reality, however, the EU has regarded ASEM as a supplementary vehicle by which to pursue market opening and barrier reducing opportunities in East Asia. This multi-dimensional approach issued from a European desire in particular to establish a wide range of discussions with Asia, and follows from a growing overlap of political and economic interests in formal EU agreements. The apparently extended scope of relations may be interpreted, therefore, as a result of the European (particularly by DG1 of the European Commission and its successors, DG Trade and DG External Relations) realization that it needs to work more closely with others (environment, social, competition, marine, transport, energy) in light of the emerging "new economy."[18] In addition, the EU also uses ASEM as a means of gaining support for activities in international fora such as its pursuit of common cause towards establishing a WTO Millennium Round. Much of the scope of issues is concerned with issue- or sector-specific interests, as the multitude of ministerial and senior official meetings on issues as diverse as immigration, tax, and intellectual property rights attest.[19]

The adoption of TFAP and IPAP is similarly issue-centric, and in the case of IPAP is split in its remit between the two goals of investment promotion and investment regulation. Since different issues are raised by each aspect and therefore require the participation of quite different constituencies, it is no surprise that the IPAP has focused almost uniquely on investment regulation and has had little impact on national approaches to investment. Investment policy tends to involve bureaucrats, who prepare legislation on the registration of businesses, taxes, and so on, while investment promotion is directly applicable to business interests, with the result that the bureaucrats attending the AEM may not be the most appropriate participants. In the Investment Expert Group, the Asian side tends to send investment promotion representatives hoping to attract investment to their countries, but Europeans tend to send regulators involved in discussing issues such as the legal framework and transparency of agreements. This situation simply results in a dialogue of the deaf. In the field of trade and investment ASEM has not been used, as foreseen, as a vehicle for co-ordinating the range of bilateral exchanges.

The scope of actors involved in ASEM is also diverse on paper, but in practice tends to be limited to a number of lower-level officials. ASEM's agenda so far have been dominated by economic concerns, which are negotiated by a combination of ministers (treasury, economic, finance, customs) as well as by the AEBF, which is in place to ensure close links with the private business community. On a number of occasions, ministers have sat in for heads of state and ambassadors have replaced senior ministers, particularly from the European side. This suggests that actors across the EU regard ASEM mostly as the preserve of the bureaucrat.

There are three levels at which ASEM is relevant for EU actors. The first concerns the projection of a greater European "voice" on a global scale, and is in the interest especially of the European Commission, but also of the Council, which uses the EU as a means of enhancing national (economic) presence in Asia and beyond. The second level concerns intra-EU debate, and is an important feature of ASEM given its overlapping remits. While the European Commission is mandated to represent the interests of the Union on matters pertaining to the single market, CFSP matters are to be dealt with by the Council. In reality, ongoing debates about the nature of the European project within Europe align with institutional conflicts between the (Euro-level) European Commission and (intergovernmental) Council of Ministers to produce a multi-headed European position. In the case of ASEM, which is not limited to economic relations – for which the European Commission would hold a representative mandate – this situation is made more complicated by the scope and range of activities across its three pillars. In ASEM this distinction is blurred, as it might examine human rights and aid, or immigration and terrorism as part of distinct packages requiring the input of a range of actors and thereby strengthening the hands of the European Commission. The third level is the extended role of nonstate representatives, from business and NGO communities, who have taken their place clearly alongside (in the case of NGOs) or within (for business) the formal ASEM structure. This factor has precipitated a strengthening of the Parliament's role in pushing for greater human rights, social welfare, and citizen participation. With the admission of new EU members – which in some cases compete directly with their Southeast Asian counterparts, and with democratic institutions still in the process of consolidation – pressure for the separation of such interests may intensify. This type of non-structural basis of power within the international political economy has recently been highlighted by a number of scholars, especially with the changes brought about by the globalization of patterns of trade and production, the rise of nonstate actors into key positions influencing national conditions, and the emergence of new civil society movements reconfiguring the nature and role of the state.[20]

This broad range of relevant actors has been fundamental to the type of process established within ASEM and, as a result, the process is more than simply a "recondite hobby for the elite,"[21] or an elite-driven (epistemic) community. While elites organize and attend the summits and function as part of the Vision Group and CAEC, ASEM also accommodates a range of actors not conventionally associated with similar institutions. The resulting set-up is a cobweb of disparate interests and actors, drawn together by the overarching label of "ASEM" activity. So far, the key interpreters[22] of the institution of ASEM have been those actors already equipped with skills to act in other such settings, principally the European Commission. However, there is clearly a residual duality on the EU side, between "EU-level" actor capacity and the interests and behavior of EU member states. On the one hand, the growth of the EU as an actor, especially in the eyes of a collective "Asia," which may choose to see it as a coherent unit in order to justify its own closer cooperation, is supported by the tangible evidence of the euro and CFSP. On the other hand, a lack of coherent policy towards Asia (such as the *ad hoc* recognition of North Korea prior to ASEM 3), as well as a general lack of interest in Asia, means that there is no real collective discussion regarding Asia and, as a result, the European Commission and individual Council member representatives tend to design and negotiate policies left to their charge.

4 Counterpart coherence and the Asian Ten

The ASEM process provides an interesting case study in the construction of regional identity. Interregional arrangements are especially important in creating *de facto* assumptions about the very notion of region. Prior to the Bangkok summit, the so-called "Asian Ten" (the then seven member states of ASEAN, alongside China, Japan, and South Korea) had not met in a formal gathering on a regular basis. To some extent, then, the ten states constituted themselves as "Asia" for the purpose of dealing as a region in an explicitly region-to-region arrangement of "equal partners." On the other side, as noted above, the EU now entertains in its statistics the category of "Asian ASEM." While it is difficult to measure the direct implications of this identification, growing interaction of intra-East Asian representatives is likely to have contributed to the development of the APT process, which now exists beyond the confines of ASEM. Other activities have also been established such as the Initiative on ASEAN Integration (IAI) launched by the ASEAN Leaders during the Fourth ASEAN Informal Summit in Singapore in 2000. APT meetings are now used to promote better use of ASEM such as through the "Asia–Europe Partnership for Prosperity and Stability in the New Millennium."[23] For the Asian contingent, the apparent failure of the IMF and APEC in the wake of the financial crisis and the Seattle fiasco of the WTO have served to reinforce a need to find alternative collective solutions to regional issues.

In terms of economic exchange, there are a number of reasons for the East Asian grouping to respond collectively to Europe. Not only is EU enlargement a potential hindrance to Southeast Asian competition that requires joint pressure on the EU, but the growth of European FDI and trade with the region is also important for East Asia. In addition, many states within East Asia also wish to fend off competition with China and to deal collectively with the need for economic reform within Japan. While intraregional trade remains central to the AFTA mechanism, the effects of the globalization of competition simultaneously exercise the need to function on a broader canvas. Ongoing discussions about the future of a wider East Asian economic community also influence this need. In terms of institutionalization, however, in spite of the presence of ASEAN, there remain only loose agreements within the region to cooperate on a regular basis. In this regard, ASEAN lobbied hard for ASEM, as a means of asserting its own central role in a new forum, in order to re-affirm its own regional relevance. However, there remains considerable economic disparity among the states of ASEM, with the practical effect that several Asian states cannot afford to fund adequately the proposals they might otherwise champion within ASEM, thereby further embedding in fact the inequality of the two regions.

Asian responses to apparent European neglect during the Asian crisis ranged from collective criticism to a recognition of the need to find regional solutions to regional crises. Although IMF conditionality was also targeted, in many ways the EU became both model and counter-model for the articulation of collective Asian interests. On the one hand, proposals for some kind of Asian "euro" became popular. For example, Joseph Estrada of the Philippines at Manila in July 1998, and Joseph Yam, the Chief Executive of Hong Kong's Monetary Authority in 1999, both declared themselves in favor of some kind of Asian currency unit, in order to establish region-level initiatives to "help maximize the benefits of globalization while minimizing the disruptive effects of global financial markets."[24] Interestingly, several European representatives have joined these calls, as can be seen from the joint French and Japanese proposal in Frankfurt in early 2001 to promote an intermediate currency band arrangement, based on a basket of currencies including the euro, the U.S. dollar, and the yen.[25] Presumably, this move is designed as much to rally the euro and promote its adoption as a reserve currency in Asia as it is to create a currency to balance the role of the dollar and to anticipate any future yen bloc. Nevertheless, "Europe's example of closer economic integration has planted the seed in many Asian minds that their region too must forge closer ties and coordinate exchange rate regimes."[26]

On the other hand, Europe became more of a counter-model than model – there have been very few suggestions that any Asian currency alignment should follow strictly in the euro's wake. Rather, Europe's regional activities as a clearly determined region prompt Asian representatives to respond with a collective regional voice, suggesting that eliciting a response is more important than the nature of that response. As Japanese Finance Minister Kiichi Miyazawa noted in early 2001, "talks with Europe are helping us build up our own Asian identity."[27] At the same time, ASEAN was recognized as a forum which, given the informal pragmatism that underpins it, could never have been designed to deal with this kind of crisis. As a consequence, it was clear that a future ASEAN would be one that was linked more closely than ever to its significant East Asian allies. It has become evident, therefore, that Asia needs to raise a stronger collective voice, but not one which imitates the EU's approach or intensity. Finally, the crisis underlined the fact that "Asia" and "Europe" frequently come to be located at opposite ends of the spectrum: western capitalism faces Asian "crony capitalism," as distinct units with irreconcilable modes of economic activity.

An intensified perception of a notion of an ever-strengthening "fortress Europe" provided the main spur for a collective Asian response to Europe. The competitive limitations of Asian firms, their preference for other locations, regulations, and language barriers, the costs of investment, and home country policies have always made Europe a difficult place to penetrate. What is more, many businesses within East Asia have long been suspicious of the EU's development of trade and competition policy, trade-related investment measures, and environmental and labor clauses, since they tend to redound to the advantage of Europe and function to the detriment of Asia.[28] While there are available incentives for foreign investors to enter the EU, restrictions on certain sectors such as telecommunications, as well as general local content requirements and access to R&D and visas, make investment difficult. The fragmented and differentiated nature of the European market and its procedures make it less attractive than the United States, while the fact that the policy framework in Europe is often set nationally makes it hard for outsiders to decipher. For these reasons, and despite the regional core networks established by firms such as Toyota within Europe, FDI from developing Asia between 1990 and 1993 accounted for only one percent of inward FDI into the EU.

During the 1990s, several states such as Singapore and Thailand took greater interest in Europe, seeing, in particular, investment in Central and Eastern Europe as a way of overcoming levels of current and projected protectionism. The geographical proximity of these potential host countries to the EU market as well as their preferential arrangements with and imminent entry into the Union made them targets for investment. Moreover, while local demand continued to increase, labor and raw material costs made it cost effective to locate production plants there. These advantages, if not secured within an institutionalized framework, however, were soon to be lost with the growth of Central and East European rivals for similar products (such as chemical and low-technology manufactures).

Until recently, many Asian countries (and especially those of ASEAN) had shown more interest and concern in APEC than in Europe, given more immediate economic interests and the former's accommodating non-binding "open regionalism." This regionalism is amenable to the Asian (and especially ASEAN's) way of doing business, in contrast to what are often perceived as incompatible rigid rule-based negotiations by the EU. However, a rash of high-profile European trade missions to Asia in the early 1990s (for example, by German Chancellor Kohl, Belgian Prime Minister Jean-Luc Dehaene, and British Prime Minister John Major) combined with preparations for the 1999 launch of the euro and greater EU political and economic consolidation (notably after the European Maastricht summit in 1992) to raise the international credibility and attractiveness of Europe to external traders and investors. The euro, in particular, was initially welcomed as a possible alternative to the role of the dollar in the region and as a means of facilitating more effective access to the European market.[29]

ASEM clearly offers its Asian participants greater bargaining power than each state, or even ASEAN, could muster alone, while also benefiting them individually. Member states of ASEM, and in particular those of ASEAN, recognized in its origins the opportunity to enhance national interests, particularly on a regional level. At its origins, Thailand and Singapore took the opportunity to spotlight their own (economic) development by hosting media-rich events (ASEM 1 and the location for ASEF, respectively) on their own territories. For the additional three East Asian states, ASEM also offers project benefits (such as the information network of Korea), but, more importantly, provides them (especially Japan and China) with a new forum in which to demonstrate their international credentials.[30] More interestingly still, China has used the forum as a channel for presenting its global citizen credentials in a period when it began to seek support for its entry to the WTO. ASEM has even been the channel used by Beijing to propose and organize seminars on (Asia–Europe) human rights, in a conscious attempt to address some of the criticisms leveled at it regarding this issue. For this reason, ASEM may in fact be a useful vehicle for the enhancement of closer regional ties. There is, however, also a cognitive level on which it is important to ponder this issue: since the Asian side of ASEM does not possess a "rival narrative" to the structural framework in which both regions must interact, the dominance of the rules-based system, to which the EU subscribes and which forms (through the WTO and other key international organizations) the backdrop for ASEM, continues to prevail and leaves the EU (with the European Commission at its core) in the driver's seat in establishing economic dialogue.

5   Driving forces for EU participation

There is no straightforward account of ASEM's origins: explanations based uniquely on notions of hegemonic pressure, a perceived need for cooperation, historical or cultural convergence, or the accumulation of well developed public or private networks do not on their own adequately represent the timing, key actors, and structural framework of its foundations. Rather, a somewhat confused combination of factors served to stimulate its establishment and to prepare the ground for the key initiatives to be adopted in its name. It is also worth noting that ASEM was not the first opportunity for the EU to engage formally with its East Asian partners.

Structural factors

Most broadly, factors for the establishment of ASEM can be distinguished as structural and actor stimuli, which encapsulate the various impacts of a changing global environment in the 1990s, growing intraregional debates, and specific national and regional interests. The two most identifiable structural factors for initial European interest in ASEM pertain to a changing geopolitical global environment and the rise of "Asia" on a global scale during the 1980s and 1990s.

First, ASEM was a product of the immediate post-Cold War period, which witnessed not only the disintegration of geostrategic and psychological barriers between regional units, but also saw the burgeoning effects of a rapid globalization of networks of production, finance, investment, and commerce alongside the expansion of global market forces. Within both Europe and Asia, the perceived changing global role of the United States was also an important factor. Together, these factors rendered imperative a collective rethink of the role of the state and the recognition of other potentially significant actors.[31] To begin with, the ending of the cold war affected a number of key relationships, including those outlined above. While the EU drove forward its program of closer intra-European cooperation, many of its representatives also proposed the development of closer intraregional linkages in the political and military fields. Against this background, it became both more common and more palatable for the EU as a region to cooperate within formal or informal regional unions, in order to secure economies of scale and greater political leverage within a changing economically disparate and politically uneven global environment. Moreover, as the various processes of globalization continued, calls for a more manageable sub-global framework were also iterated and the suggestion was voiced that region- and issue-specific fora (for example on investment) could offer a less unwieldy forum for debate.[32] This structural change pushed EU representatives to contemplate an increase in the number of its cooperative associations at a range of levels, which included closer scrutiny of the use of interregional dialogue. The absence of a pre-existing regional interlocutor (as in East Asia) would be no obstacle: Asia could behave as a region for the purpose of interregional cooperation and in any case ASEAN (as the APT would later testify) lay at its heart. Later disillusionment with the WTO process, particularly with the failure to reach agreement in Seattle, further reinforced among many practitioners the need to diversify levels of engagement.

ASEM promised to serve as a minilateral forum in which to develop common understandings and possibly "embryonic accords" prior to participation in larger fora, while also acting as a channel for reinforcing the rules of the global regime.[33] It was no coincidence that economic ministers from ASEM discussed in their first meetings how to solidify mutual support prior to the WTO ministerial meeting in December 1996.[34] Moreover, in this way, ASEM, like other regional agreements, served to codify rules and practices and to "constrain national discretionary power."[35] What is more, the WTO also shapes the economic agenda of the newer forum, to the extent that much of the language and substance is drawn from the larger framework, and WTO-consistency (or "nesting") underpins ASEM agreements.[36] In addition, larger fora such as the WTO also balance and mediate (potential) differences in Asian and European economic traditions and interests, by providing external pressure to resolve potential region-to-region conflicts. The EU has seen ASEM as an additional means of soliciting Asian support for a new round of trade talks, and utilized negotiations over WTO entry to anchor China to domestic adjustments conducive to all ASEM member states.

Discussions over China's GATT/WTO membership have been a central issue since 1987, one year after China's formal application to join. EU businesses still face market barriers in China, but multilaterally the EU, having lifted in 1998 the label of China as a non-market economy, actively supported China's admission to the WTO, most vocally in the person of EU Commissioner Leon Brittan. For the European Commission, China's accession to the WTO was predicted to enhance the transparency and predictability of dealing with Beijing and to reduce levels of Chinese tariffs and non-tariff barriers (NTBs). The EU signed an agreement on China's entry to the WTO in Beijing in May 2000 (following the U.S.–China agreement of November 1999), in which it included demands for about 50 percent of foreign ownership in joint ventures of telecommunication services (compared with the 49 percent negotiated by the United States), as well as greater market access for the telecommunications and insurance industries.[37] Highlights of EU–China WTO negotiations included the acceleration of a timetable for market opening in mobile telecommunications, the opening of China's leasing market within three years (to allow foreign firms to rent and resell from Chinese operators), and a number of concessions in the field of insurance, import/export restrictions, and tariffs.[38] This need to "engage" Beijing was important both to the Europeans and the Asian group itself.[39] The EU on the whole has welcomed the pace of China's implementation of its commitments since its accession to the organization.

In specific sectors such as e-commerce, ASEM has drawn heavily from the ongoing initiatives in different bodies of the WTO. These global and trilateral rationales have appealed in different ways to the constituencies of each region. These utilize the principle of diffuse reciprocity facilitated by a broad-based regime structure. Thus, subjects similar to those aired within the WTO process (such as SPS and technical barriers to trade) are important items on ASEM's own agenda. Other WTO issues, like public procurement and investment, can be addressed in a less daunting environment within ASEM. In fact, to date the most important link between ASEM and the WTO has been in terms of pushing forward a new trade round.

However, nesting has not been a primary concern in the evolution of ASEM. The need to make agreements compliant with Article 24 of the WTO does not affect relations between the EU and Asia in the same way as the other groupings addressed in this book. In part, this is due to the very fact that ASEM only began in 1996, and was therefore established with the explicit purpose of being consistent with WTO principles. It does not therefore affect the actual and potential strength of the emerging regime between Europe and Asia. At the same time, Asian partners' familiarity with multilateral trade agreements derives to a large extent from participation in APEC. For this reason, they are accustomed to negotiating in a forum that emphasizes open regionalism. One reservation pertains to the lack of openness associated with the Chinese economy, but its own entry into the WTO is likely to engender there, too, a long-term enforced commitment to this principle. The nature of the regime is therefore not affected by this requirement. Finally, the low level of attention paid by the EU to East Asia in general, and the loose nature of the regime more specifically, further suggest that EU treatment of East Asia is unaffected by this need for WTO compliance.

The second identifiable structural factor for initial European interest in ASEM was the economic rise of East Asia itself. By the 1990s the "Asian miracle," combined with historical linkages, set in the European consciousness an idea of "Asian" growth, which began to affect trade with Europe. According to UNCTAD figures, in 1995 Asia accounted for 23.2 percent of the EU's external trade, compared with 17.4 percent the previous year. This explosion was part of a growing Asia–Europe trade pattern that outstripped the EU's trade with Eastern Europe between 1988 and 1994. Indeed, "Asia" became an increasingly attractive market for European trade and investment during the 1980s and 1990s (despite the financial troubles of 1997), representing a rapidly expanding and dynamic arena for mergers and acquisition (M&As), joint ventures, and investment, and a place where the rise in per capita gross domestic product (GDP) and disposable income offered, and continues to offer, new opportunities for European manufacturers.

By the end of the 1990s, Asia as a whole had become the EU's second-largest regional trading partner, with total EU exports to the region in 2000 of some €197.4 billion, and total imports of €318.9 billion. Asia thus accounted for 21.1 percent of the EU's total exports, and 26.4 percent of its total external trade in that year.[40] Total EU trade with Asia grew annually by 10.5 percent between 1995 and 2000 (slowing partially due to the financial crisis). EU imports from Asia continue to exceed exports, and 2000 witnessed a €121.5 billion trade deficit (see Table 3.1).

A key factor in re-engaging European interest in ASEAN was the decision in 1992 to establish an ASEAN Free Trade Area (AFTA) by 2003 (with extensions for Vietnam, Myanmar, and Laos). This project aims, principally through its Common Effective Preferential Tariff (CEPT), to liberalize intraregional trade and reduce intraregional tariffs, as well as to eliminate NTBs and establish cooperation in customs procedures. Even though some observers question AFTA's prospects,[41] growing economies of scale in this fourth largest trading area of 400 million people make it a potentially attractive target for trade and investment. These changes have been accompanied by a concerted Asian attempt to attract inward investment and European technological know-how, supported by a wave of liberalization of outward FDI flows.

The EU is also an important investment partner for Asia, with total EU FDI flows to Asia in 1999 amounting to €18.8 billion.[42] Among the EU's

Table 3.1   Regional trade by the EU

Region	Share of EU exports (%)	Share of EU trade (%)	Trade balance (€ billion)
Northeast Asia	13.0	17.4	– 96.4
Southeast Asia	4.3	5.6	– 29.3
South Asia	1.9	1.9	– 2.6
Australasia	1.9	1.55	+ 6.7
Total Asia	**21.1**	**26.4**	**– 121.5**
Europe outside EU	30.9	29.2	+ 6.7
NAFTA	28.4	24.9	+ 43.1
Mediterranean	5.4	4.9	+ 5.9
S & C America	4.3	4.2	– 1.0
Gulf	3.3	3.0	+ 2.7
ACP	4.1	4.1	– 4.9

Source: Eurostat

major Asian investment destinations in 1999 were Japan (€8.9 billion), Hong Kong (€4.5 billion), Thailand (€2 billion), South Korea (€1.6 billion), and China (€1.1 billion). Although the financial crisis temporarily reduced EU investment in Southeast Asia, total EU FDI flows to Asia nevertheless doubled between 1995 and 1999. For Lamy, "EU investment in Asia and indeed intra-Asian investment clearly is below potential. Some of this of course reflects the Asian crisis, but it will only bounce back to full potential if investors find a clear, transparent, nondiscriminatory, and predictable investment regime in the host country."[43] Nevertheless, the expansion of European FDI in Asia has been unevenly distributed: for example, while the EU's share of FDI in South Korea has grown, the figure in China has declined. In terms of investment into the EU, at present only Japan and South Korea are major contributors from Asia.

The Asian market offered trade and investment in a range of different goods, not least opportunities created by a burgeoning arms race, while more favorable deregulatory and liberalization trends in many parts of Asia fed this interest. In recognition of the greater importance of Asia, the European Commission published a policy paper in 1995, entitled *New Strategy Towards Asia*. This paper stressed the need to open markets, and to enhance economic and security stability in the region to ensure that investors and traders would become and remain interested. It also proposed concrete initiatives such as the Asia-Invest program to promote two-way trade and investment flows and an annual Asia-Invest Conference. The paper dealt with all fields of dialogue and in terms of security, too, noted that the EU "should seek to make a positive contribution to regional security dialogues."[44] As Tables 3.2 and 3.3 illustrate, moreover, the increasing trend toward viewing East Asia as the third side of a global economic triad put Asian interests more firmly into the international realm.

Notwithstanding phenomenal economic success within Asia, however, the region has consistently failed to become a priority area for the EU and its member states. European businesses on the whole have been slow to seize opportunities in Asia, and have focused for the most part on new enterprises in Central and Eastern Europe. Reasons for this neglect also include continuing problems with Asian tariff and non-tariff barriers; the lack of transparency, harmonized laws, protection and enforcement, intellectual property rights (IPR) provisions, and control over business enterprise in general;[45] the lack of familiarity with Asian business practices and distribution systems; and structural differences in economic organization. What is more, since European investors and traders perceived Asia's potential much later than did those from Japan and the United States, their transnational corporations cannot compete easily within Asia, where those firms are already established. While Japan enjoys a competitive advantage due to its geographical placement and intra-Asian networking, U.S. firms also have a longer tradition of links with Asia and better access to information about Asian markets, particularly through JETRO and the U.S. Department of Commerce. The EU *per se* has no investment promotion agency, but since the 1980s has operated a number of promotional instruments to partially rectify these imbalances. Moreover, the requested entry of China into the GATT/WTO and the potential for consolidating economic and political relations with its various Asian partners also provided incentives for the promotion of a collective European approach to East Asia.

Table 3.2 Share of world* trade (1998 as % total)

	Commercial services	*Goods*
EU*	24.9	18.9
Asian ASEM	19.4	21.0
US	20.1	18.9

Notes: *Excludes intra-EU trade
Source: Eurostat

Table 3.3 Foreign direct investment (FDI) (1998 and % total)

	Inflows	*Outflows*
EU*	19.4	45.0
Asian ASEM	14.4	8.0
US	37.4	28.0

Source: Eurostat

Concern over Asia continued into the second half of the 1990s, notwithstanding the dampening effects of the financial crisis. The EU's growing trade deficit with Asia led the EU Madrid summit declaration to declare: "the EU will be anxious to hear from Asian countries of progress in their own efforts to open their markets. The Summit will also make the EU and its Member States better placed to encourage European companies to pay closer attention to investment prospects in Asia."[46] The EU's Economic and Social Committee (ECOSOC), taking a position on relations with ASEAN, also insisted on the need to "emphasize quality rather than the size of the European presence."[47]

At the same time, the promotion of the euro within East Asia provided an additional incentive for European interest in this potentially huge pool of currency trading and reserves. From an Asian perspective, the role of the euro as a potential model (or even anti-model) for East Asian economic integration combined with a heavy Asian dependency on external trade to offer signs of welcome for European interest. However, the effects of the Asian crisis "dwarfed the forces which the euro [was] expected to create."[48]

In addition to attracting Asian interest in Europe in general, the EU also began to target key sectors in which to develop links with East Asia. These included in particular the environment, energy, telecommunications, and vocational training. At the same time, it was clear that tangible benefits from Asia could be gained for Europe through increased cooperation: "Member States of the EU are particularly interested in sharing the expertise and know-how of Asian countries in the rapid transformation of technological breakthrough into industrial production processes."[49] These specific areas of concern were to form an important basis for ongoing discussions within the ASEM process.

Actor responses

One of the major initial European incentives for involvement in ASEM was the opportunity for the EU to extend its global profile to complement its ongoing internal evolution through deepening (particularly through the launch of the euro and further development of the CFSP) and widening (negotiations for expansion to the states of Central and Eastern Europe). In addition, the EU had come to behave as a coherent international actor on a number of levels, and gained a degree of structural power over "new" trade agenda concerning Asia in the 1990s, largely through developments within its own internal structure and the changing nature of conditions within Asia.[50]

Positional considerations, both in the international system and in East Asia, are certainly at play for the EU in its activities in ASEM. While the United States retains a high level of structural power (the ability to shape and determine systemic structures within which other actors must operate), the fight for relational power (leverage over another) may be seen to depend increasingly upon belonging to ever-larger units of actors.[51] Despite the fact that the United States does not participate in ASEM and is not a subject for discussion, the trilateral framework in which ASEM is so often represented (on official and academic levels) reinforces the fact that the United States remains a key underlying presence in terms of both structural and relational power. It may be regarded as a driving force for action, to the extent that the U.S. rejection of EU observer status in the APEC process also made ASEM a desirable means of linking the two most distant poles of that triangle. In this way, ASEM acts as a global-supporting mechanism, depending for its own existence upon the overarching conditions set by the United States and upon a static reading of the nature of the three supposed poles of the triangle.[52]

In fact, ASEM cannot simply be read as a means of either fulfilling trilateral aims or posing a direct challenge to the superior power of the United States.[53] Rather, a focus on post-Cold War determinants imposed by the actions of a lone superpower obscures the impact of the tenets of a new political economy, which gives salience at different moments to a range of actors and alliances. What is clear is that if APEC is frequently regarded as a vehicle for Washington,[54] hegemonic stability theorists are unlikely to find similar power structures in ASEM, although, like APEC, it might represent the ongoing development of hegemonic multilateralism, in which a hegemonic state underwrites cooperative behavior. In many ways, the trilateral discourse emanates from a concern to delineate the effects of globalization upon Asia–Europe relations.

The key EU actors involved in ASEM have been the (rotating) Council Presidency, the European Commission, and the European Parliament (EP), with additional participation by ECOSOC. A number of papers have been produced by the European Commission, examining cooperation in specific sectors such as energy. For example, the 1996 Europe–Asia Cooperation Strategy for Energy[55] followed a European Commission White paper on energy policy for the European Union.[56] It aimed to increase the security of energy supply in Asia and Europe, to gain entry for EU firms into Asian markets, and to take measures to protect the global environment. Another important area is that of the environment, about which the European Commission produced a Communication in the wake of the 1994 European Council at Essen.[57] It was noted in this Communication that Europe is a "world leader in environmental technologies and services [and] is well equipped to work with Asia to address its problems in this field, particularly on the urban environment and pollution reduction and prevention." This sector provides an additional incentive for European economic involvement, by facilitating market-based approaches to environmental concerns and promoting joint research.

The most comprehensive Commission statements on East Asia were presented in the 1994 "towards a New Asia Strategy" document and its revised version in 2001.[58] The New Asia Strategy was proffered as the basis of European approaches to the ASEM proposal.[59] Although intended as a way of negotiating economic relations with key actors in East Asia, it was also designed as a means of establishing a broader set of relations and was linked closely with the further development of the CFSP.[60] The issues outlined in this strategy paper – such as sustainable development, environmental protection, economic stability, and joint research – are the bases upon which the agenda for ASEM would subsequently be formed. The strategy also sought to enhance and promote the EU's inclusion of the 1991 resolution to insert a human rights clause into the text of economic cooperation agreements with third parties, against which ASEAN had voiced its collective concern. While EU agreements with Vietnam (in 1995) and Laos and Cambodia (in 1997) did indeed include human rights clauses, disputes over Myanmar raged on. As a result of the latter's poor human rights record, the EU refused to deal with Myanmar or to invite its representatives to attend EU–ASEAN meetings. Tensions increased when Myanmar gained observer status to ASEAN in July 1996, and full membership in July 1997. This delicate issue was effectively bypassed by the establishment of ASEM, which does not – for this very reason – have the latest three ASEAN member states as members. If this situation continues, it could result in a mutual blockage of new members altogether, with negative consequences for the ASEM process as a whole.

The strategy document was also used to delineate the very existence of "Asia," into East, Southeast and South Asian sub-regions.[61] By contrast, the 2001 updated version set to establish a clear set of partnerships with the different economic and political units of Asia, with the aim of raising the EU's political profile "to a level commensurate with the growing global weight of an enlarged EU."[62] Following many of the same goals of the original strategy, the 2001 paper stressed the need to set ASEM activities within the broader international fora in which it is located.

The Council has taken a number of actions *vis-à-vis* Asia, and its representatives take part in all levels of ASEM engagement, while the European Parliament has been active particularly in the area of social welfare, human rights, and civil society participation. The question of human rights has exercised the EP, especially with regard to concerns over Myanmar,[63] where it has promoted linkages also between human rights and sustainable trade.[64] In its response to the European Commission document on ASEM in 2000, the EP emphasized the need to increase dialogue over conflict prevention on the Korean Peninsula and between China and Taiwan, as well as to establish a "wider social dialogue" among sub-state actors. For this reason, it has also advocated the inclusion of the Asia–Europe People's Forum (AEPF) within the main forum of ASEM.[65] Although beyond the scope of this chapter, it should be noted that the AEPF represents an increasingly significant channel attached (albeit unofficially) to the ASEM process. ECOSOC has also produced a number of opinions on EU activities towards Asia, and has in particular been a champion of private sector involvement.[66]

Also fundamental to the origins of ASEM was the role of the business sector, as represented in particular through the Asia–Europe Business Forum, which, unlike the AEPF, was integrated fully into the ASEM formal structure in the context of the SOMTI. However, while a number of seminars have been held, business participation in ASEM is currently waning. In part this is reflection of a downturn of economies within Asia, slower growth in Europe, and the imminent opportunities presented by EU enlargement. It is unclear as to what role the business sector will play in the future of ASEM.

The ASEM process, then, offered for the EU the discussion of political dialogue, the deepening of economic relations, and the reinforcement of cooperation in other areas. However, the EU wanted from its initial involvement something it did not get: a final statement reflecting "substantive agreements reached in ASEM."[67] What was eventually produced was, rather, a "pragmatic approach, based on an individually tailored analysis of its relations with each country or group of countries."[68]

6 Conclusion

This chapter has sketched the contours of a developing interregional dialogue among the states of the EU and East Asia. This fledgling forum has begun to strengthen the weak side of the perceived triangle of the international economy and has served to facilitate trade and other interests among the two participating groupings. At the same time, however, the broad spectrum of issues addressed by ASEM, its lack of institutional procedures, and the inchoate nature of the Asian region in this putative partnership of equals have all served to diminish ASEM's capabilities. The problem with this association to date is that it has tended to set Asia–Europe relations on a course to economic Asia versus political Europe, with their respective leaders setting out how Asian and European approaches differ inherently by embedding apparently dichotomous fundamental market and political values.[69] This difference is reinforced by the absence of formal institutional mechanisms. The problem to date with this loose regime is that it lacks the comprehensive discussion and implementation of "deliverables," or tangible evidence of cooperation.

The ASEM process, taking as its core a number of bilateral and other interregional channels for dialogue that had already been established for some years, originated from the confluence of changing systemic, intraregional, domestic, and sub-national interests. Thus, while the end of the Cold War and the rapid globalization of certain aspects of production, investment, trade, and communications combined with a growing discontent with the mechanisms of global regimes, the development of new regional roles and identities simultaneously prompted a new conceptualization of the most appropriate site of agency from which to articulate the interests of differentiated sets of individuals. This case study does indeed suggest that we are witnessing "an emerging synthesis in the dialectic of market-driven globalism and politically driven regionalism."[70]

The different hypotheses presented at the start of this book are each instructive in their own way in explaining the status of ASEM. First, the interest group hypothesis would appear to offer the most compelling explanation for the early development and sustenance of this forum to date. It was, after all, as a result of business lobbying that Singapore originally proposed the meeting, while nongovernmental lobbyists in the AEPF have shadowed the summits. The latter have exerted pressure upon the EP, itself trying to augment its own position within the structures of the EU to lobby on its behalf. Similarly, East Asian business representatives have been concerned about the impending effects of enlargement upon the relative competitiveness of East Asia. European SMEs were also initially interested in utilizing ASEM to promote their activities in East Asia. However, ASEM has proved to be an insufficient vehicle for harnessing these concerns and business interests, in the form of the AEPF.

Second, the bureaucratic hypothesis expounds a competition of interests among policy networks within and around the formal mechanisms of the EU. Although the French government, on behalf of the EU, agreed to the original Singaporean proposal for ASEM and the coordination for much of the agenda has been in the hands of the European Commission in an arena left vacant by uncommitted state leaders and their Council representatives, there is not sufficient primacy attached to East Asia – particularly since the financial crisis of 1997 – for it to register to a significant degree on any bureaucratic list of priorities. Indeed, the fact that the ASEM process itself lacks a secretariat delivers the European Commission into the *de facto* role of ASEM executive. Notwithstanding this role, and with the exception of a few figures of the caliber of Leon Brittan and Christopher Patten, meetings for ASEM are frequently attended by low-level officials and the corridors of the Commission and Council have never been abuzz with East Asian themes. Indeed, given the constitution of the European Commission, there are also very few officials who are able to gain an overarching appreciation of all the Asian participants of ASEM.

Third, the balance of power hypothesis inspires many scholarly reviews of ASEM, as it can be neatly accommodated within explanations of trilateral bargaining and by proponents of various schools of thought on globalization. Indeed, external threats have been crucial in the making of ASEM; it has been touted as a counterweight to APEC, offering balancing behavior cast in the dye of the triad. These assertions were particularly pertinent in the wake of the Seattle *débâcle*, but have withered somewhat with promises of a new WTO trade round and ASEM's embrace of the Doha Development Agenda. It remains to be seen whether ASEM can play a fruitful and interactive minilateral part in promoting the new round. Moreover, the relative coherence of the EU allows it a dominant actor role in this interregional relationship. Important in this respect, however, is that ASEM does not offer an alternative forum so much as a complementary channel by which to pursue ongoing goals. In this way, multidimensionality is not confined to the substantive issues of the forum, but extends to its positioning within the global network of international engagements.

Fourth, the constructivist hypothesis is important in illustrating how the EU and its counterpart seek to finesse and develop an external identity and to promote the utility of regions as optimal units for organizing the global economy. ASEM has been able to locate in one forum a comprehensive and overlapping debate over political dialogue and economic affairs. It is therefore able to situate the European Commission's trade mandate alongside ongoing redefinitions of the role of the CFSP and express globally a comprehensive regional profile. In the context of the ASEM process, moreover, it is able to project onto its embryonic counterpart an ideal-type regional institution. In these ways, ASEM provides a novel learning environment for region-to-region interaction and for defining the very meaning of "region" itself.

The substantive measurements set out in the introductory chapter also bear witness to the confusion over ASEM's future direction. First, the strength of this arrangement, in terms of its ability to constrain actor behavior, remains low. The open and nonbinding aspects of ASEM are enshrined in the official documents that determine its four key characteristics. These comprise its informality, multidimensionality, emphasis on equal partnership, and high-level (top-down) focus, all of which obstruct the development of a more compelling regime. Second, the degree of institutionalization is low and the continuity of the process is maintained primarily by the European Commission with additional support from the rotating East Asian coordinators. Without even an APEC-style mechanism for disseminating information and providing constancy, and given the fact that it is not a negotiating forum, it is difficult to see how ASEM will be able to function in the long term in an effective manner. Third, the nature of the regime remains liberal and WTO-supporting, with the effect that it remains hard to see the value-added of ASEM itself. The issue scope is broad but unequal, as the examples of IPAP's unifocal attention to investment regulation and the downgrading of working groups in a number of policy areas both illustrate. Current global events have placed greater weight on the political pillar of ASEM, but it remains to be seen whether its participants are willing and able to make a distinct contribution to ongoing issues of political salience. Fifth, the scope of the actors is similarly diverse, especially on the East Asian side, and is linked closely to the sixth point, regarding the changing counterpart coherence.

These apparent shortcomings demonstrate that ASEM fails to measure up positively to common criteria for regional and interregional effectiveness and continues to suffer from "problems of self identification."[71] It may, however, be too soon to judge its efficacy, and a longer time-scale may reveal alternative benefits to this novel form of interregional linkages. As the AFTA mechanisms take root and new models for regionalism are constructed in East Asia with the development of the APT process, a complex set of overlapping networks may situate ASEM at the core of hybrid interregionalism. This structure reflects an "informal reallocation of responsibilities" within one of the now numerous structures, rather than a formalization of arrangements.[72] In this model, sitting alongside the further development of bilateral and intraregional structures, ASEM could also promote the EU's external identity and strengthen the sub-unit of "ASEM Asia" as a convenient marker against its external interests. The key to this structure, then, rests in the power distribution of the EU *vis-à-vis* other regions and in the context of an increasingly unwieldy global economy.

The effect of these maneuvers will be to move from hybrid interregionalism (which reflects and is founded upon interaction at multiple levels of engagement) to a form approaching pure interregionalism, in which the very development of a region of East Asia enables it to exist in other circumstances. In both forms, the EU acts as carbon copy or alternative model, and the legitimacy of its own regional identity continues to be strengthened by this kind of interregional engagement.

Notes

1. See introduction to this volume for the definitions of different types of interregionalism.
2. Camroux and Lechervy 1996; Gilson 2002; Serradell 1996.
3. The three newest member states of ASEAN – Myanmar, Cambodia and Laos – are not participants in ASEM.
4. *Daily Yomiuri*, 29 February 1996.
5. Cited on http://europa.eu.int/comm/commissioners/lamy/ speeches_articles/ spla95_en.htm.
6. See http://europa.eu.int/comm/external_relations/asem/asem_summits/ asem4/ sec02.htm.
7. Lee 1998.
8. See http://europa.eu.int/comm/external_relations/asem_ipap_vie/texts/links.
9. Peña 1997, pp. 8–10.
10. Palmujoki 1997, pp. 284.
11. Lawrence 1995, p. 414.
12. CAEC 1997.
13. The Asia–Europe Environment Technology Centre (AEETC) was a further initiative in this vein, but most ASEM partners have now ceased their funding for it.
14. Ravenhill 1998.

15. Higgott 1998b.
16. Pelkmans and Fukasaku 1995, p. 163.
17. Rosamond 1997, p. 14.
18. Dent 1999a, p. 35.
19. See, for example, Bull-EU 4-2002, p. 78, 1.6.69; Jung and Lehmann 1997, p. 57.
20. See, for example, Higgott et al. 1993, p. 5.
21. Nuttall in Maull et al. 1998, p. 174.
22. See Sikkink 1991, pp. 249 and 251.
23. See http://www.aseansec.org/12259.htm.
24. *Financial Times* 13/14 January 2001; see also 25/26 July 1998 and 6 January 1999.
25. *Financial Times* 15 January 2001.
26. *Financial Times* 16 January 2001.
27. *Financial Times* 16 January 2001.
28. Dent 1999b, pp. 387–8.
29. According to Lee (1999, p. 70), "With the introduction of a single currency, Asian countries can enter one coherent market free from impediments to its internal trade and with an impressive growth potential."
30. Gilson 1999.
31. Higgott 1998a, p. 345.
32. *Financial Times*, 3 March 1996.
33. Dent 1999b, p. 389.
34. Bull-EU 12-1995, p. 43, I.79-Annex 14 Council report on ASEM preparations.
35. Woolcock 1996, p. 125.
36. Aggarwal 1998, pp. 5–6.
37. *Financial Times*, 17 May 2000, and 15 May 2000.
38. In addition, the EU designed a number of cooperation projects with a budget totaling around €24 million. Their package deal also included the pledge that both sides remove their respective quotas by 2005.
39. Bull-EU 6-1996, p. 16; 5–2001, 1.6.89, p. 82.
40. Within this, the developed countries in the region (Japan, Korea, Hong Kong, Taiwan, Australia, New Zealand) accounted for 10.6 percent of total EU exports, and the developing countries (South and Southeast Asia, China) for 10.5 percent. Major trading partners within the region include Japan (4.8% of EU exports in 2000), China (2.7%), Hong Kong (2.2%), South Korea (1.7%), Australia (1.7%), Singapore (1.6%), Taiwan (1.6%) and India (1.4%). ASEAN as a group accounted for 4.3% of EU exports.
41. Stubbs 2000, p. 312.
42. This was still a relatively limited proportion of global EU FDI. Asia accounted for 6.8 percent of total EU outward FDI in 1999, compared to 67.5 percent going to the NAFTA countries, 15.1 percent to Central and South America, and 7.5 percent to Europe outside the EU.
43. See http://europa.eu.int/comm/commissioners/lamy/speeches_articles/spla95_ en.htm.
44. COM (96) 4, 2.
45. Lee, C. 1998, p. 21.
46. Bull-EU 1/2-1996, p. 111,
47. Ibid.
48. Lee 1999, pp. 63, 72.
49. Bull-EU 12-1995, p. 45, I.79-Annex 14 Council report on ASEM preparations.
50. Dent 1999b, p. 388.

51. Strange 1994.
52. Gilson 2001. See also, *inter alia*, Dent 1999a and 1999b; Lee Dong-hwi 1998, p. 119; Maull et al. 1998; Tanaka 1999.
53. Bobrow 1998; Ullman 1976, p. 3.
54. Nesadurai 1996.
55. Bull 7/8 1996, 1.3.140, p. 58.
56. COM(95) 682.
57. Bull 10-1997 1.2. 185, p. 53.
58. COM (94) 427; COM (2001) 469 final.
59. Dent 1999b, p. 394.
60. Gilson 2002.
61. McMahon 1998, p. 233.
62. COM (2001) 469 final.
63. Bull-EU 1/2 1997, 1.3.115, p. 95.
64. Bull-EU 3-1998, 1.3.113, p. 92.
65. COM(2000)241; Bull-EU 6-2001, p. 100, 1.6.78.
66. Bull-EU 1/2 1997, 1.3.115, p. 95.
67. Bull-EU 12-1995, p. 43, I.79-Annex 14 Council report on ASEM preparations.
68. Bull-EU 9-2001, pp. 78–9, 1.6.51.
69. Zakaria 1994; *Far Eastern Economic Review* 10 December 1992.
70. Quoted from the introduction to this volume.
71. Lee Dong-hwi 1998: 115.
72. Cohen 1995, p. 531.

References

Aggarwal, Vinod K. (ed.) (1998). *Institutional Designs for a Complex World*. Ithaca: Cornell University Press.

Bobrow, Davis B. (1999). "The US and ASEM: Why the hegemon didn't bark." *The Pacific Review* 12, 1: 103–28.

CAEC (1997). *The Rationale and Common Agenda for Asia–Europe Cooperation*. Tokyo: Japan Centre for International Exchange.

Camroux, David and Christian Lechervy (1996). "Close encounter of a third kind? The Inaugural Asia–Europe Meeting of March 1996." *The Pacific Review* 9, 3: 441–52.

Cohen, Benjamin J. (1995). "Toward a mosaic economy: economic relations in the post-Cold War era," in Jeffrey A. Frieden and David A. Lake, 3rd ed., *International Political Economy: Perspectives on Global Power and Wealth*. London: Routledge, pp. 519–31.

Communication of the European Communities (COM), Brussels 4.9.2001 COM (2001) 469 final Communication from the Commission "Europe and Asia: a strategic framework for enhanced partherships."

Dent, Christopher M. (1999a). *The European Union and East Asia: An Economic Relationship*. London: Routledge.

Dent, Christopher M. (1999b). "The EU – East Asia economic relationship: the persisting weak triadic link." *European Foreign Affairs Review* 4, 3: 371–94.

Gilson, Julie (1999). "Japan's role in the Asia–Europe Meeting: establishing an inter-regional or intraregional agenda?" *Asian Survey* 39, 5: 735–52.

Gilson, Julie (2001). "Breaking the triangle? The U.S. ghost at the ASEM feast," in Bert Edström (ed.), *Interdependence in the Asia Pacific*. Stockholm: Swedish Institute of International Affairs, pp. 155–72.

Gilson, Julie (2002). *Asia Meets Europe*. Cheltenham, UK: Edward Elgar.

Higgott, Richard (1998a). "The Pacific and beyond: APEC, ASEM and regional economic management," in Grahame Thompson (ed.), *Economic Dynamism in the Asia–Pacific: The Growth of Integration and Competitiveness*. London: Routledge, pp. 335–55.

Higgott, Richard (1998b). "The Asian economic crisis: a study in the politics of resentment." *New Political Economy* 3, 3: 333–56.

Higgott, Richard, Richard Leaver, and John Ravenhill (eds.) (1993). *Pacific Economic Relations in the 1990s*. St Leonards: Allen and Unwin.

Jung, Ku-Hyun and Jean-Pierre Lehmann (1997). "The economic and business dimension," in CAEC, *The Rationale and Common Agenda for Asia–Europe Cooperation*. Tokyo: Japan Centre for International Exchange, pp. 49–73.

Lawrence, Robert Z. (1995). "Emerging regional arrangements: building blocks or stumbling blocks?" in Jeffrey A. Frieden and David A. Lake, 3rd edn. *International Political Economy: Perspectives on Global Power and Wealth*. London: Routledge, pp. 407–16.

Lee, Chong Wha (1998). "ASEM Investment Promotion Action Plan (IPAP) revisited: establishing the groundwork for regional investment initiative," Working Paper 98-06, Seoul, Korea Institute for International Economic Policy (KIEP).

Lee, Dong-hwi (1998). "ASEM after APEC? A comparative assessment." *Korean Institute of Foreign Affairs and National Security (IFANS) Review* 6.

Lee, Sahng-Gyoun (1999). "EMU and Asia–Europe economic relations: implications and perspectives." *Journal of East Asian Affairs* 8, 1: 51–72.

Maull, Hanns, Gerald Segal, and Jusuf Wanandi (eds.) (1998). *Europe and the Asia Pacific*. London: Routledge.

McMahon, Joseph D. (1998). "ASEAN and the Asia–Europe Meeting: strengthening the European Union's relationship with South-East Asia?" *European Foreign Affairs Review* 3, 2: 233–51.

Nesadurai, Helen (1996). "APEC: a tool for US regional domination?" *The Pacific Review* 9, 1: 31–57.

Palmujoki, Eero (1997). "EU–ASEAN relations: reconciling two different agendas." *Contemporary Southeast Asian Studies* 19, 3: 269–87.

Pelkmans, Jacques and Kiichiro Fukasaku (1995). "Evolving trade links between Europe and Asia: towards 'Open Continentalism'?" in Kiichiro Fukasaku (ed.), *Regional Cooperation and Integration in Asia*. Paris: OECD, pp. 137–74.

Peña, Fortunato T. de la (1997). "The role of SMEs in technology exchange between Asia and Europe." Paper presented at the Manila Forum on Culture, Values and Technology, Shangri-La's EDSA Plaza Hotel, 10–12 December.

Ravenhill, John (1998). "The growth of intergovernmental collaboration in the Asia–Pacific Region," in Anthony McGrew and Christopher Brook (eds.), *Asia Pacific in the New World*. London: Routledge, pp. 247–70.

Rosamond, Ben (1997). "Reflexive regionalism? Global life and the construction of European identities." Paper for the Annual Convention of the International Studies Association, Toronto, 18–22 March.

Serradell, Victor Pou (1996). "The Asia–Europe Meeting (ASEM): a historical turning point in relations between the two regions." *European Foreign Affairs Review* 1, 2: 185–210.

Sikkink, Kathryn (1991). *Ideas and Institutions: Developmentalism in Brazil and Argentina*. Ithaca: Cornell University Press.

Strange, Susan (1994). *States and Markets*. London: Pinter.

Stubbs, Richard (2000). "Signing on to liberalization; AFTA and the politics of regional economic cooperation." *The Pacific Review* 13, 2: 297–318.

Tanaka, Toshiro (1999). "Asia–Europe relations: The birth and development of ASEM." *Keio Journal of Politics* 10: 31–51.

Ullman, Richard (1976). "Trilateralism: 'partnership' for what?" *Foreign Affairs* 55, 1 (October).

Woolcock, Stephen (1996). "Regional integration and the multilateral trading system," in Till Geiger and Dennis Kennedy (eds.), *Regional Trade Blocs, Multilateralism, and the GATT: Complementary Paths to Free Trade?* London: Pinter, pp. 115–30.

Zakaria, Fareed (1994). "Culture is destiny: a conversation with Lee Kuan Yew." *Foreign Affairs* 73, 2: 109–126.

Websites

www.asemconnect.com.sg
www.aseansec.org
www.asef.org
www.asem2.fco.gov.uk
www.asem3.org
www.asemconnect.com.sg
www.asem.inter.net.th
www.asem.vie.net
www.caec-asiaeurope.org
www.cordis.lu/asem/home.html
www.eias.org
www.europa.eu.int
www.mofa.go.kr

4
Why the Euro–Med Partnership? European Union Strategies in the Mediterranean Region

Beverly Crawford

1 Introduction

The Mediterranean is the world's most volatile region. In the area that ties together southern Europe, North Africa, and the Middle East, the cultural cleavages between the West and Islam and the economic gap between North and South collide. From this collision between the "clash of civilizations" and extreme economic inequality emerge the central threats of the post-Cold War era: militant religious fundamentalism, the proliferation of weapons of mass destruction, international terrorism, migration, drug trade, instability in energy supplies, and interstate military conflict. A central issue for the international community is the creation of stability in the region.

The EU strategy to create stability in the Mediterranean has been a strategy of interregionalism – the pursuit of formalized relationships between the EU and a distinct Mediterranean region that both overlaps with the territory of the European Union and extends beyond it. The EU was moved to create this set of relationships because its members feared immigration and security threats arising from North Africa and the Middle East. EU foreign ministers also recognized a need to respond to "new" security issues emanating from the region, such as drug trafficking, human rights violations, and environmental degradation.[1] Furthermore, many EU officials regarded the building of a region and the creation of interregional relationships as a strategy to compete with other trade blocs without having to invite non-European Mediterranean countries to join the EU. Finally, EU ministers believed that interregionalism would be an important component to Europe's overall intervention in the effort to settle the Arab–Israeli conflict.[2]

This paper describes this set of relationships, called the "Euro–Mediterranean Partnership" or EMP. It demonstrates that, while the goal of creating a region and establishing interregional relationships in terms of "partnership" exists ostensibly, the results in the last eight years have been dependency relationships shaped by inequalities in power. No partnership has been created, whether formally, operationally, or in the minds of the participants. While the liberal goals of the EMP expressed new ideas about power, cooperative security, community building, and regional identity, disappointments emerged because of asymmetries in power and the threat to ruling coalitions and interest groups posed by the establishment of a region governed by liberal principles of freedom, openness, democracy, and the rule of law.

The EMP can be succinctly defined and its brief history easily recounted. In 1992, the European Council Summit recognized for the first time that "the southern and eastern shores of the Mediterranean and the Middle East are both areas of interest to the Union, in terms of security and social stability." In November 1995, the Spanish presidency of the EU organized a conference in Barcelona, with the fifteen members of the EU and twelve countries of the South Mediterranean. The outcome was the Barcelona Declaration or Euro-Mediterranean Partnership Initiative. Backed by the largest EU financial commitment ever made outside the Union, the Declaration launched a set of economic, political, cultural, and social programs, intended to reinforce one another in an open-ended process of regional integration with the assistance of the EU. The stated purpose of this process was to extend southward the European area of stability. It relied on the notion of "partnership" to signal the intent to create more symmetrical interdependence between the EU and non-EU Mediterranean countries, and it saw that partnership leading to a distinct Mediterranean region.

The Barcelona Declaration explicitly used the language of regional community building to express its goals, and it treated security as an "organic" and intrinsic aspect of regional development.[3] The Declaration asserted that the best way to achieve security, political stability, and economic welfare in the Mediterranean was neither by an elaborate system of alliances, collective security systems, or mere functional economic integration schemes. Rather, security and prosperity would be achieved by inventing a region that pools its resources and offers a shared social identity that could be a partner to the European Union.

From the vantage point of 2003, eight years after the signing of the Barcelona Declaration, progress toward these goals has been disappointing. At best, the arrangement can be described as one of hybrid interregionalism, a smattering of agreements between the EU and a group of countries defined by their proximity to the Mediterranean Sea.[4] And although the scope of the Euro–Med partnership is wide and the developmental focus clear, the interregional Euro–Med regime is weak. Lofty multilateral intentions have resulted in only a handful of bilateral agreements creating a hub-and-spoke relationship between the EU and the Mediterranean non-EU member countries (MNMCs); instability has increased in the region, liberalization and democracy have failed to thrive, and regional development is disappointing.

Furthermore, the economic gap between the EU and the MNMCs is widening at an alarming rate. The trade dependence of the MNMCs on the EU has increased in recent years from 43 percent in the 1970s to 52 percent in the late 1990s, while Europe's trade dependence on the MNMCs is negligible and consists primarily of dependence on energy supplies. Even that dependence is likely to weaken as the EU enlarges and begins to look eastward to the former Soviet Union to fill its energy requirements.

Why has the Barcelona Process stalled? Why has little progress been made toward a shared regional identity, toward multilateralism, toward development, and toward a more pure form of interregionalism? I address these questions in three parts. I begin with a description of the EMP, its evolution, and its current state. In particular, I examine the strength of the partnership, its nature, and the EU's commercial treatment of the non-EU member Mediterranean countries. I then turn to an examination of the MNMCs and their inability to be a true "partner" in the region-building process. Finally, I explain the emergence of the EMP and its lack of progress.

2   The Euro–Med Partnership as an interregional regime

Background: evolution of the Euro-Med Partnership

In the 1970s, concerns over terrorism and oil defined the European Union's key interest in the stability of the Mediterranean region.[5] Terrorism had been on the rise in Europe, spilling over from the Arab–Israeli conflict, and all member states began to tighten immigration controls to prevent terrorist networks from taking root in European soil. The oil shock of 1973 jarred Europeans into a reconsideration of their dependence on Arab oil, and the need for secure supplies and the maintenance of good relations with Arab countries. Driven by these two concerns, the EU launched the Global Mediterranean Policy (GMP).[6] The GMP offered trade concessions for the MNMCs in their economic relations with the EU, aid, and social provisions for migrants from the Maghreb in Europe. It also offered agricultural concessions and eliminated its own tariffs on industrial imports originating from the MNMCs while allowing them to retain their own tariff barriers.

Driven by the concern over terrorism and the need for regional stability, the Conference on Security and Cooperation in Europe (CSCE) (now the Organization on Cooperation and Security in Europe, or OSCE) identified a Mediterranean component to its program, and throughout the 1970s and 1980s it called together regional experts in economics, science, culture, and the environment to explore interregional cooperative measures that would build mutual trust and contribute to regional stability. The meetings accomplished little, however, and did not attract the attention of the United States, which was focused primarily on the East–West conflict.

In 1974, European energy concerns gave birth to the Euro–Arab Dialogue between the European Union and the Arab League, a weak form of interregionalism. The Action Plan for the Mediterranean – the creation of a "miniregion" around a specific narrow issue – was formulated within the framework of the Barcelona Convention of 1976 to combat pollution of the Mediterranean Sea. As an interregional arrangement, it was indeed successful, but the focus of cooperation remained limited to technical environmental issues, without "spillover" effects on other areas of concern.[7]

In short, all of these efforts remained limited in the context of the Cold War and by the insistence of the Arab League that the Palestinian issue be placed on the agenda, a condition that was then unacceptable to the Europeans. In a post-war world dominated by East–West confrontation, the creation of an interregional regime – a Mediterranean area of cooperation and stability – was clearly a low priority for the world's powerful states.

The end of the Cold War, however, promised to eliminate the obstacles to inter-regional cooperation, and in 1990, the CSCE initiated the Conference on Security and Cooperation in the Mediterranean (CSCM). Like earlier efforts, the aim was to boost regional economic development through cooperation, and to increase regional trust and transparency. The Western European Union (WEU) and the Council of Europe were involved in interregional trust promoting activities. In addition, the French put forward in 1990–1991 a plan for a Western Mediterranean CSCM, and NATO formulated a Mediterranean policy in 1994, promising to work with nonmembers to strengthen regional stability.

In the immediate post-Cold War period, the EU actively participated in the Middle East peace process, underwriting the emerging Palestinian economy.[8] Between 1994 and 1996, the Middle East/North Africa Economic Conferences provided a forum for discussions about economic development within the region. These discussions raised expectations that privatization would draw in foreign direct investment (FDI), which would in turn lead to industrialization and development.

Encouraged by success in these efforts and progress in the Arab–Israeli peace process, the European Union became formally involved in the project of creating regional stability in the Mediterranean. The Euro–Med Partnership was established in 1994, and in 1995 a Euro–Mediterranean Conference was convened in Barcelona to establish a framework for cooperation in the Mediterranean region, encompassing a population of 700 million in twenty-seven countries on both sides of the Mediterranean Sea. In addition to the fifteen EU states, the EMP includes Algeria, Cyprus, Egypt, Israel, Jordan, Libya, Malta, Morocco, Syria, Tunisia, Turkey, and the Palestinian Authority.[9]

The basic premise of Barcelona was that the Euro–Mediterranean area constituted a "common space," or at least that it possessed enough of the precursor elements of a region (geographic contiguity, common values, traditions, or interests) to make regional building a possibility. Stephen Calleya writes that "from this premise flowed two other assumptions: that the member-states or regimes were equally committed to the goal of regional cooperation as a tool to promote peace, stability and prosperity; and that they were also receptive to the kinds of political, economic and social liberalization that makes transnational (as opposed to intergovernmental) cooperation possible."[10]

The political element of the Barcelona declaration includes a list of principles concerning respect for democracy and the rule of law, human rights, the rights of self-determination, noninterference in the internal affairs of other states, and the settlement of disputes by peaceful means. It also contains cooperative measures for fighting terrorism. On the economic front, the Barcelona document provides for a regional partnership to promote economic development by means of a free trade zone to be created by the year 2010.

In the period since the EMP was initiated, however, the development, integration, and security gap between the EU and the nonmember Mediterranean states has grown. The EU has undertaken two major constitutional reforms. It has convened a constitutional convention that promises a common security policy, and it has successfully completed the creation of the single market with a common currency. The EU is also proceeding with its fifth enlargement, to be completed in 2004. Yet during this same period, the nonmember Mediterranean states have experienced growing poverty and decreased security. There has been little effort toward increased integration, and there have been precious few successes in the effort to liberalize their economic and political systems.

Furthermore, little has come of the five EMP ministerial conferences since the initial one in Barcelona. The objectives of the Barcelona Declaration were slated to be confirmed by twenty-seven Mediterranean states in Malta in 1997. But the stalled Middle East peace process and ensuing tensions overshadowed the meeting and cast grave doubts on the partnership's success. Subsequent meetings, including those at Stuttgart and Marseille, did very little to get the EMP out of its failing path, or worse, irrelevance. True, some economic agreements were signed, and the idea of having a free-trade area by the year 2010 still stands. Moreover, there has been activity at the level of civil society in the region, specifically the promotion of common cultural and security understandings, including EuroMeSCo, a security think-tank, which has become an important example of "track two diplomacy" in the region. Furthermore, in April 2002, the Euro–Med partners adopted the Valencia Action Plan, making sustainable development the guiding principle of the Euro–Med Process. The action plan includes reinforced credit facilities for Mediterranean partner countries through the European Investment Bank (EIB) and the creation of a Euro–Mediterranean Foundation to promote cultural exchange.[11] However, the conference made no progress in other areas such as trade liberalization in agriculture and linkage of European aid to the progress made by aid recipients in the fields of democracy and human rights, one of the key aspects of tying security to political and economic liberalism expressed in the Barcelona Declaration.

3   Assessing the EMP

In short, progress toward the creation of a strong interregional partnership between the EU and the nonmember countries of the Mediterranean region has been disappointing. In this section, I gauge the level of that disappointment by looking at the strength and nature of the partnership and the commercial relations that have developed, measuring these realities against the goals set forth in the Barcelona Declaration.

The strength of the partnership

The Barcelona Declaration established an equal partnership between the EU and the MNMCs in the project of region building and interregionalism. But the reality is one of EU control over the pace and content of the Barcelona process. Coordination and management of all EMP activities takes place in Brussels. The EMP has no independent secretariat, and those in Brussels responsible for Euro–Med issues are scattered throughout the Commission.[12] Clearly, the management of the EMP by the Commission perpetuates and recreates an asymmetry between EU member states and the rest; there is no equivalent management structure among the nonmember partners of the EMP. The EuroMesCo Joint Report of 1997–98 suggested that while the Commission should retain this role, stopping short of the creation of a Secretariat, a "ProMed" group of civil servants from the MNMCs could be constituted to act in a management capacity as a partner of the Commission. However this form of institutionalization has yet to be implemented or even discussed.[13] Furthermore, as we shall see below, there is little counterpart coherence among the MNMCs. On economic issues, all decisions are in the hands of the EU, where decisions on trade and aid are reached through compromises among the fifteen members.

There is no voting mechanism for EMP decisions. Although the European Parliament proposed the establishment of a Euro–Mediterranean Parliamentary Assembly at the Velencia meeting,[14] no concrete decisions have been taken to create one. Decisions in the EMP on political and cultural issues are made by consensus. There is no formal voting. Veto power by any of the twenty-seven EMP members is the rule.[15] Before any EMP ministerial summit, each EMP member country prepares its national position on the different items on the agenda. Positions are shaped by a combination of business lobbies and member state conceptions of the national interest. While each state fashions its own position, the position of the EU member states is coordinated by the Commission. Although member state ministers represented their own countries at the EMP biannual intergovernmental summit, there is almost no leeway for a state to negotiate its position once in the summit.[16]

The association agreements between the EU and MNMCs lack credibility. Because there is no judicial review mechanism, either side can backtrack from the agreement with impunity. Without oversight, EU commitments are weak – for example, the EU commits itself to "exploring" an issue, and then explores it for years without making a formal commitment. When the EU does make a commitment, it is often reversible.[17] There is no dispute settlement mechanism to redress grievances if case association agreements are not fulfilled. Although many of these agreements link progress in political and economic reform in the MNMCs to trade concessions from the EU, there is no oversight mechanism to ensure that these aspects of the agreements' conditionality are being fulfilled. In short, without a secretariat, without a parliament, without judicial review of the association agreements, without oversight and a dispute settlement mechanism, without a voting mechanism among the twenty-seven, and with essential economic decisions imposed on the MNMCs by the EU, the "partnership" can be characterized as weak.

The nature of the regime: scope and focus

The scope of the EMP is in inverse relationship to its strength. Following the CSCE model of the Helsinki Accords, the Barcelona Declaration consists of three pillars (called "baskets") on which partner states are to construct a peaceful Mediterranean region: economic reform, adherence to common political principles, and cultural cooperation.

Economic proposals in the Barcelona Declaration included the establishment of a free trade area between the Union and MNM countries by 2010. The EU would provide economic aid to benefit the MNMCs' private sectors and to encourage structural reform and privatization. The underlying objective of this economic pillar was to help MNMCs adapt to an increasingly freer and more globalized economy in the belief that such transformation would also help resolve political crises, undermine rent seeking authoritarian regimes, and provide an economic basis for social stability in the region.

The political element of the Barcelona declaration emulates the 1975 Helsinki Final Act in its adoption of a "code of peace"[18] – i.e., a set of principles that set the normative guidelines around which the prospective region is supposed to be constituted. These principles include respect for international law and human rights, nonintervention, respect for the territorial integrity of states, cooperative measures for countering terrorism, and the settlement of disputes by peaceful means. The EMP also adopted "soft" security practices, such as regular political and security dialogues, security expert meetings, "seminar diplomacy," and Partnership Building Measures with the aim of creating trust and collective security understandings between EU members and partner states. One of the most important initiatives in the security field was the drafting of a "Charter for Peace and Stability," which, modeled after the 1993 "European Stability Pact" in Central and Eastern Europe, aims to increase regional security and stability by means of enhanced political dialogue, preventive diplomacy, crisis management, and post-conflict rehabilitation measures.

The third pillar is contained in the cultural basket, which is intended to break the barriers between cultures around the Mediterranean and promote a dialogue between civilizations. High on the negotiation agenda of the EMP is a "Declaration of Principles of the Dialogue of Cultures and Civilizations" and the establishment of a Foundation for the Dialogue of Cultures. Based primarily on civil society networks of academicians, students, and religious authorities, this basket aims at building the long-term conditions for the future development of Mediterranean social stability based on transnational social links and the understanding of diverse Mediterranean cultures.

The central focus of the EMP is its economic pillar. As Alfred Tovias has argued, two principles were behind the construction of the economic program. First, the improvement of the economic conditions in the MNMCs was seen as crucial to deter migration to the North. Second, the MNMCs would have to be "anchored" in a relationship with the EU through the deepening of economic interdependence between the EU and the countries of the region.[19] As noted above, initiatives to realize these principles were the creation of a Euro–Mediterranean free trade zone and an increase in EU financial assistance to MNMCs. The creation of a free trade zone was intended to shift the adjustment costs of trade to the MNMCs, ending twenty years of EU trade concessions enshrined in the GMP. Through the agreement to create a free trade zone, the Keynesian ideas of development contained in the GMP gave way to the neoliberal ideas of the Washington Consensus.[20]

Nonetheless, the economic pillar contained an aid component. Because the creation of a free trade zone will erode tariff revenues and trigger a rise in unemployment in the nonmember Mediterranean countries, their budget deficits will grow. To ease the transition to free trade by financing budget deficits, the EU's Council of Ministers, in 1996, approved a new EU regulation called MEDA (Measures d'Accompagnement) dealing with all MNMCs under a unified framework, doubling its pre-Barcelona Declaration aid to nonmember countries in the region. Approximately one billion euros per year would be distributed from the EU budget to eight of the twelve MNMCs (including the Palestinian Authority) on a bilateral basis. All eight belonged to the Arab world.[21] To the annual one billion euros of aid drawn from the EU budget, the

European Investment Bank put another one billion euros at the disposal of the same eight countries in the form of loans.[22]

Commercial treatment: degree of uniformity and treatment type

What are the guidelines by which this aid is disbursed and association agreements negotiated? The EU's treatment of the nonmember Euro–Med partners is not fully uniform, but rather mixed, and movement toward uniform treatment is stalled. Nonuniform treatment is expressed in four ways: 1) in terms of conditionality requirements, 2) in terms of the issues at stake in the agreements themselves, 3) in terms of "preference erosion," and 4) in terms of the EU's aid policy, which is unilateral.

First, aid and trade concessions are tied to the pace of economic reform in the nonmember countries. Cyprus, Malta, Israel, and Turkey have all geared their internal policies toward the accession criteria for EU membership. Cyprus and Malta are slated to join the EU by 2005 and are thus striving to meet the strict terms of the Copenhagen criteria; Turkey has completed its customs union with the EU and is attempting to accelerate its economic and political reforms to fully meet the Copenhagen criteria. Israel strengthened its links with the EU during the peace process of the 1990s; those links weakened as the peace process stalled. All association agreements with the remaining nonmember Middle East–North African (MENA) countries are bilateral – between individual EU member governments and governments of the nonmember countries, negotiated under the umbrella of the EMP. Association agreements stipulate steps in the liberalization of the economies of individual countries. Since the MNMCs vary in terms of their degree of liberalization, the association agreements are tailored to each country.

Second, the agreements vary greatly in their uniformity depending on the issue at stake – such as trade in goods and services or migration and labor – and the stage of economic liberalization that the country has reached. The most uniform treatment is in the agreements reached over trade in goods. Trade policy of the member states is almost exclusively in the hands of the Commission and thus trade concessions offered by the EU and the rules of access to the European market are uniform. This means that the degree of "politicization" and possibility of variation in interpretation of EU laws is limited.[23] Presumably, with the completion of the Mediterranean Free Trade Area by 2010, this uniformity will increase, and the scope of uniformity will expand.

Treatment on other issues is nonuniform in the sense that the agreements themselves do not call for any "adjustment" on the part of the EU. For example, as Tovias writes:

> [N]one of the agreements signed provide for the automatic removal of significant technical barriers faced by MNMCs' exports to the EU, such

as obligatory testing or certification of conformity by local EU authorities for many goods, because mutual recognition agreements (MRA) are not part of the present deals. MRAs on standards are not even contemplated. There is some talk of future standards harmonization, but in fact the idea is that MNMCs shall accept the *acquis* as far as standards are concerned. Participation in European standards institutions is a privilege reserved apparently to present and future EEA [European Economic Area] members only. This and other second-generation issues are not only important for Israel or Turkey (as one is tempted to think *a priori*), but for Maghreb and Mashrek countries. Take for instance norms and standards relating to fish canning or relating to fishing methods. It is well known that Portugal, Spain, and Morocco compete in the same canning products and in the same markets. Whereas Portugal and Spain are key decisionmakers in the EU in these matters, Morocco is not even consulted.[24]

Third, variation among the terms of the association agreements is partly due to the erosion of agreements over time. Indeed, as Tovias argues, preference erosion has been invoked frequently by MNMCs to justify their deviation from commitments throughout the life of Europe's economic relations with the region.[25] For example, in 1963, the EU negotiated an Association agreement with Turkey, stipulating the free movement of labor between Turkey and the EU. Migration, however, was (and still is) the reserved domain of member states. Thus Germany vetoed the part of the association agreement in 1986 that stipulated liberal migration of labor. Turkey used this issue – in which the EU did not hold to its association commitment – to backtrack from its own commitments under the agreement.

Fourth, aid is disbursed directly from the EU budget on a bilateral EU–MNMC basis. Tovias notes that the term "bilateral" is a misnomer because all aid is given on a unilateral basis from the EU to the MNMCs. There have been no negotiations between the EU and MNMCs within an EMP forum over how that aid is disbursed or how much aid will be offered to each MNMC. Before the Velencia meeting in April 2002, Spain advocated the creation of a Euro–Mediterranean Bank that would place EU members and nonmembers on an equal footing, a suggestion that found favor in several countries of the Maghreb. But because of opposition from the northern European countries, the idea was diluted into increased credit provision via the European Investment Bank, where decisions on aid would continue to be made unilaterally by the EU.[26]

The amount of aid and means of disbursement are negotiated among the fifteen EU members. There is no contractual obligation with each of the Arab MNMCs to disburse a given amount. MEDA is an EU regulation, not part of the bilateral association agreements. In trade, the negotiations can be considered bilateral between the EU and the MNMCs. The Commission stated from the beginning that it was prepared to engage in constant dialogue with the MNMCs on a wide range of trade and invest-ment-related matters, such as indirect taxation, standards, and customs procedures, but little progress in a change in pre-Barcelona procedures has been made.[27]

4   Counterpart characteristics

The lack of uniformity in treatment, the bilateral nature of the association agreements, and the unilateral EU decisions on aid can all be partially explained by the characteristics of the non-EU member partners to the EMP. There is no overarching self-definition of the region that encompasses the non-EU member countries; while most of the MNMC trade is con-ducted with Europe, most of Europe's external trade is conducted with other regions of the world. The entire North African market is only equival-ent to the internal Portuguese market. And the Maghreb market is frag-mented into a number of even smaller markets, and internal transaction costs remain very high. Stephen Calleya writes that "the cost of shipping a container from Tunisia to Marseilles is higher than the cost of sending the same container from Marseilles to Asia."[28] Intraregional trade in the Maghreb represents only 5 percent of the Maghreb's total external trade. Intraregional trade in the Mashreq[29] is only slightly higher at 7 percent. These small and fragmented markets go a long way in explaining why the MENA countries have managed to attract only 2 percent of all international FDI.[30]

Weak and non-institutionalized multilateral regimes govern the various subregions, offering little in the way of a regional negotiating partner for the EU or an institutional structure that would reduce the transaction costs of intraregional trade. Conflict has hindered closer cooperation between countries in the Balkans, the Maghreb, and the Mashreq. Both the Balkans and the Mashreq include countries that do not border on the Mediterranean and are not members of the EMP. Relations among coun-tries in these subregions are largely confined to the intergovernmental level, with cross-border interaction limited to the issues of energy, Islam, and agriculture.[31] A handful of specialized subregional NGOs exist such as AARINENA, the Association of Agricultural Research Institutions in the Near East and North Africa. Each of these subregions follows its own trajectory, and there is little indication that they are on a path toward inte-gration into a single region.

Relations among the MNMCs of the EMP are both multilateral and bilateral. The Gulf Cooperation Council (GCC), in existence since 1981, is the most effective of the multilateral regimes. It is comprehensive, cover-ing issues from trade to education, from foreign and military policy to cultural cooperation. The GCC is governed by a Supreme Council with a rotating presidency and administered by a Secretary-General. Decisions are taken both by consensus and majority voting and are binding on the member states. A dispute settlement mechanism supports those decisions. However, it includes countries outside of the EMP and is thus seldom a negotiating partner for the EU within the EMP. Furthermore, it has not served as a model for the creation of other groupings in the Arab world. The Arab Maghreb Union, a North African customs union, and the Arab Cooperation Council were formed in the late 1980s, but exist largely only on paper.

In April 2000, Chris Patten, the EU Commissioner for External Relations, in an effort to build reliable regional negotiating partners, advocated the creation of subregional free trade areas, offering EU support for any efforts to establish multilateralism as a principle of South–South cooperation. In 2001, the Arab League established an Arab Free Trade Area to be completed by 2007. In addition, the Agadir Declaration of May 2001 announced the establishment of a free trade area between Morocco, Tunisia, Egypt, and Jordan. The EU offered technical assistance to the "Agadir Process," and the Valencia Action Plan should facilitate efforts on the part of North African countries to revive the Arab Maghreb Union.

Finally, a number of bilateral agreements also exist in the MNMCs. Turkey and Israel have negotiated a free trade agreement as a corollary of the Turkey–EU customs union. Syria and Lebanon engage in bilateral cooperation, but the relationship is clearly dominated by Syria, a kind of "imposed" cooperation and thus unlikely to serve as a model for similar arrangements among the EU's EMP partners.[32]

In short, small and fragmented markets, combined with few and weak subregional regimes that would make suitable negotiating partners for the EU in the EMP, add up to low counterpart coherence. MNMCs compete with one another for EU aid and loans, thus limiting their incentive to join a bargaining coalition. Any region-wide regime is out of the question at the present time: potential accession countries have a different relationship with the EU than with the other Mediterranean countries, and the Arab–Israeli conflict, which at times can be subdued by the larger EMP project, prevents a common negotiating front from being forged between Israel and the rest of the Arab states. Finally, as we have seen, even the Arab MENA states have not found enough common ground to create a negotiating coalition.

5   Explaining the shape of Euro–Med interregionalism

Are there underlying factors that drive these outcomes? What explains the EU initiative in creating a Mediterranean region? Why did the EU seek a transregional "partnership" with states around the Mediterranean basis?

And why have the results been disappointing? I argue that the realist perspective best explains the incentive of both the EU and the MNMCs to create a region and to create an interregional relationship. Constructivist and bureaucratic politics approaches best explain the nature of the regime, but interest group and realist approaches best explain disappointments in terms of strength, commercial treatment, and weak counterpart coherence. Below, I discuss and weigh these explanations.

Explaining the birth of the Euro–Med Process: neorealist perspectives

The realist paradigm of international relations provides cogent explanations for region building. As Brooks and Wohlforth have remarked:

> States often build regional partnerships in order to balance against the overwhelming power of another state. Indeed, region building is likely to be a common occurrence in the coming years. The nineteenth century international system featured six to eight poles among roughly thirty states. In the early Cold War there were two poles, but the number of states had doubled to just over seventy. Today there is one pole in a system in which the population of states has trebled to nearly two hundred. Inevitably then, much activity will take place at a regional level, and it can often be in the interests of the parties involved to use balancing rhetoric as a rallying point for stimulating cooperation, even if that is not the chief driver of their actions.[33]

Within this wider perspective, the Barcelona Process is part of the EU's strategy to expand its own political influence in the region to meet three balance of power goals: 1) countering the United States in the region, especially in the Middle East, 2) controlling the region through the creation of asymmetrical dependency relationships, and 3) containing political Islam.

First, from this perspective, the Euro–Med process was triggered by European uncertainties about power balances in the aftermath of the Cold War. Indeed, with the Cold War's end and Germany's achievement of unity and sovereignty, France feared that Europe would drift eastward; the EMP would help achieve a new power balance between France and Germany.[34] It would also be part of the EU's effort to balance the influence of the United States. Indeed, the EMP has all the hallmarks of an increasingly ambitious EU foreign policy. If the EU could not yet aspire to be world hegemon, it could be a regional one, a power that would assert its preeminence over the United States in North Africa and the Middle East. This preeminence would not be induced by direct political action, mediations, and missions, but rather by a systematic use of economic tools to create a region for political ends. And the wars of Yugoslav succession reminded Europeans that the postwar peace on the continent could again be threatened.

Second, as noted above, critics pointed out that the project was devised to protect EU member states from the adverse consequences of large-scale migration flows and from an uncontrolled flood of competing agricultural products that might enter the European market under WTO agreements – an effort on the part of the EU to control the region for its own benefit by exploiting its asymmetric relationship with North African and Middle Eastern States. Indeed, recall that the origins of the EMP can be located in a pronouncement made by EU foreign ministers at an EU Summit. Institutionally, it is defined, administered, and funded from Brussels. There are no headquarters or civil servants dedicated to this project outside EU structures and thus no symbolic venue with which it can be identified. The very fact that the timeline for appraisal of the process is successive EU presidencies is telling. From the South, the enterprise is interpreted more often through the core-periphery paradigm than as an instance of positive-sum liberalism: a (friendly) takeover rather than a joint venture.

Finally, the neorealist perspective is bolstered by the fact that the impetus for EMP was clearly a strategic response to the rise of political Islam. As early as 1992, the European Council of Lisbon had expressed its unease at the "advance of extremist forces... in various North African countries." Two years later, the European Council of Essen elevated the Mediterranean to a "priority zone of strategic importance to Europe." And at the behest of France, Italy, and Spain, NATO began lobbying the EU early in 1995 to concoct a new policy towards "Islam."

All of these goals could conceivably be met, however, through a construction of alliances in the region and a strengthened EU security architecture. Instead, however, the EU linked the goals of political and economic reform, cultural convergence, and security in a new package that defined the nature of the EMP. Realist explanations fall short when they attempt to account for the relatively revolutionary nature of the Euro–Med Partnership enshrined in the Barcelona Declaration. Indeed, the Barcelona Declaration is a constructivist's dream.

Explaining the birth of the Euro–Med process: the constructivist approach[35]

The Barcelona Declaration is grounded in the literature on what constructivists have recently called the EU's revolutionary approach to security, a set of tightly linked norms and practices that define a particular approach to security that departs significantly from the realist paradigm. As Nicolaidis has argued, the EU has chosen to be weak in military capabilities because it has adopted a "Kantian" culture.[36] Many have argued that the EU's power rests on the ability to attract states to become members or partners of a political community, the access to which depends on the adoption of a set of norms, practices, and institutions. In the words of Graham Fuller, Europeans have "forged their homelands into a new cooperative whole," and taken their power to be "the power of a gradually expanding international community of consent."[37]

For constructivists, Europe practices "normative power" and this notion of power is codified in the Barcelona Process. Normative power can be defined as the ability "to shape conceptions of 'normal'"[38] or the ability to tame anarchy with civilian practices.[39] In the eyes of constructivists, this normative power is what drove Europe's success in bringing stability, security and well-being to the region.

Normative power can diffuse in time and space (geographically and functionally) and thus "conquer" other states and cultures. Whereas material power-related practices often require bypassing and overruling the rule of law, normative power depends on the diffusion of the rule of law. Whereas states that use material power may only be able to force democracy, the rule of law, and human right practices onto other states (and hope for the best), normative power, if effective, may be able to achieve the same outcome by means of learning processes, which rely on endogenous rather than on exogenous changes, and thus, it is likely to be more effective and durable. Normative power is exercised in "partnerships," not empires, in the diffusion of ideas, rather than forcing the acceptance of a normative hegemonic order.

Europeans also tend to believe that security is best achieved through the enlargement of a liberal democratic security community.[40] This conception of security can be described as "cooperative security." Based on concepts of pluralistic integration and inclusion, cooperative security is comprehensive, for it links classic security elements to economic, environmental, cultural, and human-rights factors. It is also indivisible, in the sense that one state's security is inseparable from that of other states. Most important, it is cooperative: security is based on confidence and cooperation, the peaceful resolution of disputes, and the work of mutually reinforcing multilateral institutions. Cooperative security has not only become an important policy tool, but also part of the EU's self-identification. Because the EU is constituted on a normative basis, this predisposes it to act in a normative way in world politics.[41] Thus, whereas material power has historically been conducive to understanding political reality from a national and international point of view, normative power is conducive and consistent primarily with a transnational and supranational point of view.

A quick glance at the EU today shows that "Europeans already wield effective power over peace and war as great as that of the United States, but they do so quietly through 'civilian power' [which] does not lie in the development of battalions or bombs, but rather in the quiet promotion of democracy and development through trade, foreign aid and peacemaking."[42] The EU as civilian power obtains security by instilling expectations and dispositions in near abroad states, to the effect that adoption of EU norms and values will gain them inclusion into the ranks of the EU.

A civilian power, thus, wields influence via EU accession, "perhaps the single most powerful policy instrument for peace and security in the world today."[43] It also provides civilian development assistance, builds global trust needed to manage crises, and works through multilateral means and world public opinion.[44] Most important, however, through "the propensity of the EU to seek to reproduce itself by encouraging regional integration around the world," the EU's civilian "power" rests mainly in it becoming a "'laboratory' where options for politics beyond the state are generated, for the taking," and thus, also in it becoming a normative and practical model of regional or even global governance.[45]

The Euro–Med process is such a laboratory. Region building such as in the case of the Barcelona Process and the recent initiative of a "Wider Europe-Neighborhood" works by means of the social construction of collective regional understandings, especially the development of new and encompassing social identities, which, rather than canceling deeply seated cultural and national identities, pools those identities into a larger "we." Like the CSCE did in the past, EMP partner states are invited to belong to a region of peace and stability that does not exist, but which is supposed to develop because people collectively believe that promoting region building is mutually beneficial.

In sum, for constructivists, the process of region building in the Mediterranean is consistent with Europe's practice of normative power and cooperative security. As such, the Barcelona Declaration suggests a move toward a more holistic understanding or conceptualization of the causal linkages between economic and political development and security and stability. In fact, the Barcelona Declaration represented an important shift from the sectoral approach of the GMP of the 1970s to a holistic approach based on the simultaneous launching of a set of economic, political, cultural, and social initiatives that were supposed to reinforce each other. For the EU, the Barcelona Declaration is the most coherent expression to date of the link between economic liberalism and political liberalization as an EU foreign policy tool. Only with the EMP do we see the expression of a clear external political objective associated with this link, the "transformation of the region into a zone of peace and stability."

Explaining the birth of the Euro–Med process: bureaucratic politics in the EU

The perspective of bureaucratic politics presents a much more humble explanation of the birth of the EMP. It suggests that the European Union's incentive for the construction of the Euro–Med Partnership is a direct result of the Commission's drive to expand its own authority and influence within the EU.[46] From this perspective, the Commission is a key actor, with its own set of bureaucratic interests. The EMP effort, in this light, has implications for the division of labor within the EU. In the period leading up to the Barcelona Declaration, individual member states had significant leeway to influence EU policy. Indeed, the EMP was conceived in Brussels at a time when some member states were still keen to pursue their own Mediterranean policy.[47] Since then, however, the Latin EU states have increasingly given up their Mediterranean policies. Spain, Italy, and Greece all scaled down their external policymaking ambition in their bid for EMU membership.

Furthermore, EU officials have argued that the management of the EMP by the Commission helps to soften perceptions of neocolonialism within the MNMCs. The EMP brings a greater degree of political scrutiny, especially as the European Parliament starts blocking financial protocols in the name of human rights. Such sensitive moves may be more acceptable on the part of EU institutions than individual member states.

Together, the realist, constructivist and bureaucratic politics approaches suggest a confluence of forces that provide a plausible explanation for the birth of the EMP. Clearly, after the end of the Cold War and the reorganization of the international system, Europe may well have sought a way to balance the power of the United States and contain political Islam. But the EMP is not a traditional power balancing mechanism. Many observers have argued that Europe's stern opposition to the U.S. invasion of Iraq is a clear indicator of the EU's adherence to the concepts of normative power and cooperative security. The bureaucratic politics explanation is more tangible, but it does not explain the broad and integrated scope of the Barcelona Declaration. It explains the Commission's drive to steer the Barcelona Process, but does not explain the decision to build a "region" in the Mediterranean, and the linking of democracy, economic liberalization, and security. Thus I believe that constructivists are on rather strong ground in explaining the nature of the regime. What they cannot explain, however, is the disappointing progress in realizing the concept of "partnership," in providing the EMP with institutional strength, and the lack of uniformity in the EU's commercial treatment of the MNMCs. Certainly constructivists cannot explain the disappointing results in terms of development, human rights, democratization, and security in the MENA countries. For an explanation of those results, I turn to a discussion of the role of interest groups and then again to realist hypotheses.

Explaining disappointing progress: interest group hypotheses

The Euro–Med process called for sometimes drastic economic reform in the MNMCs. In that reform process, new political coalitions have emerged that have undermined the progress toward region building and interregionalism.[48] As Solingen puts it, "politicians worldwide rely on material and ideal aspects of internationalization to broker political coalitions across constituencies that respond differently to the opportunities and constraints of internationalization."[49]

Directly in response to constructivist arguments, Solingen argues the following:

> Different coalitional combinations in different regions create regional orders, "identities," and shared expectations about conflict and cooperation and, conversely, are affected by them. Interregional comparisons suggest that where internationalizing coalitions gathered strength in a given region, there was a better chance that zones of stable peace might develop. In these cases ruling coalitions relied more on concerts, collective security, and multilateralism... avoiding aggressive steps towards each other and mutually adjusting to resolve outstanding disputes.[50]

We can assume that liberalizing coalitions in the MNMCs will push the Barcelona Process forward. Indeed, a piece of evidence for this is the EuroMeSo Report cited above which recommends that a "'ProMed' group of civil servants from the MNMCs could be constituted to act in a management capacity as a partner of the Commission."[51] Certainly liberal coalitions in Cyprus and Malta have been able to liberalize the economies of those two countries to the extent that they are on track to qualify for EU membership. Morocco has achieved a higher degree of liberalization than other MNMCs, possibly as a result of Spain's effort to expand economic ties. In the last twenty years, Spanish business has moved from having a handful of affiliates in Morocco to possessing more than eight hundred companies there.[52] Solingen suggests that liberalizing elites have gained strength in Tunisia and Jordan; both promoted exports through preferential trade agreements with the EU and governments in both countries have stimulated private sector and foreign investment. "Tunisia's President Zine al-Abidine Ben Ali deepened liberalization in financial markets and foreign investment, promoted tourism, and reduced maximum tariff rates from 220 percent to 43 percent in the early 1990s."[53]

While these examples suggest that progress in liberalization and partnership should have been made, a closer look at Morocco reveals the weakness of liberalizing forces. Spanish business expansion in Morocco was onesided, created through diplomatic initiatives rather than market incentives, and accompanied by aid packages that have decreased over time leading to a reduction in operations. Joint ventures have proven unpopular with Spanish businessmen, who cite differences in business culture as the impediment to expansion. There are similar experiences reported in the effort to build "civil society." Far fewer Spanish NGOs are involved in the Maghreb than in Latin America, and without the constant stimulus of financial resources, attempts to develop a cultural dimension to Morocco's relationship with Spain have proved unsuccessful.[54] My suspicion is that liberalizing coalitions are weak in the other Arab MNMCs as well.

In the years since the signing of the Barcelona Declaration, what Solingen calls "backlash" coalitions have also grown, in the form of Islamic fundamentalist groups opposed to both peace and foreign investment, and in the form of populist movements. Ruling coalitions such as the Baathist Assad regime in Syria resist liberalization, seeing it as a threat to their power. In Syria "public sector managers (as well as military and security) bureaucrats have countered the nascent power of private commercial and industrial groups."[55] In general, it would appear that "backlash" coalitions control the state apparatus in many of the MENA countries. They reject the liberal orientation of the Barcelona process and resist any kind of "conditionality" imposed upon them. As Calleya writes, "many of the requirements of free trade and greater foreign investment (abolition of monopolies and licensing arrangements, reduction of customs and excise fees, legal security and transparency, autonomous civil society organizations and institutions) threaten the revenue base and even the power base of neo-patrimonial authoritarian regimes."[56] The power of backlash coalitions leads to a divergence of expectations and goals that they bring to the table. While Europe seeks stability through the "careful Westernization" of the MENA countries, or the "convergence of civilizations" toward the European model, these coalitions are content with preferential access to European markets and development aid. Given the weaknesses of the EMP regime described above, they can abrogate an agreement to liberalize at any time.

Within Europe as well, backlash coalitions have emerged with the rise of right-wing politicians. Their nationalist rhetoric and xenophobia have had an important negative impact on the EMP and its multilateral agenda. Their decidedly anti-liberal stance and commitment to territoriality, sovereignty, and self-reliance spell a rejection of multilateralism, openness, and construction of a regional identity that lie at the heart of the Euro–Mediterranean process.[57]

Economic interest groups will also seek to realize their interests in the EMP, and they have a fairly strong influence, as observed in the negotiating process at the EMP biannual Ministerial Summit. An MNMC minister in charge might reach a political compromise with the EU representatives, knowing he might be opposed by a domestic interest group. He must decide if he can cope with the pressure exerted by the latter on the government.[58] The pressure often results in negotiating paralysis. Tovias provides the following example: The EU and Israel locked horns over Israel's application of the rules of origin, treating the occupied territories as part of Israeli customs territory. Under the prevailing rules, goods originating in settlements were shipped to the EU duty-free. As political tensions increased, the EU decided to apply the association agreement to Israel in its frontiers of 4 June 1967. Negotiations to look for a compromise are in the offing. The Israeli minister in charge is obliged to negotiate a compromise knowing that business interests in the territories (e.g., Golan wine-makers) or in Israel will strongly oppose it.[59]

Without the strength of binding rules in the EMP, the direct linking of political conditionality to aid and loans and a voting mechanism that can overcome the paralysis of consensus, backlash coalitions and interest groups that would lose from EMP decisions will have the power to block progress toward the Barcelona goals.

Realist explanations for disappointing progress in the EMP

Realists would argue that the Euro–Med Partnership cannot fully succeed as a partnership because of the imbalance of power between the "core" of the European Union and the "periphery" of the MNMCs. The economic inequality between Europe and the rest of the Mediterranean has created a structure of asymmetrical interdependence, giving the EU the upper hand in all negotiations in the Euro–Mediterranean process. As noted above, the trade dependence of the MNMCs on the EU has increased in recent years to 52 percent, while Europe's trade dependence on the MNMCs consists primarily of dependence on energy supplies – and that dependence is likely to weaken as the EU enlarges and begins to look eastward to the former Soviet Union to fill its energy requirements.

Indeed, EU enlargement will greatly exacerbate this asymmetry. Trade dependence of MNMCs on the EU will increase, leading them to perceive the EU as a more formidable trading bloc. And as the EU looks eastward for products that currently come from MNMCs, EU trade sanctions will bite more than before.[60] This will deepen Arab suspicions of European neocolonial intentions in the Euro–Med process. The realist approach would suggest that as the EU turns its focus eastward, interest in the Mediterranean will continue to wane, and the Barcelona process will lose steam.

Furthermore, as the EU enlarges, most FDI will flow to Eastern Europe. Without an infusion of capital, the MENA countries will remain low-wage raw materials suppliers and export platforms for the EU's industrial machine. To the extent that FDI flows into the region, it will be attracted by low-cost labor and will concentrate in labor-intensive production methods across the industrial spectrum. In modern sectors, plants in these countries might be simply "screwdriver factories" – assembling final products, importing key components, and using few local suppliers. Other foreign investments might be in services – sales, marketing, and distribution outlets for imports produced in the EU. Or investments will flow to low-technology extractive sectors, like oil and gas. All innovative activity would continue to be concentrated in the EU as the "core." This means that prospects for rapid economic development of the MNMCs are bleak.

The structural imbalances and their consequences have a pernicious effect on the Barcelona process. The agenda of Barcelona is liberal, the practices are meant to be liberal, but the imbalance distorts and discredits the liberal agenda.

Finally, the Middle East conflict has undermined the Barcelona Process. Since the EMP's inception in 1995, the Middle East peace process was halting and uncertain, and the higher the tensions, the more the EMP was disrupted and weakened. The Israeli–Palestinian conflict thus helped to produce a deep cleft, not only between Israel and moderate Arab countries that were promoting the Barcelona Process, but also between Israel and Europe. The triangular partnership between Europe, the Arab world, and Israel, is now in turmoil.

While a realist approach explains the emergence of the Barcelona Process as a means by which Europe intended to balance American power, it also suggests that a failure in that effort can mean a failure of Europe's project of region-building and the interregionalism implied in the EMP. The global preeminence of the United States means that America can interfere with the effort. Indeed, American hegemonic power poses one of the strongest obstacles to the Barcelona Process. For example, in its effort to transform the Middle East, Washington proposed a free trade agreement in April 2003 between the United States and Middle East countries that directly challenges the EMP's goal of setting a free trade zone in the Mediterranean by 2010.

Institutional reconciliation and nesting

Despite this rather pessimistic view, the EMP is likely to be further institutionalized, no matter how shallow and partial that institutionalization will be. The EMP project must be seen within the broader framework of international economic institutions. Non-EU Mediterranean countries have expressed disappointment with EU economic proposals, which fell short of any significant economic relief of the kind that might result from lowering the barriers to their agricultural exports. Integration into a global trading and investment regime has inherent advantages, particularly if accompanied by sensible and equitable privatization procedures and safety nets. FTAs are not compatible with a full commitment to global multilateralism. This does not imply that Euro–Med cooperation should be placed on hold until global cooperative agreements are reached, but rather suggests that the true engine of Euro–Med cooperation is global integration. Shallow institutions in the region are relatively easy to "nest" within global institutions.

6 Conclusion

As a first cut at the evidence supporting each of these hypotheses, it is my suspicion that the institutionalization of EMP and the effort to construct a "region" is likely to remain weak and develop slowly if at all. Significant activity is likely to be confined to the economic chapter with little spillover to the other areas of concern. Continued conflict in the Middle East is likely to prevent progress in social, political, and cultural integration, as well as progress in the institutionalization of the EMP. Given the current focus of U.S. foreign policy on rooting out terrorism, the United States is likely to be deeply involved in the region, and if the EU is attempting to create its own region to balance U.S. power, this effort is likely to fail, at least in the short run. Furthermore, economic integration in the region as a whole is likely to be partial, halting, and shallow, given agricultural protectionism in the EU, the economic chasm between rich and poor countries in the region, the weakness of democracy, and the potential growing strength of political Islam. To date, the political will to overcome these roadblocks to regional integration is weak, and therefore the EU strategy of region building and interregionalism in the Mediterranean is likely to remain weak for some time.

Notes

1. Joffe 1998.
2. Solingen 2002.
3. Spencer 2002.
4. See Aggarwal and Fogarty's introduction to this volume for definitions of the different types of interregionalism.
5. Like other chapters in this volume, I use only the term European Union, rather than identifying the bloc's various historical incarnations, for the sake of convenience.
6. Bicci 2002, pp. 4–5.
7. Haas 1990.
8. Solingen 2002.
9. In 1999, at the Euro–Med III meeting of Foreign Ministers held in Stuttgart, Germany, participants agreed to accept Libya as a partner once it agreed to the terms of the Barcelona Declaration and once UN sanctions were lifted.
10. Calleya 2002, p. 7.
11. The plan aims for 2 billion euros per year in EIB loans by 2006. The economic and financial provisions of the EMP seek to achieve a Euro–Mediterranean Free Trade Agreement by 2010 and to promote regional development by attracting foreign direct investment.
12. Interview with EU officials not for attribution.
13. Vasconcelos 2002, p. 2.
14. Gillespie 2002, p. 12.
15. Lannon et al. 2001, pp. 117–18.
16. Tovias 2002.
17. Tovias 2002, p. 12.
18. Jones 1991.
19. Tovias 2002, p. 2.
20. Tovias 2002, p. 3.
21. Turkey, Cyprus, and Malta, candidate countries and also beneficiaries of some MEDA funds, were to receive much pre-accession aid through other channels, whereas Israel was not supposed to receive any bilateral aid from the EU in view of its own development level.

22. Tovias, 2002, p. 2.
23. Tovias, 2002, p. 9.
24. Tovias 2002, p. 7.
25. Tovias 2002, p. 9.
26. Gillispie 2002, p. 12.
27. Tovias 2002, p. 3.
28. Calleya 2002, p. 10.
29. The Mashreq includes Cyprus, Jordan, Iraq, Lebanon, Palestine, and Syria.
30. Calleya 2002, p. 10–11.
31. Calleya 2002, p. 6
32. Callaya 2002, p. 13.
33. Brooks and Wohlforth 2002, p. 29.
34. Remarks by Claude Weinber, Director of the Heinrich Boell Foundation, Jerusalem on "Constructing a Mediterranean Region: Cultural and Functional Perspectives," November 19, 1999.
35. This section is adapted from Adler and Crawford 2003.
36. Nicolaidis 2003. See also Wendt 1999.
37. Fuller 2003.
38. Manners 2002, p. 240.
39. Duchêne et al. 1973; Whitman 2003; Moravcsik 2002; Nicolaidis and Howse 2002.
40. Deutsch et al. 1957; Adler and Barnett 1998.
41. Manners 2002, pp. 240, 252.
42. Moravcsik 2002, p. 12.
43. Moravcsik 2003.
44. Moravcsik 2003. See also Whitman 2003.
45. Nicolaidis and Howse 2002, pp. 768, 771, 782.
46. Interview with EU official not for attribution May 31, 2003.
47. While Spanish interest in the Mediterranean is deeply rooted in history and has been the subject of considerable engagement since the late 1970s, Portugal only began to develop a Mediterranean policy by virtue of entry to the European Union in 1986 (see Gillespie 2000; Vasconcelos, 1996a, 1996b; Silva and Pereira 1998, pp. 86–87). The Mediterranean has been a priority for post-Franco Spain, particularly under Felipe González and the Socialist Party (in office 1982–96), who grasped the opportunities for international influence to be derived from developing a European–Mediterranean–Spanish triangle as a focus of diplomatic activity (Gillispie 2002, p. 5).
48. Solingen 1998, 2001. Internationalization involves increased openness to international markets, capital, investments, and technology but also to an array of political and security regimes, institutions, and values.
49. Solingen 2002, p. 4.
50. Solingen 2002, p. 5.
51. Vasconcelos 1997.
52. Gillespie 2002, p. 7.
53. Solingen 2002, p. 6.
54. Gillispie, 2002 p. 8.
55. Solingen 2002.
56. Calleya 2002, p. 7.
57. Interview with EuroMedSco official.
58. Tovias 2002, p. 10.
59. Tovias 2002, pp. 10–11.
60. Tovias 2001.

References

Adler, Emanuel and Michael Barnett, eds. (1998). *Security Communities*. Cambridge: Cambridge University Press.

Adler, Emanuel and Beverly Crawford (2003). "Normative power and the European practice of region building: the case of the Euro–Mediterranean Partnership (EMP)." Unpublished manuscript (May).

Bicci, Federica (2002). "From security to economy and back: Euro–Mediterranean relations in perspective." Paper prepared for the conference "The Convergence of Civilizations? Constructing a Mediterranean Region." Lisbon (6–9 June).

Brooks, Stephen G. and William C. Wohlforth (2002). "American primacy in perspective." *Foreign Affairs* (July/August).

Calleya, Stephen (2002). "The Euro–Med partnership and sub regionalism: a case of region building?" Paper prepared for the conference "The Convergence of Civilizations? Constructing a Mediterranean Region." Lisbon (6–9 June).

Deutsch, Karl W., Sidney A. Burrell, Robert A. Kann, Maurice Lee, Jr., Martin Lichterman, Raymond E. Lindgren, Francis L. Loewenheim, and Richard W. Van Wagenen. (1957). *Political Community and the North Atlantic State*. Princeton: Princeton University Press.

Duchêne, François (1973). "The European Community and the Uncertainties of Interdependence." In Kohnstamm, Max and Hager, Wolfgang (eds.) *A Nation Writ Large? Foreign-Policy Problems before the European Community*. London: Macmillan.

Fuller, Graham (2003). *The Future of Political Islam*. New York: Palgrave.

Gillespie, Richard (2002). "Regionalism and globalism in the EMP: the limits to Western Mediterranean co-operation." Paper prepared for the conference "The Convergence of Civilizations? Constructing a Mediterranean Region." Lisbon (6–9 June).

Gillespie, Richard. (2000). *Spain and the Mediterranean: Developing a European Policy toward the South*. Basingstoke: Macmillan.

Haas, Peter (1990). *Saving the Mediterranean: The Politics of International Environmental Cooperation*. New York: Columbia University Press.

Joffe, George (1998). "The Euro–Mediterranean Partnership: Two Years after Barcelona," Middle East Programme, RIIA, BRIEFING No. 44 (May).

Jones, Dorothy (1991). *Code of Peace: Ethics and Security in the World of the Warlord States*. Chicago: The University of Chicago Press.

Lannon, E., K. Inglis, and T. Haenebalcke (2001). "The many faces of EU conditionality in pan–Euro–Mediterranean relations in Maresceau." In M. and Lannon, E. (eds.), *The EU's Enlargement and Mediterranean Strategies*. London: Macmillan.

Manners, Ian (2002). "Normative power Europe: a contradiction in terms?" *Journal of Common Market Studies* 40, 2: 235–258.

Moravcsik, Andrew (2002). "In defence of the democratic deficit: reassessing legitimacy in the European Union." *Journal of Common Market Studies* 40, 4 (November).

Nicolaidis, Kalypso and Robert Howse. 2002. "'This is my EUtopia...': narrative as power." *Journal of Common Market Studies* 40, 4:767–92.

Nicolaidis, Kalypso. 2003. Greek EU Presidency. Contribution on the issue of EU–USA relations to the informal General Affairs and External Relations Council, May 2–3. http://www.eu2003gr/en/articles/2003/5/1/2623. Accessed May 22, 2003.

Silva, M., and Pereira, P. (1998). "A política portuguesa para o Mediterraneo," *Janus* 98 (Universidade Autónoma de Lisboa), special supplement on 'As Forças Portuguesas no novo contexto internacional.'

Solingen, Etel (2002). "Europe's Mediterranean strategy: an asymmetric equation." Paper prepared for the conference "The Convergence of Civilizations? Constructing a Mediterranean Region." Lisbon (6–9 June).

Solingen, Etel (2001). "Mapping Internationalization: Domestic and Regional impacts." *International Studies Quarterly* 45, 4 (December).

Solingen, Etel (1998). *Regional Orders at Century's Dawn: Global and Domestic Influences on Grand Strategy.* Princeton: Princeton University Press.

Spencer, Claire (2002). "The EU as a security actor in the Mediterranean: problems and prospects." *The Quarterly Journal* 2, 2: 135–40.

Tovias A. (2002). "The political economy of the partnership in comparative perspective." Paper prepared for the conference "The Convergence of Civilizations? Constructing a Mediterranean Region." Lisbon (6–9 June).

Tovias, Alfred (2000). "From 15 to 21: The Impact of the Next EU Enlargement on Mediterranean Non-Member Countries." Marseilles, FEMISE Research Program, (October).

Vasconcelos, Alvaro (2002). "Europe's Mediterranean strategy: an asymmetric equation." Paper prepared for the conference "The Convergence of Civilizations? Constructing a Mediterranean Region." Lisbon (6–9 June).

Vasconcelos, Alvaro. (1996a). "Portugal: A Case for an Open Europe." In F. Algieri and E. Regelsberger (eds.), *Synergy at Work: Spain and Portugal in European Foreign Policy,* Bonn: Europa Union Verlag.

Vasconcelos, Alvaro (1996b). "Portugal: Pressing for an Open Europe." In C. Hill (ed.), *The Actors in Europe's Foreign Policy.* London: Routledge.

Wendt, Alexander. 1999. *Social Theory of International Politics.* Cambridge: Cambridge University Press.

Whitman, Richard. nd. "The fall and rise of civilian power Europe." http://fes-portal.fes.de/pls/portal30/docs/FOLDER/POLITIKANALYSE/PAXAMERICANA/WHITMAN.PDF. Accessed June 1, 2003.

5

Back to the Nest? Europe's Relations with the African, Caribbean and Pacific Group of Countries

John Ravenhill

1 Introduction

Europe's association with African, Caribbean, and Pacific (ACP) countries was the first of its interregional relationships. In the nearly half century since the signature of the Treaty of Rome, it developed into Europe's most institutionalized and multidimensional interregional relationship. It embraces not only trade and investment issues but also a development "partnership" that includes what has traditionally been the EU's largest single aid program, a joint parliamentary assembly, meetings of organizations representing civil society, and a dialogue on human rights. This chapter examines the factors that have shaped this relationship over the last four decades. The principal focus is on the trade regime, not just for consistency with the other contributions to this volume but also because it is in its trade dimension that the relationship has changed most dramatically over time.[1]

Historically, the relationship has not been one of pure interregionalism, as defined by Aggarwal and Fogarty in their introductory chapter to this volume, because the ACP Group is not a region as defined either by geography or by law (in the sense of a WTO-sanctioned regional preferential trade agreement under Article XXIV of the General Agreement on Tariffs and Trade (GATT)). The ACP Group was a creation of the European Union at the time of the signature of the first Lomé Convention in 1975 and has had little presence outside of the interregional partnership, one of the problems for the unwieldy grouping.[2] That the relationship is one of hybrid interregionalism caused increasing problems for the EU with the strengthening of the rules of the global trade regime when the World Trade Organization (WTO) replaced the GATT. EU efforts to bring its trade relations with members of the ACP Group back into the nest, that is, to make them compatible with WTO rules by signing regional preferential trade arrangements with ACP sub-groupings under Lomé's successor, the Cotonou Agreement, may well ultimately undermine the ACP Group.[3] This chapter concludes by demonstrating how this strategy is complicated by the lack of counterpart coherence on the ACP side.

2   Yaoundé and the road to Lomé

The relationship between Europe and the ACP Group had its origins in the Treaty of Rome, which included provisions (Arts. 131 and 136) for the then colonies of the EU's founding members to be included within the customs union. When most of these colonies gained their independence at the beginning of the 1960s, the EU negotiated arrangements to provide eighteen of them with continued preferential access to the common market, arrangements codified in the first Yaoundé Convention of 1963, the provisions of which were renewed in the second Yaoundé Convention of 1969. Under these agreements, the former colonies in principle were obliged to provide preferential access (so-called 'reverse preferences') for European exports to their markets. The EU claimed that these reciprocal preferences made the Conventions compatible with GATT's Article XXIV as "an interim arrangement leading to the establishment of a FTA," although it never sought GATT approval of them (asserting that its relations with its former colonies were covered by the "grandfather" provisions of the GATT).

Britain's accession to the EU in 1973 posed particular problems in how to accommodate the special arrangements that Britain had previously provided for trade with its former colonies and dominions. These had included not only preferential tariffs but also purchase arrangements for certain commodities, the most significant being the Commonwealth Sugar Agreement. Meanwhile, the EU had come under increasing criticism from trading partners and from the development lobby for its insistence on reverse preferences in its relations with a group of the world's poorest economies. The U.S. government viewed the reverse preferences of the Yaoundé Conventions as one of the last vestiges of the preferential colonial trading arrangements that it held responsible for much of the havoc in international trade in the interwar years. One reason why the United States had supported proposals for the introduction of Generalized System of Preferences (GSP) schemes within GATT was to move away from regimes such as Yaoundé that accorded preferential access to industrialized countries' markets other than on developmental criteria.

An extension of the EU's special relations with former colonies was part of the understanding on the terms of UK accession. Moreover, bureaucratic interests in the Commission – the Development Directorate, which managed the Community's relations with its former colonies – favored an extension of its informal empire. And the external context provided additional reasons for the EU to construct a new interregional arrangement: the negotiations for the first Lomé Convention took place in a period of unprecedented upheaval in the postwar economy – the immediate aftermath of the first round of OPEC-induced oil price rises of 1973. Lomé, or at least the rhetoric if not much of the substance of the first Convention, was one of the few concrete outcomes of the demands from less developed economies for a New International Economic Order (NIEO). European fears about the future security of raw materials supplies added to pressures from the United States, less developed countries, and the development lobby to lead the EU to propose an agreement that was more comprehensive and more generous in its provisions that its predecessors. The EU abandoned the insistence on reverse preferences: Lomé instead provided for non-reciprocal concessions on trade, the ACP countries being obliged merely to give imports from the EU treatment at least as favorable to that provided to the most-favoured industrialized country source.

What would be the geographical scope of the new relationship? This was a potentially problematic issue because Britain's former colonies included economies such as India and Pakistan, which, while low-income, were of a size and diversity that posed a much greater competitive threat to European economies than that from the Yaoundé associates. In the end, a happy coincidence of geography and development provided a solution to the dilemma: the EU would make the Lomé relationship available to Europe's former colonies in Africa, the Caribbean and the Pacific, and to countries of "comparable economic structure." This formula ruled out the more diversified and larger economies of South Asia, and enabled Europe to claim that it was creating a new relationship that not only extended beyond colonial legacies (because it included countries such as Ethiopia that had not been European colonies) but one that was also contributing to promoting integration in the three component geographical regions of the ACP Group.[4]

3   Lomé: regime characteristics

Regime strength

The Lomé Conventions were far more institutionalized than their predecessors. It created five joint EU–ACP institutions. The ACP–EU Council of Ministers is the ultimate decisionmaking authority on issues relating to the interregional partnership. On a day-to-day basis, the relationship is managed by the ACP–EU Committee of Ambassadors, to which the Council of Ministers delegates specific powers. The ACP–EU Joint Assembly consists of a representative from each ACP state and an equal number of members from the European Parliament. It meets twice a year but has consultative status only. Finally, the Convention created two functional joint institutions: the Center for the Development of Industry, financed by the EDF, aims to encourage and support the creation, expansion, and restructuring of industrial companies in ACP countries; and the Technical Center for Agricultural and Rural Cooperation develops and provides services that improve the access of ACP countries to information on agriculture and rural development.

In principle, the negotiation of the successors to the original Convention was to take place on an interregional basis – between the Commission and the ACP Secretariat,[5] and at the ACP–EU Committee of Ambassadors and ACP–EU Council of Ministers. In practice, the desire of individual ACP governments to push for special concessions for products or projects of particular interest to them, and the willingness of European countries to champion the cause of traditional clients, ensured that significant negotiations also took place on a bilateral basis. Moreover, a favourite negotiating ploy of the Europeans was to go over the head of the Brussels-based representatives of ACP countries to appeal directly to national capitals for them to rein in their ambassadors and to ensure that they be more accommodating of European perspectives. With the exception of the separate bilateral trade agreement that was negotiated with South Africa when it acceded to the Convention, the treaties, however, were always interregional in nature.

The EU over the years was keen to highlight the benefits that the Lomé trade provisions gave to the ACP compared with those available under alternative arrangements. In particular, it emphasized the contractual nature of the provisions (unlike the GSP, which is a unilateral grant by the EU), the security provided by the length of the agreements (the fourth Lomé Convention ran for ten years from 1990; its three predecessors were each of five years duration),[6] and their comprehensiveness. The reality of the matter was more complex. Although the trade concessions were negotiated with the ACP and embodied in the Conventions – that is, in documents with legal standing – no specific provisions existed for dispute settlement, which was a matter for discussion between the ACP Secretariat and the Commission or, if they failed to resolve the issue, by the ambassadors or ministers. Nor was there a provision for compensation in the event that the EU took measures that were contrary to the Conventions' letter or spirit. For instance, the EU was able to resort unilaterally to safeguard action if it deemed ACP exports to threaten European interests. The mere possibility of such action could serve as a significant deterrent. Early in the Lomé relationship the EU threatened Mauritius, a relatively small source of its textile imports, with safeguard action unless it accepted voluntary export restraints.[7]

Although the relationship was said to be contractual,[8] the EU insisted that its obligations toward the ACP did not tie its hands in its external commercial policies in any way. Accordingly, throughout the life of the Conventions, the EU unilaterally took various actions that reduced the value of the trade preferences enjoyed by the ACP. Such actions included the extension of its GSP scheme, a lowering of its MFN tariffs, the signature of preferential agreements with other countries, and what amounted to a unilateral abrogation of the rum protocol through its agreement on distilled spirits tariffs with the United States at the WTO ministerial meeting in Singapore in 1996. The ACP, meanwhile, were placed in the somewhat awkward position of trying to encourage the EU to maintain trade restrictions on third parties in an attempt to preserve the major sources of advantage that the Convention conferred on them.

The inability of the ACP to constrain EU actions was symptomatic of the asymmetries in the relationship. Although the Convention embodied the NIEO rhetoric of a partnership among equals, the principle of a contractual relationship based on equality was undermined not only by the disparities in economic power of the parties but also by the lack of reciprocity in the relationship. A fundamental problem for the ACP was that they came to the relationship only as *demandeurs*. The only concession the ACP made in the relationship was to agree to participate as beneficiaries of EU largesse. Once the fears of raw materials scarcity evaporated, the ACP had few weapons in their bargaining armory – not least because of their unwillingness to grant any form of reciprocity. In negotiations, their weakness was their principal strength – they were able to appeal to EU development constituencies, argue that their economic frailty ensured that any concessions by the EU would not do any significant damage to EU domestic interests, and generally attempt to embarrass the EU into maintaining or extending the relationship.[9] I characterized the relationship as one of "collective clientelism" in which the ACP attempted through the Conventions to gain protection from its European patron not only against the vicissitudes of world markets but also against unfriendly actions by the Europeans themselves.[10] Such a strategy was viable only as long as the EU was willing to use trade preferences as a development instrument. Over the course of the four Lomé Conventions, European interests in the relationship changed substantially.

For most of the twenty-five years of the Lomé Conventions, the ACP were fighting a rearguard action to maintain the "*acquis*" of the Conventions against European attempts to claw back the NIEO provisions that it had conceded in the frenzied atmosphere of 1973–74. In particular, the EU attempted to undo the automaticity of provisions such as financial transfers under the STABEX scheme. Because the EU was the provider of benefits, it could take unilateral action to punish what it perceived as defections from the regime's provisions (primarily political conditionality). Until the inclusion of the more specific clause on human rights in Lomé IV (bis), however, such interpretation occurred outside of the formal framework of the interregional treaty. In terms of its effect on constraining the behaviors of its participants, the formal rules of the interregional regime therefore must be judged as weak.

A former Director-General for Development of the European Commission, Dieter Frisch, provides an insight into the political relationship from an official European perspective. For the period of the first two

Conventions, he asserts, "we use to set great store by Lomé's 'political neutrality'" by accepting ACP states "into the Lomé 'club' without passing judgment on their ideological, political or economic choices."[11] ACP countries were given a great deal of discretion in how they chose to use money provided by the EU. From Lomé III (1985–90) onwards, however, following various embarrassments when, for instance, ACP military governments used STABEX funds to purchase military vehicles, the EU insisted on "policy dialogue" in which instruments of cooperation would be implemented "on the basis of duly negotiated and formulated mutual undertakings." With each Convention, political conditionality became more explicit.

Regime nature

The Lomé Conventions were by far the most comprehensive of the EU's interregional agreements and avowedly developmental in orientation. Over various iterations (Lomé was renegotiated on five occasions), the political dimensions of the Convention were made more explicit. Whereas the first two Conventions began with articles pertaining to trade cooperation, Lomé III (1984) and Lomé IV (1990) began with a "body of doctrine" comprising twenty articles specifying the objectives, principles, and guidelines of the Convention. Lomé III made reference to human dignity and to economic, social, and cultural rights. Lomé IV added civil and political rights and was the first development agreement to incorporate a human rights clause (Article 5) as a "fundamental" part of cooperation. The revised version of Lomé IV (1995), known as Lomé IV (bis), used the language of the Maastricht principles in referring to democratic principles, the consolidation of the rule of law, and good governance.[12] An updated clause confirmed human rights as an "essential element" of cooperation; any violation could lead to partial or total suspension of development aid by the European Union after prior consultation of other ACP nations and the abusing party.

The Conventions provided for duty-free access for 95 percent of the tariff lines of members of the ACP grouping (originally numbering forty-six, a figure that grew to seventy-one at the time of the negotiation of the Cotonou Agreement, and subsequently to seventy-eight – see Table 5.1). The Conventions established more than just a trade relationship. They also included protocols for preferential access to the European market for four ACP exports, programs to provide compensatory finance to ACP states for revenue downturns in exports of specified primary products (STABEX) and to help maintain production of certain minerals (SYSMIN), and a substantial enhancement of the aid program provided through the European Development Fund (EDF) that had been established in the Yaoundé period.

The comprehensiveness of the trade concessions placed the ACP at the apex of the EU's pyramid of privilege: they were Europe's "preferred

Table 5.1   ACP states at the time of the Cotonou Agreement (71)

Angola*	Gabon*	Saint Kitts and Nevis*
Antigua and Barbuda*	Gambia*	St. Lucia*
Bahamas	Ghana*	Saint Vincent and the Grenadines*
Barbados*	Grenada*	Samoa
Belize*	Guinea*	Sao Tome & Principe
Benin*	Guinea Bissau	Senegal*
Botswana*	Guyana*	Seychelles
Burkina Faso*	Haiti*	Sierra Leone*
Burundi*	Jamaica*	Solomon Islands*
Cameroon*	Kenya*	Somalia
Cape Verde	Kiribati	South Africa* §
Central African Republic*	Lesotho*	Sudan
Chad*	Liberia	Suriname*
Comoros	Madagascar*	Swaziland*
Congo (Brazzaville)*	Malawi*	Tanzania*
Congo (Democratic Republic of)*	Mali*	Togo*
Côte d'Ivoire*	Mauritania*	Tonga
Djibouti*	Mauritius*	Trinidad and Tobago*
Dominica*	Mozambique*	Tuvalu
Dominican Republic*	Namibia*	Uganda*
Equatorial Guinea	Niger*	Vanuatu
Eritrea	Nigeria*	Zambia*
Ethiopia	Papua New Guinea*	Zimbabwe*
Fiji	Rwanda*	

Note: These countries have subsequently been joined by the Cook Islands, Cuba#, Marshall Islands, Federated States of Micronesia, Nauru, Niue, and Palau.

* WTO members (total 55)
§ Lomé/Cotonou trade provisions not applicable.
# Not a signatory to the Cotonou Agreement
Least developed countries (UN list) in italics. (total 39)

Source: Adapted from Commission of the European Union 2001b.

partners."[13] The duty free access accorded to ACP tariff lines compared favorably with the average of 80 percent of tariff lines in other regional trade agreements to which the EU was a party, and to the 54 percent included within the EU's GSP.[14] The value of the trade arrangements to the ACP lay not just in the duty free access but also in the exemption of their exports from the MultiFiber Arrangement, in (limited) concessions on some agricultural products that competed with European production under the Common Agricultural Policy, and in the special protocols for bananas, beef/veal, rum, and sugar. These protocols provided for duty free access for fixed quantities of exports of commodities that would otherwise be uncompetitive or face prohibitive tariff or quota restrictions, and, in the case of beef/veal and sugar, guaranteed ACP producers prices prevailing in the (heavily protected/subsidized) European market. The European beef price, for instance, is usually more than 50 percent above world market prices while ACP sugar exporters have consistently received an EU price that is two to three times that prevailing in world markets. Although these protocols cover products that constitute only 9 percent of total ACP exports, their value to beneficiary ACP states is much higher than this figure suggests. Purchases of imports from the ACP under the sugar protocol alone, for instance, were estimated to cost the EU one quarter of all of the money spent on the relationship annually.[15]

EU commercial treatment of ACP countries

The special provisions for certain ACP exports meant that the EU's treatment of commercial relations with its partners was not entirely uniform. Least developed, landlocked, and island countries also benefited from privileged treatment under the STABEX and SYSMIN arrangements. With the exception of the ACP exports covered by specific protocols, however, the EU gave uniform commercial treatment to all ACP countries.

4   The evolution of the interregional regime

The commercial relationship

Perhaps the most striking feature of the twenty-five years of the Lomé relationship was the secular decline in this period of most ACP economies – many in absolute terms but all, and the ACP collectively, in terms of relative importance as economic partners for the EU. The share of the ACP in EU imports fell from 6.7 percent at the beginning of the Lomé partnership to 2.8 percent in 1999. Despite their position at the apex of the EU pyramid of privileges, the ACP fared substantially worse in the EU market than did other developing countries: the ACP share of EU imports from developing countries fell from 14.8 to 4.1 percent over the same period.[16] ACP exports decreased not only as a share of European imports – they actually fell in absolute terms. In the 1990s, they were consistently below the level of the mid-1980s.[17] EU imports from all members of the ACP grouping amounted to less than those it purchased from Russia. Falling trade shares were symptomatic of the economic problems of many ACP countries: by 1993, overseas development assistance accounted for 11.5 percent of the total GDP of sub-Saharan Africa, 80 percent of that of Mozambique, and 40 percent of that of Tanzania.

Data on the declining ACP share of the European market are widely quoted by the EU as evidence of the ineffectiveness of the Lomé provisions. Perhaps of even greater significance for European attitudes toward the relationship are data that seldom appear in the EU's discussion of Lomé: the share of the ACP in European exports. Over the period 1995–98, the ACP

Group accounted for an average of 3.0 percent of EU exports.[18] This is barely half the figure for the Association of Southeast Asian Nations (ASEAN) (5.9%), and substantially less than that for the countries that are candidates for EU membership (an average of 14.1 percent over the four-year period).[19] In most years, the EU runs a trade deficit with the ACP. As the EU Commission's Trade Directorate commented, "trade between the ACP and the EU has remained important for the ACP, but marginal for the EU."[20] Not surprisingly, the relationship with the ACP has not come high on the list of the EU's commercial priorities.

The strategic context

Meanwhile, other developments had also undermined the significance of the relationship for the EU. The ending of the Cold War had not only largely removed the few remaining geopolitical considerations in Europe's relations with members of the ACP Group, especially its African component, but had produced a pressing problem for the EU in how to accommodate the countries of Central and Eastern Europe. Similarly, the Mediterranean, with its greater commercial opportunities and, no less important, various threats to the EU as an actual or potential source of illegal migration, drugs, and terrorism, had assumed far greater significance than the more remotely located ACP economies.

Developments within the EU

EU expansion had brought into the Union new members that lacked historical ties with the ACP Group. The admission of Spain and to a lesser extent Portugal had added countries whose historical ties were primarily with Latin America rather than with the African, Caribbean, and Pacific areas favored by Lomé. The accessions in 1994 added Nordic countries that, while often sympathetic to the EU playing a significant role in development, saw little logic in this role being shaped primarily by colonial legacies rather than developmental needs. Moreover, the new members had few economic interests in the ACP: in 2000, the combined share of Austria, Denmark, Finland, and Sweden in the EU's exports to the ACP was less than that of Belgium.[21]

The Amsterdam Treaty (Article 177) had identified the priority of the Union's development cooperation policy as fostering "the sustainable economic and social development of the developing countries, and more particularly the most disadvantaged among them" and "the smooth and gradual integration of the developing countries into the world economy." Both phrases carried danger signals for the ACP: although many of their countries were among the least developed, the grouping remained defined primarily by geography and history rather than by level of development. And reference to integration into the world economy potentially provided ammunition for those critics of Lomé who asserted that the maintenance of preferential access for the ACP had merely encouraged their governments to put off necessary structural adjustment and thereby contributed to their poor economic record. Moreover, the Amsterdam Treaty committed EU development cooperation policies "to the general objective of developing and consolidating democracy and the rule of law, and to that of respecting human rights and fundamental freedoms" – a signal that the EU would not allow the rhetoric of "equal partnership" of the Lomé relationship to stand in the way of the imposition of political conditionality in the future.

Developments within the world trading system

The precipitant for the demise of the Lomé arrangements was a challenge to their legality within the WTO in the context of complaints from Central American countries and the United States about the Convention's banana protocol. The Lomé Conventions had not been challenged in the GATT before the Uruguay Round. The ACP and EU had not sought a GATT waiver under Article XXIV of their obligations to provide MFN treatment under GATT Article I. The belief appeared to be that the preferential treatment the Convention gave to ACP exports was legitimized by Part IV of the GATT and by the first paragraph of the "Enabling Clause" (officially the "Decision on Differential and More Favorable Treatment, Reciprocity, and Fuller Participation of Developing Countries") of 1979. The decisions of the first two GATT Banana Panels belied these assumptions.

The Lomé Convention's banana protocol was designed to maintain banana production in some ACP countries (and some of the EU's remaining overseas territories) heavily dependent on export earnings from this commodity, and to ensure the commercial survival of EU importers of ACP/overseas territory fruit. Neither category of interested party would be able to withstand open competition in the Union's banana market, the largest in the world. The Lomé banana protocol had maintained import quotas in the traditional markets of suppliers from the ACP (Britain, France, and Italy) and from overseas territories (France, Portugal, and Spain). EU markets (most notably Germany and the Netherlands) that had traditionally sourced their bananas from the "dollar zone" were largely unaffected by the policy. Imported bananas were subject to a uniform 20 percent tariff; these importing countries had lower banana prices and higher per capita consumption than those giving preference to ACP/overseas territory suppliers. The introduction of the single internal market in 1992 made the continued operation of these arrangements impossible.

In response to pressure from EU commercial interests and the ACP (supported by some EU governments), Brussels in July 1993 adopted a set of policies that seemed tailored to maximize intervention and distortion in the marketplace. Quotas on banana imports were extended EU-wide and supported by over-quota tariffs. Imports from Latin America were subject to tariffs to raise revenue. The policy also created a system of import licensing that identified three categories of operators; those marketing companies that had benefited under the previous national policies were favoured – they were effectively handed one third of the dollar banana trade and could on-sell their import licences to other traders. Companies that traditionally had marketed dollar zone fruit found their markets reduced both by the quotas and by the requirement that one third of dollar zone fruit should be handled by other importers. The net effect was to boost EU banana prices, reduce consumption, and create a system whereby quota rents were divided among EU marketing companies. The overall benefits to ACP producers were very limited.[22]

The full story of the tortuous process whereby the EU was eventually forced to bring its banana regime into compliance with the WTO is outside the scope of this chapter. (At various stages the policies were found to contravene Article I, Article III.4 on National Treatment, Article XIII on the nondiscriminatory administration of quantitative restrictions, Article XXIV on regional trade arrangements, and Article V of the GATS, as well as contravening elements of EU competition law.) The significance of the dispute for the Lomé relationship was that the judgement of the GATT dispute panels extended far beyond the specific provisions of the banana protocol. In particular, the second GATT Banana Panel in 1994 declared that the Convention itself contravened GATT's most favoured nation requirement because it treated countries at the same level of development in a discriminatory manner. Furthermore, the Panel found that the Convention did not meet the requirements (reciprocal free trade for "substantially all trade") for an exemption from the most favored nation requirement by virtue of compliance with the provisions for regional preferential trade agreements laid down in Article XXIV. The Panel also found that because Part IV of the GATT made no reference to Article XXIV, a relationship with developing countries did not obviate the conditions that regional arrangements must meet as specified in that Article if they were to receive a derogation from the most favored nation requirement.

Although the EU in principle could have ignored the Panel's findings under the old GATT dispute settlement rules, the finding sent shockwaves through participants in the Lomé relationship. The EU rushed to secure a GATT waiver for the Convention (while maintaining that it was in fact compatible with Article XXIV provisions) before the entry into effect of the new WTO rules. In one of the last acts of GATT under the 1947 rules, contracting parties in December 1994 approved a five-year waiver for the Convention for the duration of Lomé IV (bis). To gain unanimous agreement, the EU had to accept the proviso that, the waiver notwithstanding, GATT contracting parties could still have recourse to the nullification and impairment provisions of Article XXIII of the GATT if they wished to challenge the Convention. These provisions essentially opened the way for a challenge to be mounted against the operationalization of the waiver if it could be demonstrated that it was being implemented in a way that was incompatible with GATT principles – and were used to good effect by Central American countries and the United States in lodging further complaints against the banana regime.

The need to secure a waiver from the WTO for the Lomé arrangements was seized upon by those elements in the EU that wished to see a new basis established for relations with less developed economies. Their argument was that the need for a future Convention to obtain a waiver under Article IX.3 of the Marrakech Agreement, which would require approval by at least 75 percent of WTO members, and would be of a fixed duration and subject to annual review, undermined the security that the ACP had previously enjoyed through the contractual nature of the Lomé provisions. Such security could only be restored if the ACP countries entered into WTO-compatible regional trade agreements with the EU.

The logic of this argument is open to question. The objections of other countries to the banana regime, for instance, were not because it provided tariff preferences for ACP countries (who provided only 16 percent of European consumption) but because of the way in which the regime's quotas limited the access of other suppliers, and because its import licensing system discriminated in favor of European commercial interests. Indeed, the U.S. government repeatedly asserted that it was not opposed in principle to tariff preferences for ACP banana suppliers. Moreover, trade agreements between other industrialized countries and groupings of less developed economies (LDEs) discriminate among LDEs in the same way as Lomé did: the principal examples are the U.S.–Caribbean Basin Economic Recovery Act (CBERA), the Canadian Tariff Treatment for Commonwealth Caribbean Countries (CARIBCAN), and the U.S.–Andean Trade Preference Act (all of which have received WTO waivers).[23] It is uncertain for how long the WTO might have been prepared to grant a waiver of the type that the Lomé arrangements would have required but precedents existed for such a waiver to be made. Less important than the accuracy of the logic of the argument that Lomé was incompatible with the WTO, however, is that it was widely accepted throughout the EU and used as the basis for its negotiating mandate on the successor arrangements to the Lomé Convention.

From Lomé to Cotonou

The EU's lack of interest in expending further political capital to secure a continuing WTO waiver for its trade relations with the ACP was symptomatic of the low priority that the relationship held for Brussels by the mid-1990s.

The decline in the significance of the ACP as an economic partner for the EU documented in the previous section meant that there were few

European commercial interests speaking out in support of maintenance of the relationship. Those that did were decidedly "old economy" and in many instances non-competitive enterprises dependent on the protection provided by the Convention for their survival.[24] Moreover, the maintenance of the traditional trading relationships that Lomé epitomized had threatened more significant European interests. For leading European companies and indeed most officials in European governments and the EU Commission itself, the idea that the WTO should come close to being wrecked and Europe engage in a trade war with the United States over a dispute over banana imports was more than slightly ludicrous.

Among the former colonial powers, Britain had long since lost interest in Africa. Even France, which had maintained far closer political and economic links with its former African colonies, no longer appeared willing to invest significant diplomatic capital in defence of the Lomé relationship.[25] The ACP could traditionally count on support from the Development Directorate of the EU Commission; they had provided the main focus for its activities since the Commission's foundation. Here again, however, interests were changing. Commission officials, like their counterparts in the member states, had tired of the wrangling every five years over renewal of the Convention. To enable the ACP to save face in successive negotiations and to maintain its image as sympathetic to the needs of the least developed, the EU inevitably had to make some incremental improvements in the Convention's provisions (and in the trade sphere the only areas in which improvement could be made were in products, typically in agriculture, that had great domestic political sensitivity). It was to avoid such sensitivities and the investment of significant bureaucratic resources in lengthy negotiations that produced essentially trivial outcomes that the EU had decided that the trade provisions for the fourth Convention should extend for ten years.

Over the years, the share of EU aid going to non-ACP countries has risen (Table 5.2). The Development Directorate foresaw a broader role for itself with responsibilities extending beyond the ACP states.[26] Even in the EU development lobby, which had grown up largely around the Lomé relationship, support for maintaining the ACP at the apex of Europe's pyramid of privilege was waning. Again, the emphasis was on redefining European aid priorities according to the level of development of potential beneficiaries rather than on historical ties.

To the extent that trade preferences for the ACP clashed with other EU commercial objectives, tensions existed between elements of the Development Directorate (the old DG VIII) and DG I, responsible for other external relations. Of particular note here for the redefinition of the inter-regional partnership was the reorganization of the Commission that occurred in 1999, which removed trade with the ACP from the responsibilities of the Development Directorate and handed it to the Trade Directorate

Table 5.2   Regional distribution of development aid of the EU (%)

	1975/76	1980/81	1990/91	1993
Sub-Saharan Africa	59.6	60.3	58.2	45.5
Near East, North Africa,	12.3	11.7	19.6	25.6
Latin America and Caribbean	5.4	6.3	10.1	10.9
South Asia	20.8	16.9	7.2	5.3
Other least developed	–	–	–	8.1
Other Asian countries and Oceania	1.9	4.8	4.9	4.6

Source: OECD/DAC

– a clear signal of the Commission's intentions that trade with the ACP would be subordinate to the overall principles of EU external trade relations.

Given this evolution of European interests, it is not surprising that the "Green Paper" that the Commission issued on the future of the relationship favored the negotiation of trade arrangements that would be compatible with the WTO. Although the Commission identified a menu of future trade options that ran from the maintenance of the status quo through a reciprocal preferential agreement with the ACP as a single region, through the abandonment of the trade provisions of Lomé in favor of an expanded GSP, the Commission's preferred alternative was clearly the negotiation of what it termed regional economic partnership agreements (REPAs). These would be reciprocal regional preferential trade agreements "plus," that is, their trade provisions would be supplemented by the supply of EU development assistance. The EU would seek an extension of the WTO waiver to allow existing trade relations to continue for a further five years to provide an opportunity for ACP countries to take the necessary measures to prepare for reciprocal preferential agreements. Least developed members of the ACP Group, however, would benefit from trade arrangements at least equal to the status quo, provisions that the Commission proposed to extend to all UN-designated least developed countries.

The principal arguments the EU advanced in support of the REPAs were:

- they were in accordance with the overall thrust of EU commercial policy under which the Union had signed an increasing number of regional trade agreements with preferred partners, and would follow the example of relations with Mediterranean partners where, after the Barcelona Euro–Mediterranean conference, one-way preferential agreements were transformed into reciprocal arrangements;
- they would be compatible with Article XXIV of the GATT, thereby providing the ACP countries with the security that had been removed from the Lomé relationship because of the successful challenge within the

WTO to its trade provisions (and would provide more security than a waiver subject to annual review within the WTO);

- by "locking in" trade policy reforms in the ACP through the require-ment for reciprocity, such agreements would make the ACP more attractive hosts for foreign investors and thereby contribute to fulfilling the Maastricht objective of integrating developing countries more fully into the global economy;
- they would help promote regional integration among sub-groups of the ACP, a development the EU regarded as beneficial in its own right.

Moreover, because the special treatment given to least developed members of the ACP would be extended to all least developed countries, these provi-sions would be compatible with the Enabling Clause of Part IV.

Skeptical commentators saw the proposals as reflecting the new determina-tion of the EU to pursue its commercial interests in all external relations – the Commission's mandate had called for a more balanced relationship in which the "mutual interests" of partners would be taken into account. Since the EU was essentially offering no additional trade benefits to the ACP (the mandate made no promises on improved access for products subject to the CAP), merely additional hoops through which the ACP would have to jump to maintain the status quo in terms of free access to the EU market, the direct benefits of the new trade provisions would accrue overwhelmingly to EU exporters. With free access to their markets for European exports, ACP pro-ducers would not only have to compete with EU industries but also faced the prospect of CAP-subsidised EU agricultural products entering their markets on a preferred basis. In economies where import prices were already above world norms,[27] it was likely that the gains from the removal of tariffs would be cap-tured by overseas producers rather than by local consumers. Moreover, inde-pendent studies commissioned by the EU for six potential subregional groups of ACP countries found that the free trade requirements of such interregional arrangements would lead to a substantial drop in revenue for several govern-ments that depended heavily on income from tariffs, and that trade creation would be minimal and would often be more than offset by trade diversion.[28] Overall, however, the likely non-renewal of the Convention's four commodity protocols would cause greater income loss for ACP states than would the removal of any other trade preference.

Critics pointed out that a series of "hub-and-spokes" agreements would be likely primarily to benefit the EU rather than ACP countries – especially if no arrangements were made between the various ACP subregions, and that nego-tiation of free trade agreements would offer a politically convenient opportun-ity to exclude "sensitive" products (the EU mandate suggested that REPAs "will cover substantially all trade between the parties excluding no sector but taking into account the sensitivity of certain products of both parties").[29] And to confine the most generous access to the EU market to least developed countries would ensure in effect that the provisions would not be utilized: the Lomé experience had reinforced that of the GSP where only the more developed economies were able to take substantial advantage of the preferential access provisions to diversify their exports.[30]

The EU's Green Paper, with its offer of nothing for something through the negotiation of REPAs, placed the ACP Group on the defensive, not least because the new approach posed a potential threat to the grouping's very existence. Its original negotiating mandate[31] showed some confusion on the trade issue, reflecting the inability of the Group to reach consensus on the issues involved. On the one hand, it called for improved non-reciprocal trade preferences from the EU – a status quo "plus" (paragraph 39). On the other, it recognized that "under the prevailing WTO rules, the current arrangements including non-reciprocity applied to ACP states only cannot continue indefinitely" (paragraph 35). The Group also called for "a transition period which is more realistic and consequently longer" (paragraph 37) than that proposed by the EU, and for phased introduction of reciprocity.

Recognition by the ACP of the limited viability of the existing trade arrangements might be seen as indicating a degree of cognitive consensus on the issue. But few ACP governments perceived significant benefit in the EU proposals; it was more a matter of having to accept an unpalatable alternative forced on them by the power asymmetries in the relationship. The problem for the ACP was that they were attempting to maintain a clientelist relationship with an EU that was no longer willing to be a patron. The EU, however, did concede the ACP demand for greater flexibility in the implementation of the new arrangements:

- ACP governments were given an eight-year preparatory period before entering a transitional phase towards a free trade agreement with the EU;[32]
- the EU would approach the WTO for a waiver to allow the maintenance of existing trade arrangements for this eight-year period;
- negotiation of the new arrangements would begin in September 2002 and be concluded by the end of December 2007 at the latest;
- in 2004, the Union will assess the situation of the non-least developed countries which, after consultations with the Union decide that they are not in a position to enter into economic partnership agreements (the word "regional" disappeared during the negotiations) and "will examine all alternative possibilities, in order to provide these countries with a new framework for trade which is equivalent to their existing situation and in conformity with WTO rules."[33]

5   From Cotonou to confusion?

The Cotonou Agreement can be regarded as a victory for multilateralism over particularism through a return to a WTO-compatible form of interregionalism. Yet the proposal to make the relationship Article XXIV compatible is beset by a number of problems that may inhibit the realization of the stated objectives, and which may render them contrary to WTO principles.

The first set of problems relates to counterpart coherence: the absence of viable regional groupings on the ACP side with which the EU can negotiate. The recent history of ACP countries, especially those in Africa, is littered with the debris of a large number of failed regional treaties. Few viable regional institutions exist; fewer still that have realized intraregional free trade and that have the capacity to negotiate collectively with the EU. Low levels of intraregional trade (Table 5.3) provide few incentives to negotiate more formal arrangements.

In its Green Paper, the Commission foresaw regional economic partnerships being negotiated with the Caribbean (CARICOM), the Pacific, and four African groupings – EAC, SADC, UDEAC, and UEMOA – covering East, South, Central and West Africa respectively.[34] Of these groupings, CARICOM is by far the furthest advanced towards freeing intraregional trade, and has a competent regional secretariat. The problem for the Caribbean, however, is that it would risk the loss of its preferred access to the U.S. and Canadian markets under the Caribbean Basin Economic Recovery Act (CBERA) and the Canadian Tariff Treatment for Commonwealth Caribbean Countries should it grant imports from the EU more favorable treatment than that given to those from its North American partners.

Elsewhere, the lack of viable regional institutions with which the EU might negotiate is more acute. The Pacific Islands have no regional trade arrangement amongst themselves; the only regional institution is the Pacific Islands Forum, which also includes Australia and New Zealand. Again, any move to accord imports from the EU more favorable treatment than those from the two industrialized Oceanic economies would risk the

Table 5.3   Trade relations for selected ACP regional groupings, 1995

Trade (in %)	UEMOA	SADC	EAC	UDEAC	CARICOM
Intra-regional	8.7	11.5	7.9	3.2	3.3
With EU-15	49.6	36.4	36.3	52.0	24.4
With others	41.7	52.1	55.9	44.7	72.3

Note: Trade is the sum of exports and imports.

UEMOA = Union Economique et Monétaire Ouest Africaine
SADC = Southern African Development Community
EAC = East African Cooperation
UDEAC = Union Douanière et Economique de l'Afrique Centrale
CARICOM = Caribbean Community and Common Market

Source: IMF, *Direction of Trade Statistics*, 1997. Reproduced from Lecomte, 1998.

loss of preferred access that Pacific islands currently enjoy to their markets under the SPARTECA agreement.

In Africa, regional economic integration remains a distant aspiration. Moreover, the four groupings that the Commission identified are far from comprehensive: they currently exclude nineteen sub-Saharan countries.[35] An additional complication is one instance of overlapping membership: Tanzania is a member of both the Eastern African Cooperation and the SADC groupings. While European officials might credibly claim that the Cotonou Agreement provides a powerful incentive for African regions to get their act together, the possibility of their doing so in time to begin negotiations with the EU in accord with the Cotonou timetable appears remote.

A second, familiar problem further complicates matters: the lack of coincidence of geography and level of development. This is problematic because the Cotonou Agreement provides for special treatment for the least developed countries. Article 37.9 of the Agreement specifies that "The Community [EU] will start by the year 2000, a process which by the end of multilateral trade negotiations and at the latest 2005 will allow duty free access for essentially all products from all LDCs building on the level of the existing trade provisions of the Fourth ACP–EC Convention and which will simplify and review the rules of origin, including cumulation provisions, that apply to their exports." The EU has pressed ahead with implementing these commitments through its "Everything but Arms" initiative, launched in February 2001. Through this proposal, the EU provided immediate duty and quota free access for all exports from the world's forty-eight least developed countries save for armaments and certain agricultural products.[36]

The effect of this initiative has been to remove any incentive for the forty ACP economies with least developed economy status to enter into regional trade agreements with the EU: the access to the EU market they enjoyed under Lomé will be maintained (and even improved upon for agricultural products included in the CAP) without their having to offer reciprocity to the EU. Least developed ACP economies are represented in all three geographical areas of the grouping: Haiti in the Caribbean; Kiribati, Samoa, Solomon Islands, Tuvalu, and Vanuatu in the Pacific; and a host of countries in Africa (see Table 5.1). Of the regional arrangements identified by the EU as possible negotiating partners, only one – CARICOM – does not contain at least one least developed country. The EU's initiative for the least developed, whatever its merits in its own right, may therefore have the unintended consequence of making its negotiations with regional groupings among the ACP countries more difficult and, indeed, even give rise to a situation where regional groupings among the ACP are shaped more by the imperatives of negotiating with an extraregional partner than by the logic of local geography or intraregional considerations. In any event, the differences in economic structures among countries of the various regional groupings in Africa makes it highly unlikely that they will be able to reach agreement on a common approach for negotiations with the EU.[37]

For non-least developed ACP countries, the alternatives to a regional partnership agreement are bleak. In its Green Paper, the Commission did make reference to the possibility of negotiating bilateral free trade arrangements, as it did with South Africa, with "willing single ACP countries which are outside any regional integration process and are large and capable enough (examples: Nigeria, Zaire [Congo]), and provided that political conditions are right." The implication is that this option will not be available to smaller ACP economies. Already faced with the possibility of simultaneously negotiating five arrangements with ACP regions, the EU would not welcome the bureaucratic burden of entering talks with a string of individual ACP countries. Although the EU in Article 37.6 of the Cotonou Agreement, quoted above, does commit itself to examining "all alternative possibilities" that are compatible with the WTO for ACP countries unable to enter regional agreements, the only option that officially has been regarded as viable has been to provide them with the same treatment under the GSP afforded all other non-least developed LDEs. To do so would significantly reduce the advantages that these economies currently enjoy in the EU market.[38]

Whether the economic partnership arrangements the EU proposes will in fact be compatible with the WTO provisions under Article XXIV remains an open question. Two issues are particularly problematic in this context. One is the time period for entry into force of these arrangements. The second is the comprehensiveness – or lack thereof – of the product coverage. The EU has suggested that it may argue in the WTO for a longer transition period (fifteen to twenty years) than provided for in the Marrakech memorandum of understanding on Article XXIV (which specifies a ten-year period). Moreover, the EU has asserted that the partnership arrangements while covering "substantially all trade" will impose "asymmetrical" obligations and take into account the "sensitivity" of certain products. Here the free trade agreement with South Africa (described by the EU as "differentiated in coverage and asymmetrical in timing") may point to what the EU has in mind. The agreement provides for the full liberalization of 95 percent of EU imports from South Africa over a transitional period of ten years, and of 86 percent of South African imports from the EU over a period of twelve years. On agriculture, however, the asymmetry is reversed: the EU will provide duty free entry for only 61 percent of imports of South African agricultural products whereas South Africa will provide free access for 81 percent of European exports of agricultural products. Among the South African agricultural exports excluded from the agreement are beef, sugar, most dairy products, sweet corn, maize, rice, and fresh fruit, while imports of South African wine are only partially liberalized.[39] Similarly, unlike the North American Free Trade Agreement (NAFTA), the EU–Mexico free trade agreement does not provide for free trade in agriculture but excludes close to 40 percent of agricultural exports (again sugar, dairy, beef, and grains).[40]

How much "variable geometry" the WTO will tolerate in regional free trade agreements remains to be seen. At the very least, the variations from strict Article XXIV compliance that the EU is proposing for the partnership agreements will render them vulnerable to challenge within the WTO. It may yet have to seek waivers from other WTO members for any regional economic partnerships negotiated under Cotonou.

Given the lack of negotiating capacity of individual ACP states and of most of the regional groupings the EU has identified as potential partners, the emergence of a patchwork quilt of arrangements to replace the Lomé Convention is quite likely (Table 5.4). Whether they will return the interregional relationship with the ACP to the WTO nest through the negotiation of Article XXIV-compatible arrangements or fall out of it altogether will only become clear toward the end of the decade.[41]

6 Explaining the evolution of the interregional regime

Lomé differed from many of the other relationships discussed in this book in that it was not written on a *tabula rasa*. The legacy of the colonial relationship and the Yaoundé Conventions created vested interests within the Commission and member states as well as in the client countries. Moreover, it provided a set of arrangements, an *"acquis,"* that was a reference point that constrained how the relationship could evolve until the EU made a decisive break with the past in proposing to move, via the negotiation of regional economic partnership agreements, to interregional arrangements designed to comply with WTO requirements for regional trade agreements.

How do the various approaches identified in the introductory chapter by Aggarwal and Fogarty inform an explanation of the evolution of the interregional relationship with the ACP? As would be expected with an interregional partnership that has lasted for close to fifty years and which is of such a broad scope, the significance of the different explanatory factors changed over time.

The argument that the relationship was shaped in part by balance of power considerations has some relevance for the creation of the relationship and its extension with the negotiation of the Lomé Convention. At this time, the maintenance of a preferred relationship with former colonies appeared to offer an advantage to Europe both in providing an assured market for old technology products, offsetting U.S. competitiveness in other parts of the global economy, and in affording preferred access to raw materials at a time when the industrialized economies were increasingly

Table 5.4 EU's trade relations with African, Caribbean and Pacific countries

	Form	GATT/WTO compatible?	Uniform treatment of partners?
Treaty of Rome	Colonies included in custom union provisions	Yes?	Yes
Yaoundé Conventions	Agreement intended to lead to FTAs with individual countries	Yes?	Yes
Lomé Conventions	Non-reciprocal preferential access to EU market	No: did not meet requirements for an FTA. Discriminated amongst countries at similar levels of development	Uniform access to EU market except for specific products – beef, bananas, sugar, rum – which subject to country quotas
Cotonou Agreement	3 possibilities:		No
	(1) FTAs with regional groupings or large individual Economies	Yes? Comprehensiveness of product coverage?	
	(2) Non-reciprocal preferential access to EU market for least developed	Yes under Part IV of GATT	
	(3) No special arrangements: Cuba plus non least developed countries that fail to negotiate FTA	Yes – GSP or MFN treatment	

anxious about future security of supply. These concerns figured prominently in the decision to extend the scope of the commercial relationship with the ACP to include two schemes – STABEX and SYSMIN – originally designed to foster continuity of supply of raw materials to the European market. With the relative decline of ACP economies and the disappearance of concerns about raw materials supplies (no effort being made to address the ineffectiveness and underfunding of the STABEX and SYSMIN arrangements), such balance of power considerations largely disappeared from consideration – with one exception. The EU determination to transform the relationship into one in which the more developed of the ACP economies were required to offer free access to their markets for EU exports (a strengthening of the regime by imposing additional rules on ACP behavior) was driven in part by a desire to balance the treatment that the United States and Canada were negotiating for their exports to Caribbean countries.

Societal interests affected the development of the interregional relationship with the ACP in two principal dimensions. EU economic interests were dominant in determining the scope of the commercial relationship. As always, European agricultural producers and their champions in national governments and the Commission played a significant role in limiting the range of products that were given preferential treatment under the trade regime and their terms of access – causing interminable haggling over, for instance, the volume of ACP produce that would be admitted to the EU market in the off-season and the duration of such concessions, each time the Convention was renegotiated. European agricultural interests also shaped the scope of the commercial relationship in a manner beneficial to the ACP, however. If it had not been for the determination of the UK sugar refiner, Tate and Lyle, to maintain its cane sugar processing capacity, it would have been far more difficult for the ACP to prolong the purchasing arrangements that Britain had previously offered under the Commonwealth Sugar Agreement. Similarly, the regime for banana imports owed as much to pressure from European commercial interests as it did to the lobbying of ACP banana exporters.

With the evolution of European commercial interests and the decline of many ACP economies, the desire of European companies to maintain the relationship declined, particularly when it was seen as actually damaging or having the potential to do harm to relations with more significant economic partners. The Convention's banana regime found few domestic supporters once it posed a threat to transatlantic trade relations.

As European commercial interests in the relationship diminished, a new set of European societal actors grew in prominence – NGOs that focused on development issues. At first these interests worked overwhelmingly in favor of maintaining or improving the treatment provided to the ACP under the partnership. The development lobby was effective in national parliaments;

it also worked closely with members of the European Parliament to maintain pressure on the Commission and the Council of Ministers. Increasingly, however, NGOs found little merit in a development policy that privileged countries according to colonial inheritance rather than developmental status. They supported the efforts of the Commission and the member states to impose political conditionality and to claw back the "automatic entitlements" that ACP countries had won in the negotiation of the first Convention.

In a relationship as broad in its scope as that defined by the Lomé Conventions, and one that was administered by the Commission on a day-to-day basis, it was inevitable that bureaucratic interests played a significant role in defining the interregional partnership and how it evolved. A whole directorate of the Commission came into being because of the responsibility of administering the Lomé relationship. The Directorate-General for Development had bureaucratic interests in seeing the geographical scope of the interregional relationship expanded with the accession of Britain to the EU, and in broadening the issue scope of the partnership with the addition of new instruments for collaboration in Lomé I. The Development Directorate in the early days of Lomé was a promoter of the interests of the ACP, often fighting bitter bureaucratic battles with the Directorate for External Relations and the Directorate for Agriculture to attempt to secure an improvement in the terms of the commercial relationship.

With the growth in significance of Europe's commercial relations with non-traditional partners, the balance of interests in the Commission changed considerably. The end of the Cold War and the consequent possibilities for eastward expansion of the EU produced a new aid program that grew rapidly to rival that to the ACP countries. The successful conclusion of the Uruguay Round negotiations and the advent of the WTO provided new challenges for the coordination of the Union's external economic policies. Within the Commission, the "global" element, reflected in the Trade Directorate, was triumphant over the regionalist elements of the Development Directorate, which lost its responsibility for trade negotiations with the ACP partners. But even within the Development Directorate itself, twenty-five years of dealing with ACP governments on a daily basis within the Lomé relationship had produced considerable disillusionment. Enthusiasm for the heady rhetoric of the first Convention of a partnership among equals, and for a relationship in which the obligations were entirely one-sided had long since disappeared. Moreover, the interests of the Development Directorate itself had changed as an increasing share of its activities was directed towards non-ACP states. The "Everything but Arms" initiative, with its privileged treatment accorded to all least developed countries, made EU trade preferences WTO-consistent and brought them in line with the new orthodoxy in development thinking; it also broadened the mission of the Development Directorate.

Ideas and identity also figured at various times during the evolution of the interregional partnership with the ACP. Identity issues were most important at the beginning of the partnership when the maintenance of relationships established during the colonial period and the desirability of promoting *la francophonie* and the British Commonwealth continued to enjoy significant support within the former metropoles. Besides generally underwriting the desire to negotiate a partnership with the ACP, such issues of identity were significant in shaping the commercial regime through the championing by European states of the particular interests of some of their former colonies – e.g., the UK support for special provisions for ACP sugar and rum producers, and for imports of beef from Botswana. With economic decline and political decay in many ACP countries, with Europe redirecting its commercial and political interests eastwards and westwards rather than towards the South, and with the end of the Cold War removing what little geopolitical significance ACP states previously had for Europe, issues of identity largely disappeared from the relationship.

Ideas played a prominent role in shaping the commercial relationship over the course of the interregional partnership. The influence of ideas derived from the NIEO debate was evident not only in the rhetoric of the first Lomé Convention but also in some of its provisions including the asymmetrical obligations under the trade regime and the automatic entitlement of ACP economies to transfers under the STABEX system. Europe consistently promoted the idea that regionalism would be good for the ACP throughout the life of the interregional partnership – indeed, it often seemed that the EDF was more enthusiastic in funding regional schemes than were the ACP participants. And the decision to move to Article XXIV compatible regional trade partnerships in the Cotonou Agreement marked a new strategy on the EU's part for promoting regionalism within the ACP. The influence of new ideas on the purpose of development and how this might best be pursued through aid programs was prominent in changing the content of the Conventions, particularly in the introduction and extension of political conditionality.

Distinguishing ideas and interests is never easy, however, and this was as true of the interregional partnership with the ACP as of other areas of international relations. Particular bureaucratic actors in some instances adopted ideas because they forwarded their own interests. Similarly, new ideas about the purposes of development cooperation, enshrined in the Maastricht Treaty and in Article 177 of the Amsterdam Treaty, were seized upon by the states that joined the EU in the 1990s to justify their desire to see the Union extend to all least developed countries the privileged relationship previously enjoyed by the ACP. The interregional partnership provides little support for the argument that ideas can redefine interests.

7   Conclusion

The Lomé relationship was a colonial inheritance that became increasingly embarrassing for the EU as its economic interests changed and the global trade regime evolved. The decision to break the Lomé mold reflected the dominance of "global" elements within the member states and the Commission, a combination of societal interests, national governments, and bureaucratic elements. Over the years, even those member states with the strongest historical ties with the ACP countries had lost interest in the economic relationship, given the economic decline of African and Pacific countries. The accession of new member states with few historical links (with the exception of aid relationships for the Nordic countries) to the ACP strengthened the coalition among members who wished to see development policy determined by the characteristics of the recipient economies rather than by historical ties.

The Lomé relationship had always placed the ACP Group in an awkward position in that its interests lay in defending trade preferences and other economic benefits not offered to other less developed countries. These countries seldom found the Group's arguments for special treatment credible. Increasingly the ACP Group lacked European allies in the quest to defend its privileged position. Even the strong development lobby in Europe, the sophisticated network of NGOs that had grown up around the Lomé relationship, and their supporters in the European Parliament, found little merit in a development policy that privileged countries according to colonial inheritance rather than developmental status.

Whether the non-reciprocal character of the Lomé relationship would have been maintained had it not been for developments within the global trade regime, given the evolution of EU interests, is debatable. The transition from GATT to the WTO with its new dispute settlement mechanisms afforded an opportunity for those within the EU and outside desiring to do so to take the initiative to break the Lomé mold. It offered non-privileged LDCs an opportunity to attack one of the most market-distorting of the Lomé provisions, the banana regime. And in doing so, they raised the stakes in the struggle to defend the Lomé relationship. The banana dispute became a significant threat to the carefully crafted Uruguay Round bargain and to Europe's broader interests in the global trade regime.

In attempting to return the Lomé relationship to the WTO nest by turning it into several different forms of interregional arrangements, the EU faces a new set of problems. In part these derive from the incentive structure it has itself put into place: the "Everything but Arms" initiative removes for fully half of the ACP states any imperative that Cotonou would otherwise have created to form viable regional grouping to negotiate with the EU. The lack of counterpart coherence of the ACP will present an ongoing challenge in the transition to new forms of interregionalism.

Notes

1. Some would argue that the trade component of the relationship is now relatively unimportant in that the economic decline of many of the ACP countries prevents them from taking advantage of their trade preferences; meanwhile the overall reduction in EU tariffs/extension of EU preferential trade agreements has eroded the preferential margins enjoyed by the ACP. Trade relations nonetheless remain a more significant development instrument than aid. For a discussion of some of the non-trade components of Europe's relations with the ACP see Arts 2000 and Schrijver 2001.

   For stylistic convenience, I use European Union (EU) throughout this paper even though relations with the ACP originated when the EU (and some members of the ACP) were known by other names.

2. In other forums, save when forced to defend their privileged treatment by the EU, the ACP typically fragmented along various lines of cleavage including principal commodities exported, and linguistic and geographical divisions.

3. On the concept of nesting of international agreements within a hierarchy, see Aggarwal 1985.

4. The fit between geography and level of development was far from perfect, however. Least developed Bangladesh, for instance, was excluded, while the Bahamas benefited from the Lomé provisions. The problems with this correlation became acute when the post-apartheid South Africa sought membership in the ACP Group. (South Africa is a natural candidate for membership if geographical criteria applied, but is regarded as a "developed" country in the WTO.) The EU eventually agreed that South Africa should join the ACP Group but not benefit from the trade provisions of the Lomé Convention. Instead, a bilateral, reciprocal preferential trade agreement, claimed to be compatible with GATT's Article XXIV, was signed that will lead to the creation of a free trade area between the parties.

5. A small ACP Secretariat with approximately two dozen professional staff was established in Brussels during Lomé I. The EU pays a substantial portion of the budget of the Secretariat (and has recently proposed to finance an ACP office in Geneva to facilitate the Group's relations with the WTO). The Secretariat has always been hard pressed in negotiations to keep up with the mountain of paper that the much larger European Commission was able to generate.

6. Although the trade provisions of the fourth Convention ran for ten years, the amount of financial assistance to be provided was renegotiated at the halfway point of the Convention – the second period of the fourth Convention is referred to as Lomé IV (bis).

7. Besides the lack of certainty of the trade provisions, their benefits were also limited by the restrictive (and exceedingly complicated) rules of origin that govern preferential access to the EU market (to which 360 pages of the Cotonou Agreement are dedicated), and by the limited access afforded agricultural products covered by the CAP.

8. The Commission's "Green Paper on Relations between the European Union and the ACP countries on the eve of the 21st Century: Challenges and Options for a New Partnership," in referring to the "contractuality" of the trade relationship, notes that "preferences are jointly agreed, they cannot be modified unilaterally by the EU." Quote appears in Chapter II, Part 6. Available at http://www.oneworld.org/euforic/greenpap/chap2.htm

9. Ravenhill 1993.

10. Ravenhill 1985.

11. Frisch 1997.
12. For further discussion see Frisch 1997.
13. Davenport, Hewitt and Koning 1996. Bhagwati's 1992 characterization of regional trade agreements as forming a "spaghetti bowl" of preferences is particularly apt for the EU. The WTO notes that the exports of only eight of its members face MFN tariffs in entering the EU. All other WTO members benefit from some form of preferential treatment (World Trade Organization 2000). Besides Lomé and its successor, the Cotonou Agreement, the EU operates a GSP scheme that benefits most less developed economies, and by August 2001 had notified the WTO of its participation in four customs unions arrangements (all in Europe), fourteen free trade agreements with European countries and nine with economies outside Europe (with Mediterranean countries, Mexico, and South Africa). In addition, it had yet to notify the WTO of agreements with the Former Yugoslav Republic of Macedonia and with San Marino, and was negotiating agreements with MERCOSUR, Chile, Croatia, and the Gulf Cooperation Council (Commission of the European Union 2001c).
14. World Trade Organization 2000.
15. Sugar constitutes 5 percent of total ACP exports, bananas two percent, and beef and rum one percent each. For further discussion see Ravenhill 1985, chapter 5; Dunlop 1999; and ECDPM 1999.
16. Commission of the European Union 2001a.
17. Aggregate data on ACP exports have always to be treated with some care given the disproportionate influence of oil (which alone constitutes close to one quarter of EU imports from the ACP) and thus of fluctuating oil prices. Diamonds and gold constitute a further 25 percent of the aggregate figure. Nonetheless, these figures reflect the overall decline in significance of ACP member states as economic partners of the EU.
18. This figure jumped to 4.1 percent in 1998 with the accession of South Africa to the Convention. South Africa alone accounts for one third of all EU exports to the ACP grouping. Allen 2002, p. 4.
19. Figures calculated from data in Commission of the European Union 2001d.
20. Commission of the European Union 2001a. Thirty-eight percent of all ACP exports go to the EU market; for African ACP exports the figure is 48 percent. On the evolution of trade between the ACP and the EU see Moss and Ravenhill 1982, 1987; McQueen and Stevens 1989; and Davenport, Hewitt, and Koning 1996.
21. Allen 2002.
22. The problems with the EU policies are documented most fully in a series of papers by Borrell (1996; 1999; 1994). He estimates that the regime cost consumers $5.30 for each $1.00 of assistance provided to preferred banana suppliers. Approximately 60 percent of this sum was siphoned off in excessive marketing margins by European companies with another 5 percent collected as tariff revenue by the EU. Moreover, for every dollar of aid reaching preferred suppliers, other developing country suppliers were estimated to lose $0.32 because of reduced export opportunities (Borrell, 1996, p. 6). Grynberg 1997 is also useful on the background to the banana disputes.
23. And the U.S. Sugar Act applies discriminatory quotas to less developed economy suppliers. Even GSP schemes discriminate among developing countries. Sometimes this discrimination is according to political criteria – the United States, for instance, has for a long time excluded countries governed by communist parties and OPEC members from its scheme. Most schemes also discriminate among countries that identify themselves as less developed in the WTO according to level

of development: the Newly Industrialized Countries, for instance, have been "graduated" from most GSP schemes. Brazil has challenged the EU's GSP scheme in the WTO because of the inferior treatment its exports receive compared to those from Andean and Central American countries.

24. Some were concerned that access to some ACP markets, particularly in the Caribbean, was becoming more difficult for EU firms, given the signature of trade agreements between these states and other industrialized countries – hence a demand that any new arrangements should be based on "mutual obligations."

25. Posthumus 1998 provides further discussion of the views of individual EU governments.

26. Moreover, while the volume of EU aid disbursed to the ACP in the 1990s stagnated after 1992, that disbursed to Eastern Europe rose rapidly. By the end of the 1990s, disbursements to Eastern Europe were running at levels of roughly two-thirds of that to the ACP.

27. Yeats 1990.

28. McQueen 1999.

29. The trade agreement with South Africa excluded several significant agricultural exports that competed with European production (see below).

30. Least developed economies account for under 0.5% of world exports.

31. ACP Group 1998.

32. The Doha WTO ministerial meeting in November 2001 approved a waiver of WTO requirements for ACP states until December 2007. Significantly, the waiver included a more restrictive annex pertaining to bananas, suggesting that it may have been possible for the EU to have gained a long-term exemption for a Lomé-type arrangement had the banana dispute been settled.

33. Cotonou Agreement Article 37.6.

34. The membership of these regional groupings as identified by the European Commission was:

    CARICOM (Caribbean Community and Common Market) 11 countries: Bahamas, Barbados, Belize, Dominica, Grenada, Guyana, Jamaica, Saint Lucia, Saint Christopher & Nevis, Saint Vincent & Grenadines, Trinidad & Tobago.

    EAC (Eastern African Cooperation) 3 countries: Kenya, Uganda, Tanzania

    PACIFIC (Pacific Countries) 8 countries: Fiji, Kiribati, Papua New Guinea, Solomon Islands, Tonga, Tuvalu, Vanuatu, Western Samoa.

    SADC Southern African Development Community 12 countries: South Africa, Angola, Botswana, Lesotho, Malawi, Mauritius, Mozambique, Namibia, Swaziland, Tanzania, Zambia, Zimbabwe.

    UDEAC Union Douanière et Economique de l'Afrique Centrale 6 countries: Cameroon, Central African Republic, Chad, Congo, Equitorial Guinea, Gabon.

    UEMOA Union Economique et Monétaire Ouest Africaine 7 countries: Benin, Burkina Faso, Ivory Coast, Mali, Niger, Senegal, Togo.

35. These countries include Burundi, Cape Verde, Comoros, Djibouti, Eritrea, Ethiopia, Gambia, Ghana, Guinea, Guinea Bissau, Liberia, Madagascar, Mauritania, Nigeria, Rwanda, and São Tomé and Principe.

36. Thereby realizing a longstanding proposal – see Ravenhill 1986. The restriction on imports of sugar, rice, and bananas, introduced after extensive lobbying by farm groups in Europe and by Caribbean countries, has caused some to term the initiative "Everything but Farms." For a study of the possible economic effects of the proposal see Stevens and Kennan 2001.

37. For further comment see McQueen 1998.

38. For a study of the possible effects on ACP economies of dropping back to GSP treatment, see Stevens 1997.
39. Commission of the European Union 1999.
40. Schott and Oegg 2001, p. 748.
41. Meanwhile, Cuba became the seventy-eighth member of the ACP grouping in December 2000 but the EU refused to permit it to join the Cotonou Agreement. Cuba's accession could be interpreted alternatively as a positive sign that the ACP Group was beginning to take on a presence outside of the relationship with the EU or as a likely cause of further incoherence in the Group.

References

ACP Group (1998). "ACP group negotiating mandate." Accessed 9 September 2001. http://www.oneworld.org/acpsec/gb/lome/future/negman_e.htm.

Aggarwal, Vinod K. (1985). *Liberal Protectionism: The International Politics of Organized Textile Trade*. Berkeley: University of California Press.

Allen, Tim (2002). "EU trade with ACP countries." Statistics in Focus: External Trade. Theme 6–3/2002. Accessed 2 October 2002. http://europa.eu.int/comm/eurostat/Public/datashop/print-product/EN?catalogue=Eurostat&product=KS-NO-02-003-__-N-EN&mode=download.

Arts, Karin (2000). *Integrating Human Rights into Development Cooperation : The Case of the Lomé Convention*. The Hague/Cambridge, MA: Kluwer Law International.

Bhagwati, Jagdish (1992). "Regionalism versus multilateralism." *The World Economy* 15, 5 (September): 535–55.

Borrell, Brent (1996). "Beyond EU bananarama: the story gets worse." Canberra: Centre for International Economics June.

Borrell, Brent (1999). "Bananas: straightening out bent ideas on trade as aid." Canberra: Centre for International Economics September.

Borrell, Brent W. (1994) "EU bananarama III." Washington, D.C.: World Bank, Policy research working papers 1386.

Commission of the European Union (1999). "The Trade, Development and Cooperation Agreement." Accessed 6 September 2001. http://europa.eu.int/comm/development/publicat/south_africa/p05-13_en.pdf.

Commission of the European Union (2001a). "Bilateral trade relations: ACP countries (77)." Accessed 19 August 2001. http://europa.eu.int/comm/trade/bilateral/acp/acp.htm.

Commission of the European Union (2001b). "Bilateral trade relations: ACP countries: European Union requests WTO waiver for the New ACP–EC Partnership Agreement." Accessed 19 August 2001. http://europa.eu.int/comm/trade/bilateral/acp/wto_waiver.htm.

Commission of the European Union (2001c). "EC regional trade agreements." Accessed 6 September 2001. http://europa.eu.int/comm/trade/pdf/ecrtagr.pdf.

Commission of the European Union (2001d). "Trade in goods: statistics." Accessed 19 August 2001. http://europa.eu.int/comm/trade/goods/stats.htm.

Davenport, Michael, Adrian Hewitt, and Antonique Koning (1996). *Europe's Preferred Partners? The Lomé Countries in World Trade*. London: Overseas Development Institute.

Dunlop, Adam (1999). "What future for Lomé's commodity protocols?" ECDPM Discussion Paper 5. Accessed 30 August 2001. http://www.oneworld.org/ecdpm/pubs/dp5_gb.htm.

ECDPM (1999). "The future of Lomé's commodity protocols: fiddling while rum burns?" *Lome Negotiating Brief* No. 6. Accessed 30 August 2001. http://www.oneworld.org/ecdpm/lome/lnb_gb.htm

Frisch, Dieter (1997). "The political dimension of Lomé." *The Courier ACP–EU* (November–December): 78–82.

Grynberg, Roman (1997). "Negotiating a fait accompli: The WTO incompatibility of the Lomé Convention trade provisions and the ACP–EU negotiations." ECDPM Working Paper Number 38. Accessed 21 August 2001. http://www.oneworld.org/ecdpm/pubs/wp38_gb.htm.

Lecomte, Henri-Bernard Solignac (1998). "Options for future ACP–EU trade relations. ECDPM Working Paper No. 60. Accessed 20 August 2001. http://www.oneworld.org/ecdpm/pubs/wp60_gb.htm.

McQueen, Matthew (1998). "ACP–EU trade cooperation after 2000: an assessment of reciprocal trade preferences." *The Journal of Modern African Studies* 36, 4: 669–692.

McQueen, Matthew (1999). "The impact studies on the effects of REPAs between the ACP and the EU." ECDPM Discussion Paper 3. Accessed 23 August 2001.

McQueen, Matthew and Christopher Stevens (1989). "Trade preferences and Lomé IV: non-traditional ACP exports to the EC." *Development Policy Review* 7, 3: 239–60.

Moss, Joanna and John Ravenhill (1982). "Trade developments during the First Lomé Convention." *World Development* 10, 10 (November): 841–56.

Moss, Joanna and John Ravenhill (1987). "The evolution of ACP–EEC trade: the First Ten Years." *The EEC and the Third World: Survey 5* edn. Christopher Stevens. London: Hodder and Stoughton, pp. 112–32.

Posthumus, Bram (1998). "Beyond Lomé IV: preliminary views of European governments on future EU–ACP relations." ECDPM Working Paper Number 53. Accessed 21 August 2001. http://www.oneworld.org/ecdpm/pubs/wp53_gb.htm.

Ravenhill, John (1985). *Collective Clientelism: The Lomé Conventions and North-South Relations.* New York: Columbia University Press.

Ravenhill, John (1986). "Aid through trade: reforming the international trade regime in favour of the least developed." *Third World Quarterly* 8, 2 (April): 449–85.

Ravenhill, John (1993). "When weakness is strength: the Lomé IV negotiations." In I. William Zartman (ed.), *Europe and Africa: The New Phase.* Boulder, Co.: Lynne Rienner, pp. 41–62.

Schott, Jeffrey J. and Barbara Oegg (2001). "Europe and the Americas: toward a TAFTA South?" *World Economy* 24, 6: 745–59.

Schrijver, Nico (2001). "'Triple C' from the perspective of international law and organization: comparing League of Nations, United Nations and European Union Approaches." The Hague: Ministry of Foreign Affairs Policy and Operations Evaluation Department, Working Document, December.

Stevens, Christopher (1997). "From Lomé to the GSP: implications for the ACP of losing Lomé trade preferences." IDS Research Paper for Oxfam GB. Accessed 21 August 2001. http://www.oxfam.org.uk/policy/papers/lome-gsp/index.htm.

Stevens, Christopher and Jane Kennan (2001). "The impact of the EU's 'Everything but Arms' proposal: A Report to Oxfam." Oxfam/Institute of Development Studies Research Report–01/01. Accessed 16 September 2001. http://www.oxfam.org.uk/policy/papers/eba.htm.

World Trade Organization (2000). "European Union: July 2000." Trade Policy Reviews: First Press Release, Secretariat and Government Summaries. Accessed 5 September 2001.

Yeats, Alexander J. (1990). "Do African countries pay more for imports? Yes." *World Bank Economic Review* 4, 1 (January): 1–20.

Elusive Interregionalism: The European Union and Eastern Europe

Cédric Dupont and Hilde D. Engelen

1 Introduction

After the fall of the Berlin Wall, the political and economic landscape of Europe changed dramatically. Western European countries became even more integrated, as the implications of the Maastricht and Amsterdam treaties testify (e.g., European Monetary Union, European citizenship, Common Foreign Security Policy). For its part, the eastern side of Europe, until then under Soviet tutelage, de-integrated. After the Soviet Union and the Warsaw Pact fell to pieces in the summer of 1991, the Central and Eastern European countries (CEECs) were compelled to drastically reform their economies and their policies.[1] In the midst of economic, political and security vacuums in the East, Western organizations became poles of attraction for the CEECs aspiring to political stability, economic prosperity, and security. Members of the former Soviet Union, for their part, have tried to reorganize their relationships within the Commonwealth of Independent States (CIS) with Russia as the central actor.[2] They have also become economic and political partners of the European Union (EU), with Russia and Ukraine benefiting from privileged relations.

In terms of economic relations, CEECs together with the CIS member states have collectively become the second partner of the European Union, just after the United States. How have these important commercial flows been managed? In particular, has there been any effort toward an interregional regime? This paper aims to bring answers to these questions, using the various explanatory factors developed in the introductory chapter of this volume as an analytical guide. As such, it sheds new light on EU relations with Eastern Europe, most of the literature focusing on the pros and cons for membership expansion without any consideration for other alternatives. Furthermore, few studies on EU enlargement have carefully tried to assess competing explanations for EU policy.

To assess the relevance of EU–CEEC interregionalism, we consider three different sets of relationships: EU relations with countries from Central

Europe,[3] with the three Baltic states,[4] and with members of the CIS. Each provides a logical way to study attempts of EU interregionalism since all include some efforts by the EU to develop some regional cooperation. Yet, as our analysis will show, there has not been a strong and consistent mutual willingness on the part of either the EU or its partners to create more than one region. For the cases of EU–Central Europe and EU–Baltic states this has meant EU enlargement, whereas for the case of EU–CIS this has mostly meant differentiated bilateralism with multiple partners. Reasons behind this attitude range from balance-of-power considerations to normative ones, including the interests of salient import-competing groups in the EU.

The first section serves as a historical benchmark for the trade relations that prevailed before the end of the Cold War between the EU and Eastern Europe. The next section draws the general contours of EU policy toward CEEC to serve as a background for the following three sections that look at more specific developments. The third section considers the failed case of interregionalism between EU and Central European countries, whereas the fourth section focuses on the transient interregional framework between the EU and the Baltic states. Next, we turn to the case of EU–CIS relationship, before concluding on the relevance of the various explanatory factors underlying this volume.

2   Historical benchmark: the pre-1989 trade situation

Trade agreements concluded between the European Union and its Eastern neighbors predate the end of the Cold War. Despite the existence of the Iron Curtain, they were important in framing the non-negligible trade flows between the East and the West.

As can clearly be seen from Tables 6.1 and 6.2, trade relations were sharply asymmetric. In principle, this would have given the European

Table 6.1   Percentage share of Central and Eastern European countries in EC trade

	EU (12) exports			*EU (12) total imports*			*Extra-EU imports*		
	1958	*1975*	*1988*	*1958*	*1975*	*1988*	*1958*	*1975*	*1988*
USSR	1.1	2.0	1.1	1.3	1.5	1.4	2.0	3.1	3.4
GDR	0.2	0.2	0.1	0.2	0.2	0.2	0.3	0.4	0.4
Poland	0.6	0.1	0.3	0.6	0.7	0.4	1.0	1.3	0.9
Czechoslovakia	0.4	0.4	0.2	0.4	0.3	0.2	0.6	0.7	0.6
Hungary	0.2	0.4	0.3	0.2	0.3	0.2	0.3	0.5	0.6
Romania	0.4	0.2	0.1	0.2	0.4	0.2	0.3	0.7	0.6
Bulgaria	0.1	0.3	0.2	0.1	0.1	0.1	0.1	0.2	0.1

Source: Eurostat

Table 6.2   Percentage share of EC in Central and Eastern European countries trade

	EU (12) exports			EU (12) total imports		
	1985	1986	1987	1985	1986	1987
USSR	12.2	11.5	14.4	18.1	13.2	11.4
GDR	20.2	15.9	15.5	19.6	18.2	15.8
Poland	18.5	17.0	18.1	22.6	23.6	23.4
Czechoslovakia	9.5	9.7	10.6	9.0	9.6	9.5
Hungary	21.6	22.5	24.3	16.0	17.3	19.7
Romania	10.1	11.6	10.2	24.6	26.1	24.1
Bulgaria	8.4	9.4	9.5	6.4	6.4	4.9

Source: Eurostat

Union important political leverage, but the situation was not that clear cut.[5] The CEECs, under Soviet tutelage through the Council of Mutual Economic Assistance (CMEA), were not entirely free to conduct their trade relations since they were to some extent economically and politically dependent on Moscow.[6]

More generally, three main obstacles hampered EU–Eastern Europe commercial relations for three decades: a) the incompatibility between planned and market economies; b) the differences of power and areas of competence between the EU and CMEA; and c) the Soviet distrust toward the European Union, perceived as the "economic arm of NATO" and as an "organ of West European monopoly capitalism doomed to inevitable destruction because of its internal contradictions."[7] As a result, before the 1970s, no real efforts were made to establish an agreement between both organizations; only bilateral agreements were concluded between countries within the two blocs. While the CMEA did not recognize the Union, the latter was reluctant to deal with it on a bloc-to-bloc basis (i.e., on an equal level). Privileging dialogue and negotiations with individual members, the Union, after having set up its Common Agricultural Policy in 1967, began to sign agricultural arrangements with individual Central and Eastern European countries.

Eventually, after much reluctance from Union members, a more or less coherent Common Commercial Policy entered into force in 1975, rendering necessary the replacement of bilateral agreements by Union agreements. This was eased by détente, a time when both parties opened the way for official contacts and launched initiatives to establish some solid foundations. On the one hand, in May 1974, the European Council offered to negotiate trade agreements with individual CMEA members and was prepared to give them Most Favored Nation (MFN) treatment. On the other, the CMEA proposed a framework agreement in 1976 that would establish MFN and would liberalize trade. It also called for a more elaborate commer-

cial cooperation. Alas, despite lengthy talks, the proposition
rejected because of their firm irreconcilable positions on th
ments and on the type of agreement (either on a bloc-to-bl
vidual basis).

The first extensive bilateral agreements were signed by the two most
independent states of the East, Romania and Yugoslavia. Benefiting already
from the Generalized System of Preference in the 1970s, both countries
signed a cooperation agreement with the Union in 1980. Sectoral agreements (e.g., textile agreements based on the Multifiber Agreement, and
agreements on steel products) were also signed, provided they would not
challenge the CMEA position.

Starting in 1983 the CMEA adopted a more pragmatic view of the Union.
In that same year, Czechoslovakia and Hungary discussed with the Union
the possibility of extending their trade relations beyond the existing sectoral agreements. With the arrival of Gorbachev to power and the advancing ossification of the Soviet empire, Moscow finally recognized the need
to initiate relations with the Union and proposed to negotiate a mutual
official declaration. While differences were worked out (e.g., the geographical application of the declaration with the status of Berlin), the Soviet
Union finally agreed to a bilateral dialogue and to negotiations between the
Union and the individual CMEA members, and called for cooperation in
areas of mutual interest.

3   European Union and Central and Eastern European countries: general contours of an evolutionary policy

The turn of events in 1989 and 1990 forced the EU to change its policy
toward the Central and Eastern European countries, mostly because they
had common borders with EU members and because they were leaders in
economic and political reforms. The EU members had already begun to differentiate between the CEECs and the CIS, with the Baltic states having an
intermediate status. Yet there was also a broad EU approach to postcommunist Eastern Europe as a whole, whose exploration will help us identify the broader regime in which more specific ones have been nested.[8]

From Trade and Cooperation Agreement to Europe Association

Even prior to the end of the Cold War, the EU started to formally establish
stronger trade relations with selected CEECs through the conclusion of
bilateral Trade and Cooperation Agreements (TCA) (see Table 6.3). Within
these first-generation agreements, the signatories reaffirmed their commitment to granting each other MFN treatment in accordance with GATT procedures. Aiming to establish a free trade area, they each promised to
abolish within four years quantitative restrictions on imports and committed themselves to trade and commercial cooperation. The scope of a typical

6.3   Trade and cooperation agreements

Country	Signature of agreement	Entry into force of agreement	Duration	Deadline for removal of quantitative restrictions
Bulgaria	May 1990	November 1990	5 years	31 December 1995
Czechoslovakia	December 1988	November 1990	10 years	31 December 1994
Estonia	May 1992	February 1993		
Hungary	September 1988	December 1988	10 years	31 December 1995
Latvia	May 1992	February 1993		
Lithuania	May 1992	February 1993		
Poland	September 1989	December 1989	5 years	31 December 1994
Romania	October 1990	May 1991	10 years	31 December 1995
Soviet Union	December 1989		10 years	*

TCA is wide-ranging. Depending on the interests of both parties, it extended to fields such as industry, agriculture, transport, mineral extraction, energy, science, training, finance, research, tourism, the environment, and the encouragement of joint ventures. The agreement included, however, strong safeguard clauses and anti-dumping procedures, pointing toward the protectionist attitude of the EU member states.[9] Furthermore, sensitive goods (e.g., steel, coal, agricultural products, and textiles) were often not included in the first generation agreements themselves but separate agreements for textiles and voluntary restraint agreements for steel existed nonetheless. A joint committee was set up to monitor compliance, further encourage trade and cooperation, and solve eventual problems.

As a response to the decisive events of 1989 and 1990, the European Council decided to improve the terms of the bilateral trade agreements. While offering General System of Preference (allowing better export conditions for agricultural products and for textiles), the Union cancelled the transition period for the abolition of quantitative restrictions for Hungary and Poland.

Improved market access was only part of the EU policy to facilitate the reintegration of the CEECs within the world economy. To improve their economic infrastructure, CEECs depended heavily on external financial aid. Besides playing an important role in the establishment of the European Bank for Reconstruction and Development (EBRD), the EU coordinated the Group of 24 aid program, which financially assisted the transition economies, provided some specific conditions were fulfilled. That same year, pending an IMF agreement, the Union decided to help the most reformist Eastern states by agreeing to establish a stabilization fund for Poland and to bridge a loan to help Hungary overcome its balance of payment problems. This led to the establishment of an EU aid program, Economic Reconstruction Aid for Poland and Hungary (PHARE), in 1989.

In order to become a recipient, the applicant state had to fulfill a number of economic and political conditions: a) ensure the rule of law; b) respect human rights; c) establish a multiparty political system; d) ensure free elections; and e) institute a market economy. At the outset, only Poland and Hungary (the fastest reformers) benefited from the financial assistance program, but financial aid was later extended to their immediate neighbors and then eventually to the Baltic states (see Table 6.4).

Financial aid under PHARE was designed in part to promote regional cooperation among recipient countries. For instance, in 1991–92 PHARE general guidelines specified that 10–15 percent of PHARE resources be reserved for cross-national or regional projects involving two or more PHARE countries.[10] Between 1990 and 1995, 579 million ECUs was allocated to multi-country programs.[11]

TCA and PHARE, although adequate to support the short-term needs of the East, soon appeared insufficient to cope with the collapse of the Soviet Union. Eastern Europeans wanted more than what they had secured through the TCA. In an attempt to prevent a flood of new demands, the EU, together with the European Free Trade Association, launched the process for the creation of a European Economic Area (EEA) whose aim was to extend the four fundamental freedoms of the EU's internal market (freedom of movement of labor, capital, goods, and services).[12] Eastern European countries would be offered the possibility of entering the EEA through EFTA membership. Already by June 1990 declarations of co-operation in areas of trade, tourism, transport, and environment were signed between EFTA members and Czechoslovakia, Hungary, and Poland. This project, however, due in part to the stark differences between the members, quickly failed to act as a magnet for the Eastern politicians.[13]

After the multilateral solution failed, the EU subsequently reverted to bilateral responses by offering a new type of agreement that has formed

Table 6.4   PHARE assistance to beneficiary countries, 1990–1996 (in ECU million)

Country	1990	1991	1992	1993	1994	1995	Total
Bulgaria	24.5	106.5	87.5	90	85	83	476.5
Czechoslovakia	34	99	100	–	–	–	233
Czech Republic	–	–	–	60	60	110	230
Slovak Republic	–	–	–	40	40	46	126.5
Estonia	–	–	10	12	22.5	24	68.2
Hungary	89.8	115	101.5	100	85	92	583
Latvia	–	–	15	18	29.5	32.5	95
Lithuania	–	–	20	25	39	42	126
Poland	180.8	197	200	225	208.8	174	1186
Romania	15.5	134.3	152	139.9	100	66	607.6
Slovenia	–	–	9	11	24	25	69

the fundamental legal basis of the relation: the Europe Agreement (EA). The EA, replacing TCAs, has an extensive issue scope. It encourages wider economic integration (especially freer movement for people, capital, goods, and services) and more intensive and multidimensional cooperation (e.g., cultural, economic, scientific, and technical cooperation). Introduction of new taxes, or other restrictive measures affecting trade would be prohibited. Within this framework, candidate countries are encouraged to seek legal convergence in company law, company accounts and taxes, financial services, competition, health and safety regulations, consumer protection, the environment, transport, and intellectual and commercial property. It calls for the creation of a free trade area on the basis of reciprocity within ten years – six for Lithuania and Latvia, and almost immediately for Estonia – from entry in force of the agreement. The EU agreed to first lift its trade restrictions, giving time to its Eastern counterparts to become more competitive. It was expected that, in the first phase of liberalization, expected to last five years, the EU would remove all specific quantitative restrictions, and then would gradually reduce non-specific ones. Meanwhile, its Eastern European counterparts were expected to gradually eliminate their tariffs on non-sensitive products and reduce tariffs on sensitive products to bring them in line with the GSP. Then, during the remaining five years, the EU would dismantle all remaining tariffs and quotas, whereas the associates would reduce customs duties and restrictive taxes. Although quotas would be allowed, there would be preferential treatment for EU products.[14]

To aid its counterparts, the EU, through PHARE and EIB loans, channelled financial assistance through a wide range of domains (i.e., environment, transport, telecommunications, agriculture, energy, regional development, and tourism). Measures were also taken to assist small and medium enterprises in CEECs and to encourage and protect investment.

The EA also institutionalized a political dialogue, which extended far beyond the TCA's joint committees. It was based on a more intricate institutional framework, which consists of:

- the Association Council, a forum for discussion and decision. This body, which comprises the ministerial level (members of the European Council, the European Commission, and the government of the associated country) and meets at least once a year, supervises the implementation of the agreement. It may delegate decisionmaking powers to the Association Committee and may decide to establish subcommittees. The latter, specializing in a particular area, discusses technical issues in depth, then reports to the Council.
- the Association Committee, composed of members of senior officials. This institution sets the agenda for the Association Council, and reviews all areas of the agreements.

- the Association Parliamentary Committee, composed of members of parliament of the associated country and members of the European Parliament. It deepens the understanding of issues between parties and makes proposals to the Association Council.

In the event of a dispute, if no agreement can be reached between the associate member and the EU within the Association Council, three arbitrators are nominated (one for each party and one for the Council) who together make a decision by majority. This decision takes precedence over the domestic laws of both parties.

To be eligible to sign the EA, interested CEECs needed to fulfill a number of conditions related to their human rights records, political pluralism, free elections, rule of law, and liberalization of economy. Starting the discussions with the most advanced Eastern European countries in the beginning of September 1990, the EU signed the first EA in December 1991. Eventually, by 1995, even the Baltic states became associates.

EU membership: from application to accession negotiations

Initially, when the EA was offered, membership was excluded. After lengthy discussions, the EU eventually accepted its inclusion as "an ultimate, though not automatic" goal into the Preamble of the second generation agreements. Political dialogue and financial aid were further designed to help signatories reach their ultimate goal: EU membership. Since then, the EU has treated applicants on a strictly bilateral basis, although it continues to strongly recommend regional cooperation.

In June 1993, the Copenhagen summit invited interested associates to become EU members, provided they fulfilled a number of criteria. Although the Commission attempted to make the criteria seem objective,

Table 6.5 Europe agreements

Country	Signature of Europe agreements	Coming into force of Europe agreements
Bulgaria	March 1993	February 1995
Czech Republic	October 1993	February 1995
Estonia	June 1995	February 1998
Hungary	December 1991	February 1994
Latvia	June 1995	February 1998
Lithuania	June 1995	February 1998
Poland	December 1991	February 1994
Romania	February 1993	February 1995
Slovakia	October 1993	February 1995
Slovenia	June 1996	February 1999

they remain vague, and no timetable was provided. These criteria include:

- the stability of the institutions guaranteeing democracy, the rule of law, human rights, and respect for and protection of minorities;
- the existence of a functioning market economy, as well as the ability to cope with competitive pressures and market forces within the Union;
- the ability to take on obligations of membership, including adherence to the aims of political, economic, and monetary union;
- the capacity of a country's administrative and legal systems to put into effect the principles of democracy and the market economy and to apply and enforce the *acquis* in practice.

When signing an EA, a candidate country would automatically end up in membership, provided it fulfilled the Copenhagen criteria. In order to help the candidates towards their accession, a Pre-Accession Strategy was proposed in December 1994. It consists of the general framework to adopt EU requirements: Europe Agreements and the Single Market White Paper of 1995, which define key measures in each sector of the internal market and priorities of harmonization of legislation. It also includes the tools that facilitate the process – PHARE and the structured multilateral institutional dialogue.

The Madrid European Council of December 1995 sent a signal that accession negotiations ought to be launched. It confirmed the conclusion of an interim report in November 1995 on the effect of EU enlargement and stressed that the countries "will accede on an individual basis in the light of their economic and political preparedness and on the basis of the Commission's opinion on each applicant."[15] In 1997, the Commission published an opinion on the progress made by each candidate toward the fulfillment of the Copenhagen criteria. On that basis, the EU adopted a

Table 6.6   Applications for EU membership

Country	Application for EU membership
Bulgaria	14 December 1995
Czech Republic	17 January 1996
Estonia	24 November 1995
Hungary	31 March 1994
Latvia	27 October 1995
Lithuania	8 December 1995
Poland	5 April 1994
Romania	22 June 1995
Slovakia	27 June 1995
Slovenia	10 June 1996

two-track approach. Membership would be extended to a first wave of five applicants – Czech Republic, Estonia, Hungary, Poland, and Slovenia (aside from Cyprus) – leaving out Bulgaria, Latvia, Lithuania, and Slovakia.

Launched in March 1998, the reinforced pre-accession strategy incorporated existing instruments (the Europe agreements, the White Paper on the internal market,[16] and the PHARE program) and launched accession partnerships. Concluded with each applicant, the accession partnership contains a precise national program for the adoption of the *acquis* within a set timetable. Accession negotiations began on 30 March 1998 with the five most advanced CEECs. However, by 1999, in the midst of the Balkan crisis and on the basis of the progress made by the second track of candidates, the EU came back to a more unified treatment of CEECs by opening up the possibility of membership to the latecomers. The laggards were to start negotiations by February 2000.

To sum up, the EU has gradually developed an increasingly binding regime to manage its relationships with Central and Eastern European countries. That regime is broad in scope, developmental in nature, and increasingly strong and institutionalized. Generally speaking, the general regime has not offered uniform commercial treatment to counterpart countries. And the latter have not tried to organize themselves as one group. Thus, to gain more insights of interregionalism, we now turn to a more disaggregated picture, starting with Central European countries.

4   Interregionalism as a dominated option: EU and Central European countries

As we have seen above, EU policy developments have not been uniform across time and space. On the latter dimension, Central European countries have benefited from differential treatment. Common borders with current EU members and early domestic economic and political reforms have made them the leading recipients of new policy developments. From the perspective of this paper, the interesting question is to assess the collective dimension of that specific treatment. In other words, this section will explore to what extent the EU has considered Central European countries as a group with which it could conduct trade relations on an interregional basis. This, however, also begs the related question of the amount and success of efforts by the counterpart to invest in the emergence of a collective platform.

Central European efforts at intraregional cooperation: Visegrad and CEFTA

In the context of strengthening EU commitments in the early nineties, Central European countries demonstrated some collective, regional reaction. Whereas such cooperation could draw upon historical precedents, in particular various plans to develop a Danube confederation in the late 18th century,[17] the immediate cause of renewed regionalism was the radical changes that these countries had experienced in less than a decade. Of particular interest was the creation of the Visegrad group by Czechoslovakia, Poland, and Hungary. In a first meeting in Bratislava in May 1990, the heads of the three countries justified their willingness to develop a regional group as a "means for ordering both external and internal relations" of Czechoslovakia, Poland, and Hungary.[18] Concern for security and order among these countries was primary, as revealed by the declaration adopted in February 1991 in the town of Visegrad.[19] This document was a common pledge for "total integration into the European political, economic, security and legal order."[20] Countries declared their willingness to cooperate over security issues[21] – to fill the security gap in Central Europe – and on other issues such as the promotion of a transnational civil society, infrastructure in communication, ecology, minorities, and economic integration.

The Visegrad Declaration did lead to specific agreements, in particular regarding trade. Czechoslovakia, Hungary, and Poland signed in December 1992 the Central European Free Trade Agreement (CEFTA) to create a free trade zone by 2000 or 2002.[22] Trade would be gradually liberalized both for industrial and agricultural products. For industrial goods, the agreement identified three groups. For the first group, including industrial raw materials (e.g., copper, salt, sulfur), products such as chemicals, intermediate products for the pharmaceutical industry, and some types of equipment and machinery, tariffs were lifted as soon as the agreement came into effect. The second group, consisting mostly of industrial products, would be liberalized in 1995–1996. The third group, including so-called sensitive goods such as products of the metallurgical, automobile, and light and electronics industries, would follow a gradual liberalization starting in 1995 to reach free trade in 2001. The agreement also called for the abolition of non-tariff barriers. With respect to agriculture, countries could keep their commitment to a much lower level, in particular for Czechoslovakia (and later Czech Republic and Slovakia) and for Hungary. Quotas were to be maintained to protect these countries from excessive import competition, especially from Poland. Other non-tariff barriers, such as licenses, and strict phyto-sanitary regulations, would keep agriculture mostly immune to liberalization.[23]

On the implementation side, CEFTA members have explicitly rejected several times any move toward supranationalism. CEFTA has remained a strictly intergovernmental regime without even an executive secretariat. Main decisions are made during yearly summit meetings of prime ministers, whereas more specific implementation and monitoring is left to the CEFTA Joint Committee (where foreign economic ministers sit) that has been meeting between one and three times a year. Decisions in both organs require unanimity.

Despite writing down an "evolutionary" clause in the initial treaty, members have not deepened their cooperation since the creation of CEFTA.

They have agreed on a small number of amendments (mostly on the content of liberalization lists), and have accepted new members – Slovenia in January 1996, Romania in July 1997, and Bulgaria in January 1999.

In terms of achievement, intra-CEFTA trade significantly increased in the 1990s (see Table 6.7).

Table 6.7   Evolution of intra-CEFTA trade (1993–98)

Index 1998/93	CZE[24]	HUN	POL	ROM (1998/96)	SLK[25]	SLV (1998/95)
Export	149	441.7	297.8	125.7	125.1	145.8
Import	133.2	269.5	435.9	192.3	125.7	114.4

Source: Dangerfield 2000, p. 63.

Furthermore the increase in intra-CEFTA trade was relatively bigger than the general increase in trade experienced by CEFTA members (see Table 6.8).

Yet there remains a rather long list of exceptions to free trade among CEFTA countries, and significant non-tariff barriers. The absence of any delegation in either decisionmaking or monitoring has not allowed for any momentum on these fronts.

The dominance of bilateralism: EU policy toward Central European regionalism

Looking at EU policy toward Central European countries, it is hard to find evidence of a push for regional cooperation among those countries. The first steps toward an increased cooperation with Central European countries, the TCAs, were bilateral agreements designed specifically for the different countries. A multilateral treatment was then attempted through the EEA but, as we mention above, it failed to attract the interest of Central European countries. Then came the Europe Agreements, which again were

Table 6.8   CEFTA states' mutual trade as a percentage of total trade

	Export 1995	Import 1995	Export 1998	Import 1998
Czech Republic	6.2	3.4	9.1	5.5
Hungary	5.9	6.4	8.9	6.9
Poland	5.4	5.6	7.2	6.3
Romania	–	–	4.4	8.8
Slovakia	8.9	4.8	11.6	5.6
Slovenia	–	–	6.5	7.2

Source: Dangerfield (2000: 64)

bilateral and did not ask explicitly for regional cooperation among Central European countries.

On that basis, the signing of CEFTA can hardly be attributed to a strong, explicit push for such a solution by the EU. In fact, the EU went the opposite direction during the Copenhagen meeting in June 1993, when the European Council declared:

> "The associated countries in Central and Eastern Europe that so desire shall become members of the European Union... Accession will take place as soon as an applicant is able to assume the obligations of membership by satisfying the economic and political conditions required."[26]

This new policy line was a strong blow to the willingness of associate countries to pursue a multilateral road. Yet the EU policy had some ambiguities. The conclusions of the Copenhagen meeting stated that acceleration of the opening of the EU market to transition countries should "go hand in hand with further development of trade between those countries themselves."[27]

EU policy ambivalence toward regional cooperation was also manifest at the Essen European Council of December 1994. On the one hand, a Pre-Accession Strategy was developed to better prepare the countries that had signed an association agreement with the European Union. The strategy, whose aim was to guide applicants towards their accession to the Union, consists of four elements: a) Europe Agreements; b) the Single Market White Paper of 1995; c) the PHARE program; and d) the structured multilateral institutional dialogue. On the other hand, the conclusions stated that "being aware of the role of regional cooperation within the Union, the Heads of States or Government emphasize the importance of similar cooperation between the associated countries for the promotion of economic development."[28] Thus, the EU seemed to encourage regional cooperation for the purpose of economic transition and as an element of preparation for accession.

The Madrid European Council of December 1995 soon proved, however, that bilateralism was really the driving approach to relations with Central European countries. Member states confirmed the conclusion of an interim report in November 1995 on the effect of EU enlargement and stressed that the countries "will accede on an individual basis in the light of their economic and political preparedness and on the basis of the Commission's opinion on each applicant."[29] From then on, the relationship between the EU and Central Eastern European countries followed a strictly bilateral route. As an illustration, the European Council during the Luxembourg summit in December 1997 approved carrying out the two-track approach outlined by the Commission in its *Agenda 2000 for a Stronger and Wider Union*, published in July 1997. The document proposed that membership should be extended to a first wave of five applicants: Czech Republic,

Estonia, Hungary, Poland, and Slovenia (as well as Cyprus), leaving out Slovakia, one of the original Visegrad-4, and another CEFTA member, Bulgaria.

The EU came back during the Helsinki meeting in December 1999 to a uniform bilateral treatment of Central European countries. The reason behind this change was its desire to avoid the potential destabilizing effects of excluding the 'slow-track' candidates. This has allowed Slovakia to catch up with its CEFTA partners, and will allow eight former communist countries – the Visegrad-4, the three Baltic states, and Slovenia (together with Malta and Cyprus) – to join the EU in 2004. Bulgaria and Romania will remain outside for at least a couple of years thereafter.

Explaining EU–CEFTA failed interregionalism

Why was interregionalism not the path pursued by the EU *vis-à-vis* central European countries? The interest group explanation identified in the introduction to this volume seems to work well to explain why bilateralism was preferred to interregionalism. Bilateralism was the ideal solution for those groups concerned about the costs of granting free access to the Single Market. For exporters interregionalism would have been a better option primarily due to market size effects, but given the minor differences between the two options in the short term,[30] these groups did not express intense preferences on this issue.

Bilateralism was also a better way to maintain stability in the tenuous post-Cold War balance of power in Central Europe. Dealing on a bilateral basis did not convey a message of a wholesale transfer of Central and Eastern Europe into the Western sphere of influence, thereby assuaging insecurity further east, in particular in Russia. As for identity building, there was definitely a normative motive behind EU policy toward Central Europe. Yet the idea was not to keep the counterpart separate but rather to integrate them, so that they would become part of the EU regional identity.

How then can we account for the ambiguity in policy, with some transient support for interregionalism? Bureaucratic politics is a possible answer, especially in a quickly changing context. Dealing with countries on a group-to-group basis was a way to minimize transaction costs and to better control demands coming from Eastern neighbors. The EEA recipe failed, but the EU tried to redesign it on a smaller scale without greater success. While such an explanation is plausible, there were hardly intense discussions about the relevance of interregionalism. The question has rather been about the content and final goal of bilateral trade relations.

The impetus for interregionalism came mostly from the counterpart. What were the factors driving the Visegrad countries' cooperation? Multilateral responses after the signing of new bilateral tools, the Europe agreements, could appear quite puzzling at first glance. To understand the reaction, one needs to consider three main elements. First, the EU's new policy stance was not without ambiguity with respect to its ultimate objective. Initially, the second-generation agreements were not meant to automatically lead to membership. Furthermore, Europe agreements provided only restricted market access to the EU, while opening Central European markets to EU exports. In such a context, it was hard for Central Europeans to neglect the potential of intraregional trade. From this perspective, Visegrad cooperation was exogenously driven.

There were, however, other reasons for coordination among Central European countries. First, Central European countries considered CEFTA as a "fitness center" or even as a precondition for membership. Second, some countries wanted to achieve a coordinated return to the West. A regional framework would help countries not only to respond to EU demands but also to mutually constrain each other, thereby minimizing the possible externalities from a lack of coordination (such as trade and investment distortions). Beyond trade, CEFTA was considered as a kind of "self-security" arrangement. In particular, the regional framework was perceived as a good means to cope with ethnic minorities. This was especially important for Hungary, with three million ethnic Hungarians living outside national borders.

But action by the Central Europeans always lacked a strong momentum, which would have been needed to raise the interest of the EU for interregionalism. A first reason for this is economic. Central European countries needed both foreign investment and competitive export markets, two things that they could hardly get from regional free trade area. Second, there were deep national differences in approaching the EU. Poland was seeking rapid and comprehensive trade liberalization, which would link the EU and Poland irreversibly.[31] Hungary was more interested in political and economic rapprochement within a gradual approach.[32] Czechoslovakia saw the political level as primary and believed that economic aspects should follow the establishment of strong institutional commitments. After the partition, the Czech Republic distanced itself from the Visegrad grouping, with Prime Minster Vaclav Klaus in January 1993 suggesting it was "an artificial device created by the West."[33] On the contrary, from the Slovak perspective, Visegrad has been considered as an "essential lifeline" that has allowed Slovakia to stay in contact with the pace of their neighbors toward EU accession.[34] Those deep differences prevented any strengthening and deepening of CEFTA, which would have been needed to push the EU toward the interregional road. In sum, interregionalism did not emerge mostly because it was simply not the preferred option on either side.

5   From interregionalism to bilateralism: European Union and the Baltic states

A second sub-case was the relationship between the EU and the Baltic states. Unlike with Central Europe, there were initially efforts by both sides to promote an interregional approach. Yet bilateralism finally prevailed, with each Baltic country entering the road to EU membership separately.

Baltic states' regional efforts

Cooperation dates back to the interwar period, when the three modern Baltic states gained (or regained) independence. In 1934, the Treaty of Good Understanding and Cooperation was signed in Geneva, but due to growing antagonism among the parties, it failed. Regional cooperation between Estonia, Latvia, and Lithuania resumed in late 1980s after a long period of Moscow-imposed dormancy, spurred by their common drive towards independence from the Soviet Union. Their pre-independence unity was, as Mare Haab summarized, "symbolic in form, strategic in essence."[35] This was demonstrated by the August 1989 "Singing Revolution," when hundreds of thousands of Balts forwarded the password "freedom" from Tallinn to Vilnius.

This emotional side of nationalism and regional cooperation was complemented by a more formal political dimension. In an attempt to establish formal cooperation between these newly independent countries, the three heads of states signed the Declaration of Concord and Cooperation, reestablishing the Council of Baltic states originally founded in 1934, which eventually became the Summit of Baltic Presidents. From then on, the three states cooperated in an attempt to make Soviet troops withdraw as soon as possible from their territories.

Regional cooperation became official with the signature of the Agreement on Baltic Parliamentary and Government Cooperation in Tallinn in June 1994, coinciding not only with the withdrawal of Russian troops but also the sixtieth anniversary of the first Baltic agreement. The agreement comprises the following institutional framework for cooperation: a) the Baltic Assembly, created in November 1991, with declarative powers; b) the Baltic Council of Ministers, the supreme body that takes legally binding decisions and recommendations on the basis of consensus; c) the Baltic Council, a joint session between the Baltic Assembly and Baltic Council of Ministers that adopts declarations; d) the Summit of Baltic Presidents, which takes place at least once a year and promotes Baltic cooperation at the highest level. This institutional regional framework provides opportunities for policy coordination both in economic and security areas; we focus here only on the commercial aspects.[36]

Baltic regional economic integration has materialized through four main trilateral agreements whose objective is the establishment and development of a free trade area. Coming into force on 1 April 1994, the first Baltic Free Trade Agreement covers industrial products, with each party abolishing all customs duties and quantitative restrictions to trade. Its successor, which came into force three years later, covers agricultural goods – one of the few international agreements establishing terms for tariff-free movement on agricultural products. After the July 1998 agreement on abolition of non-tariff barriers to trade (which sets terms for abolition of technical barriers to trade and for harmonization of sanitary and phyto-sanitary measures), the Agreement on Baltic Common Transit Procedure in June 1999 further reduced barriers to trade such as delays in border controls or customs procedures.

Since their independence in 1991, the Baltic authorities have been discussing the prospect of a customs union, in part to increase their stature in the international economy. After some time of inaction, the prime ministers of the three countries signed a resolution on the establishment of a customs union in 1995. Yet despite a deadline for completion set in 1998, the customs union is currently still not in force. Furthermore, as the 1998 and 1999 "pork and egg war" illustrated, each country has continued to use measures to protect domestic producers from competition in the free trade area. These difficulties are reflected in the relatively low increase in intraregional trade as contrasted with a sharp increase in trade with EU members (see Table 6.9). The latter have quickly replaced Russia as Baltic states' main trading partners – a sharp turnaround from the situation in 1987, when the Soviet Union accounted for more than 84 percent of the Baltic countries' total trade and the EU merely 4 percent.[37]

EU attitudes toward the Baltic states

Until the mid-1990s, even if bilateral negotiations were conducted, the EU seemed to treat the three Baltic republics as a group and pushed for their regional cooperation. By 1997, however, with the publication of the

Table 6.9   Baltic states' trading structure

	Estonia			Latvia			Lithuania		
	1995	1998	2000	1995	1998	2000	1995	1998	2000
Exports									
Estonia	–	–	–	3.1	4.5	5.3	2.2	2.6	2.3
Latvia	7.7	8.8	6.8	–	–	–	7.1	11.1	15
Lithuania	4.5	4.1	2.7	5.5	7.4	7.6	–	–	–
Russia	17.7	10.5	2	25.3	12.1	4.2	20.4	16.5	7.1
EU	54	55	76.53	44	56.6	64.6	36.4	38	47.9
Imports									
Estonia	–	–	–	5.1	6.6	6.2	1.8	1.5	1.2
Latvia	3.3	4	3.9	–	–	–	3.2	1.8	1.6
Lithuania	2	2.1	1.9	5.5	6.3	7.6	–	–	–
Russia	15.4	7.6	8.1	21.7	11.8	11.6	31.2	21.2	27.4
EU	66	60.1	62.6	49.9	55.3	52.4	37.1	47.2	43.3

Sources: Statistical Office of Estonia; Bank of Estonia; Central Statistical Bureau of Latvia; Lithuanian Department of Statistics.

Commission's opinion on the candidates' progress toward the fulfillment of the Copenhagen criteria, the EU sent a clear signal that it intended to distinguish amongst the three Baltic republics and that it would deal with them on an individual basis.

The EU's initial reaction to the reemergence of the three Baltic states was one of explicit nondifferentiation. It recognized the independence of the three republics at the same time on 27 August 1991, and sent one ambassador for the three states in April 1992. At a time when Central Eastern European countries were concluding Europe Association Agreements, EU members appeared reluctant to extend the comprehensive agreements to all former Soviet republics. Two reasons may explain their hesitancy: the Baltic countries' lagging economic and political reforms, and the EU members' fear of jeopardizing their relations with Russia and hence the stability of the continent. Only after much lobbying by the Baltic delegations and Scandinavian candidates (eager to maintain their free trade regimes with the Baltic republics) and the slow stabilization in Russia did the European Council consider extending Europe Agreements to the Baltic states, which it eventually did – all on the same day – in June 1995.

Intra-Baltic cooperation was often supported rhetorically by key EU decisionmakers or mentioned in reports or Council conclusions. In 1993, when Baltic decisionmakers raised the issue of establishing a free trade area with the EU, the latter's response was that the three "should first improve cooperation among themselves" and that they could learn from the Benelux example.[38] As a result, the three Baltic states signed the Baltic free trade agreement in September 1993. One year later, the free trade agreements, and later the Europe agreements between each Baltic state and the EU, explicitly recognized the need for continuing intra-Baltic cooperation. At the Essen Summit in December 1994, the conclusions read that "being aware of the role of regional cooperation within the Union, the Heads of States or Government emphasize the importance of similar cooperation between the associated countries for the promotion of economic development."[39]

By mid-1990s, the EU started to differentiate among the Baltic states, but on the latter's impulse. Although the three EAs are very similar in content, an important difference exists concerning the transition period requested by the candidates in the implementation of their Agreement's provisions. While the Latvian and Lithuanian agreements mention a transitional period that is to end no later than 31 December 1999, the Estonian negotiators surprised the EU when they did not call for a transition period. (Even the Visegrad countries asked for long transition periods.) Acknowledging Estonia's very liberal economic policies and its already extensive trade relations with the EU, the Commission decided to include almost no transition period in the agreement. This marked the beginning of a more mixed treatment and bilateral approach between the Baltic states and the EU.

Meanwhile, Tallinn and Vilnius pressed Brussels to judge their applications on an individual rather than a group basis to increase their membership's prospects. Convinced that they would soon be invited to start accession negotiations, both states did not want the shortcomings of their Baltic peers to diminish their membership prospects. EU policy change became striking in July 1997 with the publication of the Commission's Opinions on the applicant countries. By identifying Estonia as a potential member, the EU, although still promoting regional cooperation, altered the dynamics of intra-Baltic relations by explicitly differentiating among the three and implicitly designating Latvia and Lithuania as slow-track countries. With the help of annual accession partnerships together with their individual national programs for the adoption of the *acquis communautaire*, Latvia and Lithuania were ultimately invited in 1999 to start accession negotiations by February 2000.

Explaining EU–Baltic relations

Several factors account for the development of the trade regime between EU and Baltic states. On the EU side, the balance of power explanation was clearly dominant. The initial preference for an interregional approach came out of the EU members' fear of the effect on relations with Russia if they were to grant former Soviet republics quick EU membership – and thereby admission into the organization's security and defense structures, notably the Western European Union (WEU).

EU attitude also fits with the interest group and identity explanations. Interregionalism was clearly seen as a way to grant fewer concessions to Baltic states, reflecting the reluctance to embrace partners that had not achieved significant economic and political reforms. Due to the economic situation of the Baltic states, there were few gains to be achieved from quick integration and therefore interregionalism was a good way to start. Yet the enlargement of the EU to Nordic countries changed the situation. The Nordic states had an important stake in the future of the Baltic Sea region and the stability of the Baltic states has constantly pleaded in favor of the Baltic states' membership to the EU. The absence of political reforms did not make Baltic states look very akin to EU members and therefore there was no good reason to keep them separate, through interregionalism, from an EU identity building process. Bureaucratic politics does not seem to have mattered significantly.

The primary factor motivating all three Baltic states' policies toward the EU was their common experience of Soviet past. Although the rankings of their motivations differ to some extent, the implications of their delicate geopolitical position have been the most important incentive in aligning with Western states. Even if the 1996 Joint Declaration of Baltic Presidents for Integration stipulates that integration into EU and NATO is motivated by the wish to be "part of a united Europe" rather than by a "fear of a third country," the Baltic endeavors to obtain Western security guarantees against possible Russian future threats are evident. Whereas in the waning years of Communist Party rule in the Soviet Union the Baltic and Russian republics were partners in the struggle against the central power,[40] from the moment Russia became the legal successor to the Soviet Union it adopted a policy toward its small Western neighbors very similar to that of its predecessor. The three republics became convinced that the ultimate threat to their security emanated from their geopolitical position, fearing that they would be stuck in a "gray zone" between East and West if they did not gain EU and NATO memberships – and that they would thus be increasingly vulnerable to Russian threats, whether veiled or explicit.

When the Baltic countries suggested forming a free trade area with the EU, the latter asked them first to create one amongst themselves based on the Benelux model. They embarked on such an endeavor without great enthusiasm, knowing that their economies were rival, to improve their chances for EU membership.[41]

This shared eagerness to become full-fledged members of the EU and NATO seems to be the main driver of – and at the same time the principal impediment to – regional Baltic cooperation. Although Baltic authorities tended to undervalue EU "soft" security guarantees at first, the fact that the prospects for near-term NATO membership were uncertain in the beginning of the 1990s increased the appeal of integration with the EU. In August 1993, the three Baltic presidents, making public their intentions to integrate their country into the EU, declared that the aim to achieve Baltic integration was a step towards integrating their sub-region within the EU. This spurred the signing of free trade agreements, which the EU noted would assist in future integration into the organization.[42]

Efforts by the Baltic states to develop a regional platform have been weakened by several factors. First, there have been important differences among the three states, in particular regarding the pace and extent of economic reforms. Despite having made headway, the Baltic states are still far from having viable economies. Disadvantaged by the burdensome legacy of the Soviet Union, their limited natural resources, and their negative trade and current account balances, they are very vulnerable to embargoes and fluctuations of the world economy. There exists a sharp contrast between Latvia and Lithuania on one hand and Estonia on the other, which led Estonia to call for no transition period in the Europe Agreements.

Second, cooperation has suffered from the conjunction of divisive objectives and low resources to achieve them. While the Baltic countries have pursued regional cooperation specifically to enhance their prospects for membership in both in NATO and EU, NATO does not admit new members in bloc, and the EU policy has also to negotiate membership bilaterally with candidate countries. Therefore, pursuing intra-Baltic cooperation has in fact been largely incompatible with these countries' ultimate objectives. What's more, regional cooperation eats up significant political resources.[43]

To increase their membership prospects, Estonia and Lithuania altered somewhat their integration strategies by mid-1995. Convinced that they would soon be invited to start accession negotiations, both states did not wish the shortcomings of their Baltic neighbors to diminish their own membership prospects at the profit of the Visegrad group. Despite EU recommendations that the Baltic states cooperate to enhance their membership prospects, Tallinn and Vilnius pressed the organization to judge them on an individual rather than on a group basis. To further increase their prospects, both states chose to cooperate more intensively with their Western strategic partners (respectively Finland and Poland) rather than solely amongst themselves. Lacking a Western strategic partner, Latvia has been the most prominent Baltic state in pushing for Baltic cooperation.

The Baltic republics are gradually being incorporated into a larger region, often referred to as the Baltic Sea region.[44] Each of them, by their culture and geographic location, differ nonetheless in their European orientation. While Estonia, and to a somewhat lesser extent Latvia, identifies itself with Northern Europeans (mainly Scandinavians and Finns), Lithuania has developed strong bonds with Central Europeans (especially Poland). This orientation is also exposed through their trade. Estonia's main trading partners are Nordic states, especially Finland. Latvia trades extensively both with Germany and the Nordic countries, but Russia's economic weight remains important. Lithuania's principal trade partners are Germany, Russia, and Poland. The area bordering the Baltic Sea (which is somewhat reminiscent of the Middle Age Hanseatic League) is becoming a promising economic market.[45]

Since the end of the 1990s, the EU has adopted a specific (originally Finnish) policy, coined "the Northern Dimension," in view of these developments. The European Council of Cologne conceived it "as a way of working with the countries of the region to increase prosperity, strengthen security and resolutely combat dangers such as environmental pollution, nuclear risks, and cross-border organized crime."[46] It is also an initiative to reduce the East–West dividing lines that are still very present in the region.[47] One may ask the question if the attempts from the part of the EU to promote a region in the Baltic Sea region are not more successful than its attempts to promote a Baltic states' region. This would mark a move from interregionalism to EU sub-regionalism plus Russia.

6   Interregionalism with leftovers? The EU framework for CIS cooperation partners

Whereas interregionalism has clearly not been a stable option to manage trade relations with Central and Eastern European countries, the case for interregionalism between the EU and former Soviet republics seems to offer better prospects. Indeed, given both the economic and political character-istics of those countries as well as the geopolitical context, interregionalism is *a priori* an interesting option. We discuss in this section to what extent, and how, the EU has used it. In contrast to our discussion of Central Europe and Baltic states, we do not, however, specifically assess the explanatory power of the various hypotheses stated in the introductory chapter of this volume. Such an effort would be, given the ongoing status of the process with CIS states, too speculative.

The buildup of a new regional platform: the CIS

After the disintegration of the Soviet Union and the CMEA in the summer of 1991, the newly independent states (NIS) sought to disentangle their economies from the collapsed Russian economy. Inspired by Western pros-perity, the NIS sought their economic salvation in the transition from a centrally planned economy to a market economy. In the midst of this complex and difficult process, several NIS attempted to provide an appro-priate framework for post-Soviet trade and economic relations. Under Russia's leadership, a number of bilateral trade agreements were concluded in the region, ultimately leading to the creation of the Commonwealth of Independent States.[48]

The CIS, initially created in December 1991 and strengthened in 1993, provides a complex institutional framework to help promote several multi-lateral agreements on regional economic integration. The framework com-bines intergovernmental and supranational modes of governance. On the one hand, member states fully control the general dynamics with unanim-ity voting in the two supreme bodies, the Council of Heads of State and the Council of Heads of Government. On the other hand, member states have entrusted a permanent secretariat, known since 1999 as the CIS Executive Committee, with permanent coordination and executive func-tions. Decisions by the Executive Committee share similar features with EU legislation. Indeed, there are three types of decisions: a) instructions that are binding on member states and directly applicable in domestic law; b) decisions that are binding but require domestic legal transposition; and c) nonbinding recommendations. The institutional framework also comprises a web of more specialized bodies as well as an Inter-Parliamentary Assembly, an Economic Court; an Economic Council, a Council of Commanders-in-Chief of Frontier Troops, and a Council of Collective Security.

In terms of policy commitments, the ultimate objective is the creation of an economic union, through the prior establishment of a free trade area. All parties signed the free trade agreement in 1994 (with significant amend-ments in 1999) but few of them have ratified it to date. More ambitiously, member states signed in 1997 an agreement to establish a common agricultural market, mimicking in several dimensions mechanisms of the EU common agricultural policy (CAP). Implementation of the agrarian market has not started yet, however.

In sum, the CIS lays down an impressive agenda within a complex institutional set-up but the machinery has not really produced many results. This is clearly reflected in the figures on intraregional trade (see Table 6.10), which have significantly declined since the end of the Soviet Union. One could, however, see positive signs in the inversion of the trend for some countries in the early 2000s. Yet it is hard to gauge whether this reversion comes from the effect of the CIS or from the conclusion of other plurilateral agreements among some CIS members. One of these agreements has been the Central Asian Economic Union (CAEU) created in 1998 including Kazakhstan, Kyrgyzstan, Uzbekistan, and Tajikistan, countries that have all experienced expansion on intraregional trade recently (see Table 6.10).[49]

EU policy toward CIS countries: from bilateralism to interregionalism?

As with the Central Eastern European countries, the first initiatives the European Union took toward the Soviet Union and ultimately its ex-constituents had a financial and technical character. In 1991, the European Union set up the Technical Assistance to the Commonwealth of Independent States (TACIS). With the aim of supporting the economic and democratic transition process, the program, tailored to individual needs, presently provides grant-financed technical assistance to thirteen countries of Eastern Europe and Central Asia.

As Table 6.11 indicates, Russia has been TACIS's most important beneficiary (it gets almost one third of the total), followed by Ukraine

Table 6.10   Share of exports and imports to the CIS countries in percentage

	Exports				Imports			
	1992	1995	1998	2001	1992	1995	1998	2001
Azerbaijan	49	45	38	10	65	34	38	31
Armenia	89	63	37	26	83	50	26	25
Belarus	66	63	73	60	76	66	65	70
Georgia	53	62	56	45	41	40	30	37
Kazakhstan	60	55	40	30	90	70	47	52
Kyrgystan	76	66	45	35	83	68	52	55
Moldova	65	63	68	61	72	68	43	38
Russia	22	19	19	15	14	29	26	27
Tajikistan	44	34	34	33	76	59	63	78
Turkmenistan	41	49	26	52	93	55	47	38
Uzbekistan	42	39	25	34	48	41	28	36
Ukraine	56	53	33	29	70	65	54	56

Source: Interstate Statistical Committee of the Commonwealth of Independent States.

Table 6.11 TACIS funds committed by country 1991–1999 (in million euros)

	1991	1992	1993	1994	1995	1996	1997	1998	1999	Total
Armenia	2.3	9.6	17.0	0.0	6.0	14.0	0.0	10.0	0.0	58.9
Azerbaijan	0.4	12.5	8.0	8.0	6.0	16.0	0.0	26.8	9.5	87.2
Baltic republics	15.0	0.0	0.0	0.0	0.0	0.0	0.0	0.0	0.0	15.0
Belarus	8.9	14.6	9.0	7.0	12.0	0.0	5.0	0.0	0.0	56.6
Georgia	5.0	9.0	6.0	8.0	6.0	16.0	0.0	16.0	0.0	66.0
Kazakhstan	7.7	20.6	14.0	14.0	15.0	0.0	24.0	0.0	16.6	111.9
Kyrgystan	0.7	9.2	10.0	0.0	8.0	0.0	13.0	0.0	8.6	49.5
Moldova	1.1	9.0	0.0	10.0	9.0	0.0	18.0	0.0	14.7	61.8
Mongolia	0.0	0.0	0.0	8.0	0.0	9.5	0.0	11.0	0.0	28.5
Russia	212.0	111.0	160.8	150.0	161.2	133.0	132.9	139.7	73.5	1274.0
Tajikistan	0.0	0.0	0.0	4.0	4.0	0.0	0.0	0.0	0.0	8.0
Turkmenistan	0.9	8.8	0.0	8.0	4.0	0.0	11.5	0.0	6.7	39.9
Ukraine	28.7	48.3	43.3	50.5	72.5	76.0	59.0	44.0	38.6	460.8
Uzbekistan	1.7	18.8	0.0	15.0	10.0	28.0	0.0	29.0	0.0	102.5
Regional Programmes (1)	106.0	88.6	172.0	131.5	124.5	152.0	135.0	155.8	129.4	1194.8
Donor Coordination (2)	0.0	34.9	21.0	24.7	40.0	43.0	37.0	43.0	64.4	308.0
Programme Implementation Support (3)	6.2	24.0	11.1	21.0	23.0	37.5	34.5	31.9	65.6	254.8
Others (4)	0.0	0.0	0.0	10.0	10.0	11.0	11.9	0.0	0.0	42.9
Total	396.5	418.9	472.1	469.7	511.2	536.0	481.7	507.2	427.6	4220.9

(1) Includes the inter-state, nuclear safety and cross-border cooperation programs
(2) Includes EBRD Bangkok Facility, Partnership and Coordination Program, International Science and Technology Centre
(3) Includes Coordinating Units, information, monitoring and evaluation
(4) Includes Democracy Programme and STAP-Likanen facility

(10 percent). Since the collapse of the Soviet Union, the EU, and more specifically Germany, has been by far the most important provider of international aid in the region. The EU provided some 59 percent of the bilateral aid between 1990 and 1995, compared to the United States, which provided less than 14 percent, and Japan 5 percent, of the total.[50]

For the last ten years, TACIS has evolved from a stand-alone activity to an integral part of the EU's bilateral relations with the thirteen countries under the frameworks provided by Partnership and Cooperation Agreements (PCAs). (See Table 6.12 for a list of PCAs with time of signature and entry into force.) Replacing the outdated 1989 Agreement on Trade and Cooperation between CMEA and the EU, the PCAs aim to establish a strong and comprehensive bilateral economic and political partnership between the EU and individual CIS members.

To speed up implementation of the trade-related provisions, interim agreements have been adopted allowing signatories to export their products at low or even zero-rated custom duties. In addition, the EU granted NIS access to the Generalized System of Preferences and lifted nonspecific quantitative restrictions on 15 March 1995.

Besides its economic and commercial nature, the PCAs have a political dimension. Emphasizing human rights and democracy, the agreements establish a multilevel political dialogue.[51] To bring about mutual understanding, signatories have institutionalized a political dialogue. Largely inspired by political dialogue clauses of the Europe agreements, the political dialogue consists of a number of consultative bodies:

- Cooperation Councils (ministerial level), which monitor the PCA implementation, provide recommendations, and settle disputes on thorny trade and political issue;

Table 6.12   Partnership and cooperation agreements

	Date of signature	*Entry into force*
Armenia	22 April 1996	1 July 1999
Azerbaijan	22 April 1996	1 July 1999
Belarus	6 March 1995	Not yet in force
Georgia	22 April 1996	1 July 1999
Kazakhstan	23 January 1995	1 July 1999
Kyrgystan	9 February 1995	1 July 1999
Moldova	28 November 1994	1 July 1999
Russia	24 June 1994	1 December 1997
Tajikistan	Covered by the Trade and Commercial Agreement with ex-USSR	
Turkmenistan	25 May 1998	Not yet in force
Ukraine	14 June 1994	1 March 1998
Uzbekistan	21 June 1996	1 July 1999

- Cooperation Committees (senior official level), which assist the Council, and are themselves assisted by a number of technical sub-committees (working level);
- Joint Parliamentary Committees, which can make recommendations to the Cooperation Council.

The European Union has been inconsistent with respect to fostering group cohesion among the counterpart. On the one hand, it favored it by clearly distinguishing, through its choice of a newly tailored framework, CIS countries from CEECS and from the Baltic states. Furthermore, the original reason for choosing bilateral PCAs was the fact that the CIS lacked legal personality to sign an agreement with the EU. On the other hand, the EU has clearly started to introduce differentiation in its treatment of the counterpart. The PCAs signed with Belarus, Moldova, Russia, and Ukraine (the EU's future neighbors) contain an "evolutionary" clause whereby the signatories agree to consider the possibility of establishing a free trade area amongst themselves. Furthermore, the EU later designed an additional policy instrument for some states. The EU recognized that more coherence was needed between itself and member states' policies *vis-à-vis* partner countries that did not ask to be included.

Introduced in the Treaty of Amsterdam, the Common Strategy is one of the instruments belonging to the Common Foreign and Security Policy (or third pillar) "to be implemented by the Union in areas where the Member States have important interests in common."[52] The first to benefit was Russia. Presented at the second EU–Russia Summit on 18 February 1999, the Common Strategy was endorsed by the European Council of Cologne in June of that same year. In December 1999, the European Council of Helsinki adopted the Common Strategy on Ukraine. While the Common Strategy aims to foster coordination, coherence, and complementarity of all EU and member states' policies and instruments, it nevertheless does not replace the PCA, which remains the core of the EU–partner relationship. The PCA is an instrument that shapes the Common Strategy, whereas TACIS provides the financial means to implement it. The Common Strategy is implemented through joint actions and common positions, instruments other than the CFSP that increase the cross-pillar dimension. Problems therefore exist of possible duplication, contradiction, and institutional clashes.

The objectives of the Common Strategies are determined in part by the EU vision of the partnership. The Common Strategy with Russia provides for an overall framework in the following priority areas: a) consolidation of democracy, rule of law, and public institutions; b) establishment of the market economy and integration of Russia into a common European economic and social space;[53] c) stability and security in Europe and beyond; and d) common challenges on the European continent (e.g., the environment and crime). In the case of Ukraine, the Common Strategy has three principal goals: a) to support the democratic and economic transition process; b) to meet common challenges on the European continent (maintain stability and security; environment; energy and nuclear safety); and c) to strengthen cooperation between the EU and Ukraine in the context of enlargement (i.e., assistance to Ukraine's integration into the regional and world economy; enhancement of cooperation in the field of justice and home affairs).

What then will be the future of interregionalism between EU and CIS countries? Two recent strategy papers indicate that the CIS–EU regime has few prospects. But interregionalism may still develop between EU and the so-called Western NIS on the one hand, and between EU and Central Asia on the other hand. In a March 2003 communication to the Council and the Parliament entitled *Wider Europe Neighborhood: A New Framework for Relations with our Eastern and Southern Neighbors*, the Commission mentions Russia, Ukraine, Moldova, and Belarus as the eastern part of a "ring of friends" of the EU, the other part being the Southern Mediterranean countries. As such they deserve special treatment, combining both the existing bilateral logic but also explicitly calling for intraregional cooperation. A few months earlier (October 2002), the EU published a *Strategy Paper 2002–2006 and Indicative program 2002–2004 for Central Asia* that covers the relationship with Kyrgyzstan, Kazakhstan, Uzbekistan, Tajikistan, and Turkmenistan and promotes regional cooperation among those countries.

7   Conclusion

Viewed from the interregional perspective, trade relations between the European Union and Eastern European countries are not a story of great success. In some sense such a result is no wonder because one could argue that we are dealing here with only one region – Europe – and thus interregionalism does not make sense. Yet understanding that regions are not simply objectively, geographically determined should warn us that failure cannot simply be inferred from a look at a map. Transient sub-regions can to some extent be constructed and one way to do it is to build up regional cooperation platforms. Focusing on trade, this paper has discussed three candidate platforms for such a trend to develop, the Visegrad group/CEFTA, the Baltic states, and the CIS. The prospects for these different platforms to anchor trade relations between the West and the East did differ but eventually all came to failure as cases of interregionalism.

Interregionalism was never considered as a serious, long-lasting solution to EU–Central Europe trade relations. In particular, the EU hardly mentioned it beyond the failed attempt to use the multilateral EEA platform. Central European countries created CEFTA as a way to facilitate entry into the EU, making the regional platform a transient one. As such the CEFTA story strikingly resembles the EFTA experience.[54] The EU had a different attitude toward a Baltic regional platform. Up to the mid-1990s, it pushed Baltic states to embark upon a regional endeavor. Those states did so but considered the Baltic regionalism as a waiting room to EU membership. When membership became an option, they quickly seized the opportunity, leaving regionalism aside. Interregionalism with the CIS countries was not a greater success. The EU clearly paid different levels of attention to different countries, whereas on the CIS side there has been a trend toward more restricted regional agreements, in particular in Central Asia, not to mention the still dominant role of Russia.

So, in some sense, interregionalism did not fail but simply was not the chosen option, or at least never a dominant option. Why? We found preliminary support for three of the four hypotheses examined in this volume. The bureaucratic politics hypothesis tells us little: discussions on the merits of interregionalism have been anything but prominent within and among EU institutions, which have focused more on the specific forms of bilateralism and the timing of membership. From an interest group perspective, bilateralism (under its various forms including association and pre-accession) dominated interregionalism. It offered more flexibility to import-competing groups, which were the groups that had the more intense preferences on EU relationships with Eastern Europe. The balance-of-power logic was clearly present but in a conservative way. The EU refrained from pushing strong interregional relationships with regions that did not include Russia, out of fear to upset too abruptly the geopolitical situation. One could also argue that there was no need for interregionalism for balance-of-power reasons given the expansion of NATO.[55] Still on the geoeconomic side, the only interregional platform that was seriously considered as a way to promote Europe's influence was the European Economic Area, but Eastern Europeans never showed any interest in it. Since then an expanded membership has clearly been considered superior to interregionalism for security and power considerations. Nesting considerations, for their part, have not been particularly relevant to EU relations with any of the sub-regions: the EU always approached Central European and Baltic countries as prospective members of the EU (whose internal provisions are not subject to WTO rules), while Russia to date has not yet become a member of the WTO. Lastly, in a constructivist vein, the foreign policy of the European Union has been one of inclusion for Visegrad and Baltic states, giving clear signs that cooperation could always be furthered until the stage of accession was reached.[56] As such, we are dealing here with cases of extension of the European collective identity, not consolidation in the current form.

Notes

1. Throughout the paper, we will use the label "Central and Eastern European Countries" for the ten current Eastern European applicants to EU membership,

that is, Bulgaria, the Czech Republic, Estonia, Hungary, Latvia, Lithuania, Poland, Romania, Slovakia, and Slovenia.

2. The members of the Commonwealth of Independent States include: Azerbaijan, Armenia, Belarus, Georgia, Kazakhstan, Kyrgyzstan, Moldova, Russia, Tajikistan, Turkmenistan, Uzbekistan, and Ukraine.

3. We define Central Europe as comprising Bulgaria, the Czech Republic, Hungary, Poland, Romania, and Slovakia.

4. The Baltic states include Estonia, Latvia, and Lithuania.

5. Similar to other authors in this volume, we use the term European Union to refer to all the Union's post-1958 manifestations (European Economic Community, European Community), for the sake of convenience.

6. The Council for Mutual Economic Assistance, established in 1949 as a response to the Marshall Plan, entered into force in 1957. Unlike the European Union, the members of the CMEA did not transfer sovereignty to the organization, and all recommendations and decisions were adopted only with the consent of the states. The organization was mainly concerned with the coordination of central plans and the setting up of certain common projects.

7. See Marsh 1978, p. 26.

8. On the problem of nesting regimes, see Aggarwal 1998.

9. In the Hungarian case for instance, a clause allowed the EU to unilaterally limit imports or impose a duty if necessary. The EU could act similarly with the Soviet Union after consultation.

10. PHARE Annual Report 1991, pp. 5 and 9.

11. Smith 1999, p. 145.

12. See Dupont 1998 for an analysis of EEA.

13. Dupont 1998.

14. The problematic fields – textiles, steel and iron, and agricultural products – would be subject to separate protocols attached to the agreements.

15. Bulletin of the EC, 11, 1995, p. 69.

16. The Single Market White Paper of 1995 defined key measures in each sector of the internal market and priorities in the harmonization of legislation.

17. Bakos 1993, pp. 1025–1026.

18. Kolankiewicz 1994, p. 483.

19. "It is the conviction of the states-signatories that in the light of the political, economic and social challenges ahead of them, and their efforts for renewal based on principles of democracy, their cooperation is a significant step on the way to general European integration." (Visegrad Declaration; available on http://www.visegradgroup.org)

20. Torreblanca 2001, p. 143.

21. For a discussion of Visegrad in a security perspective, see Kolankiewicz 1994.

22. Slovenia joined in January 1996, Romania in July1997, and Bulgaria in January 1999.

23. On CEFTA agreement, see in particular Dangerfield 2000; see also Bakos 1993, Perczynski 1993, and Biskup 1994, as well as http://www.visegradgroup.org.

24. When one excludes trade with Slovakia, the index is 365 for exports and 317.8 for imports.

25. When one excludes trade with the Czech Republic, the index is 303.7 for exports and 351.9 for imports.

26. Bulletin of the EC, 1993, no. 6, p. 3.

27. Bulletin of the EC, 1993, no. 6, p. 13.

28. Bulletin of the EU, no. 12, 1994, p. 13.

29. Bulletin of the EC, 11, 1995, p. 69.
30. As Baldwin, François, and Portes (1997) show, there were more costs than gains for the West in EU expansion. This result refers explicitly to EU enlargement but also holds for interregionalism.
31. Torreblanca 2001, p. 144. See Sachs 1992 regarding Poland's postcommunist economic policy.
32. Hare and Révész 1992.
33. Quoted in Torreblanca 2001, p. 282.
34. Kolankievicz 1994, p. 484.
35. Haab 1997, p. 3.
36. The three states have established significant military cooperation programs regarding joint training, military education, peacekeeping activities, and procurement and air surveillance projects. In an effort to pool resources, the Baltic states created the common Baltic Battalion (BaltBat) in 1994, and later Baltic Naval Squadron (Baltron), Baltic Air Surveillance Network system (BaltNet) and Baltic Defense College (BaltDefCol), but the Baltic states heavily rely on the financial support of the NATO members.
37. Bayou 2002, p. 104.
38. Cited in Arnswald 1998, p. 8.
39. Bulletin of the EU, no. 12, 1994, p. 13.
40. The Baltic republics and the Russian republic openly supported each other's demand for independence and, by July 1990, established horizontal relations without Soviet mediation.
41. Bayou 2002, p. 112.
42. The preamble of both the 1994 and 1997 free trade agreements mention that the agreement is a "means to reinforce cooperation in European economic integration."
43. Haab 1997, p. 12–13.
44. The Baltic Sea Region is understood here as consisting of Denmark, Norway, Sweden, Finland, Russia, Estonia, Latvia, Lithuania, Poland, and Germany.
45. "Launching a Region. Potentials, Possibilities and Prosperity", Baltic Development Forum, Malmö, Summit 17–19 September 2000. http://dialog.em.dk/bdf/report. htm.
46. European Council of Cologne, 3–4 June 1999, Presidency conclusions.
47. Haukkala, 2000, p. 27.
48. CIS members are Armenia, Azerbaijan, Belarus, Georgia, Kazakhstan, Kyrgyzstan, Moldova, Russia, Tajikistan, Turkmenistan, Ukraine, and Uzbekistan.
49. Other agreements are the so-called GUUAM initiative (after the name of the members, Georgia, Ukraine, Uzbekistan, Azerbaijan, and Moldova), and the Eurasian Economic Union (Russia, Kazakshtan, Belarus, Kyrgyzstan, and Tajikistan).
50. "Towards greater economic integration," p. 17.
51. The PCA preambles all explicitly indicate the prerequisites of democracy, a market economy, and human rights. If these prerequisites were not respected, the agreement might be suspended, as was the case in 1999 during the second Chechen war, when the EU suspended some PCA provisions and limited TACIS aid to very specific domains.
52. Article 13 ex J.3, Treaty on European Union.
53. The EU–Russia summit in May 2001 established a joint High-Level Group on the creation of a Common European Economic Space (CEES) with the aim to define the concept of CEES by October 2003.

54. For a detailed treatment of EFTA experience, see Dupont 1998.
55. For a detailed study on the links between EU enlargement and NATO, see Seidelmann 2002.
56. For a nice demonstration of this attitude for the case of Baltic states, see Wennersten 1999.

References

Aggarwal, Vinod K., ed. (1998). *Institutional Designs for a Complex World: Bargaining, Linkages and Nesting.* Ithaca: Cornell University Press.

Arnswald, Sven (1998). "The politics of integrating the Baltic states into the EU – phases and instruments." In *The European Union and the Baltic states*, ed. Mathias Jopp and Sven Arnswald. Helsinki: Ulkopoliittinen Instituutti, pp. 19–100.

Bakos, George (1993). "After COMECON: a free trade area in Central Europe?" *Europe-Asia Studies* 45, 6: 1025–1044.

Baldwin, Richard E., Joseph F. François, and Richard Portes (1997). "EU enlargement. Small costs for the West, big gains for the East," *Economic Policy* 24: 125–176.

Bayou, Céline (2002). "La coopération économiques des Etats baltes", in *La Baltique. Une nouvelle région en Europe*, ed. Nathalie Bland-Noël. Paris: L'Harmattan, pp. 101–116.

Biskup, Jozef (1994). "Central European free trade area." *Eastern European Economics* 32, 5: 65–71.

Dangerfield, Martin (2000). *Subregional Economic Cooperation in Central and Eastern Europe.* Cheltenham: Edward Elgar.

Dupont, Cédric (1998). "The failure of the nest-best solution: EC-EFTA institutional relationships and the European economic area." In Vinod K. Aggarwal (ed.), *Institutional Designs for a Complex World: Bargaining, Linkages, and Nesting.* Ithaca: Cornell University Press.

Haab, Mare (1997). "Baltic states' potentials and vulnerabilities. Mutual competition and cooperation." Danish Institute of International Affairs Working Paper 97/1.

Ham, Peter van (1993). *The EC, Eastern Europe and European Unity.* London: Pinter.

Hare, P. and T. Révész (1994). "Hungary's transition to the market: the case against a big-bang." *Economic Policy* 14 (April): 229–264.

Haukkala, Hiski (2000). "The making of the European Union's common strategy on Russia," UPI Working Papers 28. Helsinki: The Finnish Institute of International Affairs.

Kolankiewicz, George (1994). "Consensus and cooperation in the Eastern enlargement of the European Union." *International Affairs* 70, 3: 477–495.

Marsh, P. (1978). "The development of relations between the EEC and CMEA," in Shlaim, A. and G. N. Yannopoulos (eds.), *The EEC and Eastern Europe.* Cambridge: Cambridge University Press.

Perczynski, Maciej (1993). "La collaboration subrégionale dans le cadre du groupe de Visegrad." *Revue du marché commun et de l'Union Européenne* 369: 541–546.

Sachs, Jeffrey (1992). "Building a market economy in Poland." *Scientific American* 226, 3: 20–26.

Seidelmann, Reimund, ed. (2002). *EU, NATO and the Relationship Between Transformation and External Behavior in Post-Socialist Eastern Europe.* Baden-Baden: Nomos.

Smith, Karen E. (1999). *The Making of EU Foreign Policy: The Case of Eastern Europe.* New York: St. Martin's Press.

Svetlicic, Marjan and Andreja Trtnik (1999). "European Union enlargement. Is enthusiasm waning?" *Eastern European Economics* 37, 4: 70–96.

Torreblanca, José I. (2001). *The Reuniting of Europe*. Aldershot: Ashgate.
Wennersten, Peter (1999). "The politics of inclusion. The case of the Baltic States." *Cooperation and Conflict* 34, 3: 272–296.
White, Stephen, Ian McAllister, and Margot Light (2002). "Enlargement and the new outsiders." *Journal of Common Market Studies* 40, 1: 135–153.

7
Be Careful What You Wish For: The European Union and North America

Edward A. Fogarty

1 Introduction[1]

Since the early 1990s, the United States and the European Union have taken halting steps toward institutionalizing cooperative economic and trade relations in a bilateral framework. EU and U.S. negotiators have come up with several potential frameworks – including the Transatlantic Partnership (TAP), the Transatlantic Business Dialogue (TABD), and the New Transatlantic Agenda (NTA) – in which to cement commercial ties between these two economic giants. Each has hailed the vitality and importance of transatlantic economic relations; yet, each has failed to build momentum toward a larger goal of a Transatlantic Free Trade Area (TAFTA).

While the United States and European Union were launching these serial trial balloons of institutionalized commercial ties, Washington was simultaneously busy establishing the North American Free Trade Agreement (NAFTA), which, by promoting unfettered commerce among the United States, Mexico, and Canada, created a new North American economic bloc that would potentially rival the EU in world markets. While not as institutionally ambitious as the EU, NAFTA became a cornerstone of U.S. trade policy as a gateway to a prospective Free Trade Area of the Americas (FTAA), and a key piece of the evolving patchwork of international economic integration. Thus the establishment of NAFTA – and the prospect of a future FTAA – promised to embed EU–U.S. trade relations in an increasingly complex web of current and future relationships, involving some countries directly (Mexico and Canada) and others indirectly (potential members of NAFTA, FTAA, and the EU).

What is relevant in the context of this book is that there has failed to emerge from this hodgepodge any real momentum toward – or indeed, any hint of – transatlantic interregionalism. Simply put, there is no discernable EU–"North America" relationship, at least not in the terms in which corresponding interregional relationships have been discussed by other authors in this volume. But this state of affairs is perhaps what makes this negative case important to explore – it is just as essential to account for why interregionalism does not occur as it is to understand why it does. The EU–North America case is a particularly good negative case (as opposed to, say, EU–Central Asian relations) because all of the factors highlighted in Aggarwal and Fogarty's introduction to this volume – interest group activities, bureaucratic contention, balance of power politics, and identity concerns – are all conspicuously present in this relationship. Nowhere is this statement more true than with respect to the EU–U.S. relationship, which forms the core of this case and shadows each of the others.

This chapter does not seek to make a general evaluation of EU–U.S. relations – which are exceedingly multifaceted and evolving too quickly to make lasting assessments of anyway – but rather forces it through the given lens and focuses only on the prospects for an interregional regime between the EU and North America as a whole. It is a story of disappointment for those Altanticists who have waited expectantly for the arrival of a more formal transatlantic partnership, but, as will be suggested below, perhaps one from which a happy ending is more likely to emerge for the international political economy as a whole.

2   EU commercial relations with North America

Despite the creation of NAFTA in 1994, the EU has studiously maintained separate bilateral tracks for managing its commercial relations with the three countries of North America. Thus to assess the EU's trade ties to NAFTA as a whole, we first have to consider those with each North American country individually.

Europe and the United States

The evolution of European–American economic ties since the end of the Cold War are best understood in the context of a much longer-term history of integration (and disintegration). U.S.–European commercial relations over the last 150 years have been a consistent story – with one big blip – of ever closer union. Trade between the two sides of the Atlantic steadily increased between the latter half of the nineteenth century and the outbreak of war in Europe in 1914, with the United States entering the war for the most part because Germany's unrestricted naval warfare wreaked intolerable havoc on U.S. trade with the belligerents. Growth in transatlantic trade resumed through the end of the 1920s; the Great Depression that followed was exacerbated by policies that sharply curtailed this trade. The postwar cooperation between Western Europe and the United States in creating the liberal international economic order, with its provisions for facilitating stable and open trade relations between the two, was largely a legacy of shared dissatisfaction with the beggar-thy-neighbor policies of the 1930s – and was not simply a reaction to the threat of the Soviet Union.[2]

The two sides' commitment to the General Agreement on Trade and Tariffs (GATT) – which was formally multilateral but whose direction was determined in large part by U.S.–European collaboration – helped to liberalize transatlantic trade relations, to the effect that by the 1970s earlier levels of integration had been reached once again. Agreements in the Kennedy, Tokyo, and ultimately the Uruguay Rounds of multilateral trade negotiations formalized this creeping process of cooperation and liberalization. The point of this dash through the history of transatlantic commercial relations is simply to show that, generally speaking, both Europe and the United States have prospered when transatlantic commerce has bloomed, and both have paid a heavy price – and indeed the international economy as a whole has paid a heavy price – when it wilted.

The Europe–United States commercial relationship remains today the cornerstone of the world economy. The EU and United States represent the world's two largest markets, and each absorbs roughly 20 percent of the other's exports, with total trade in 2002 worth roughly $650 billion.[3] The relationship is similarly intimate with respect to investment: in 2001, European firms accounted for over 60 percent of FDI stock in the United States (roughly $870 billion in total), while American firms owned a similar proportion of investment stock (approximately $630 billion in total) in EU member countries.[4] In 2001, the total amount of trade and investment streaming across the Atlantic came to $36 billion *per day*.[5] The current level of economic integration is high, and is only getting higher.

Assessments of troubles in EU–U.S. commercial ties tend to suffer from a lack of a sense of proportion. Economic relations remain, despite headline-grabbing disputes about bananas or steel, almost completely trouble-free. As EU trade commissioner Pascal Lamy has asserted, less than 2 percent of total EU–U.S. trade is involved in some sort of dispute.[6] Much of this exchange is intrafirm, which underscores the fact that transatlantic "trade" is very much intertwined with investment and merger and acquisition activities. Given the extensiveness of mutual interests, both with one another and with respect to the global economy, the two have retained a broadly consonant preference for, and agenda in, multilateral liberalization of trade and investment through the WTO – despite each's participation in various regional and trans-/interregional arrangements.

In the past as now, however, growing integration and interdependence have not been synonymous with unproblematic commercial relations. During the 1940s and 1950s the United States overtly sought to undermine the systems of imperial preference Britain and France had constructed among their respective colonies. During the 1960s the United States and Europe fought the "chicken wars," and Europe chafed under American benign neglect of its role as international creditor and its export of inflation from the Vietnam War and Great Society programs. In the 1970s the two were buffeted by the collapse of the Bretton Woods system and the oil shocks, and the United States put increasing pressure on Europe (and particularly West Germany) to act as an engine of world growth. Among the problems during the 1980s were the pasta and citrus wars, as well as European progress toward a single market that made Americans nervous about a new "fortress Europe." Over the past decade, bananas, genetically-modified organisms, steel, and the tax status of U.S. multinational corporations have all tested the bilateral relationship (as well as the fragile enforcement mechanisms of the WTO), and tensions in the aftermath of the 2003 Iraq war at least temporarily injected nationalist sentiments into consumer choices on both sides of the Atlantic. But U.S.–European trade relations have always involved complex patterns of economic intercourse as well as political cooperation and contention, and these more recent developments should be seen in this light.

During the 1990s, in the wake of the cold war and in a period of ascendant regionalism, the United States and Europe struggled to recast their relations in the absence of the Soviet threat. Many analysts predicted the future of international competition to be economic rather than political-security, and policymakers in the United States and Europe sought ways to retain their partnership even in the face of a growing sentiment that their relationship would be increasingly defined by commercial competition. Accordingly, the United States and Europe announced a series of agreements during the 1990s that attempted to institutionalize economic cooperation, with varying degrees of significance and success.

In 1990, the two sides announced a Transatlantic Declaration that was intended to deepen and institutionalize commercial relations. However, this declaration was more symbolic than substantive. Its main functional purpose was to establish a framework for regular consultation, specifically a regimen of biannual summits at which U.S. and European ministers and heads of state would meet to discuss important issues on the transatlantic and world agendas.

A New Transatlantic Agenda (NTA) was unveiled in December 1995 to provide some of the substance that the Transatlantic Declaration lacked. The NTA sought to broaden the scope of EU–U.S. cooperation both on trade and investment matters as well as on transnational issues such as terrorism and the environment. On the economic front, the NTA spawned two further acronyms: the New Transatlantic Marketplace (NTM) and the Transatlantic Business Dialogue (TABD). The NTM, for its part, was to be a framework for dismantling most remaining trade and investment barriers between the two, and a building block toward a possible Transatlantic Free Trade Area. However, the NTM's broad agenda proved difficult to translate into specific commitments, and the NTM ultimately gave way to a somewhat less ambitious Transatlantic Economic Partnership (TEP) in 1998. The TEP focused on the less sexy but still quite important matters of harmonizing standards and cooperating on other nontariff barriers more generally.

The TABD, for its part, provided a forum for European and U.S. CEOs and trade officials to generate their own agenda and momentum for closer commercial ties across the Atlantic. (The United States specifically sought, and the EU accepted, the exclusion of Canadian businesses from the TABD.) Indeed, the recommendations of those working within the TABD were a major factor in the push to harmonize regulations and standards. A direct result was the set of six Mutual Recognition Agreements (MRAs) signed by the United States and the EU in June 1997, which streamlined testing and approval procedures in the sectors of telecommunications, medical equipment, electromagnetic compatibility, electrical safety, recreational craft, and pharmaceutical manufacturing practices. By some estimates, these agreements save U.S. industries alone $1 billion annually.[7]

Despite this alphabet soup of smaller agreements, no comprehensive meeting-of-the-minds has been achieved by political leaders on the future shape of transatlantic economic relations, and plenty of disagreement remains between the two on their visions for the broader international economy. Indeed, the failure to launch a new round of multilateral trade negotiations in Seattle in 1999 was more a result of the inability of the United States and Europe to cooperate than any protest activities on the streets. Subsequent trade spats have clogged both the newspaper headlines and WTO arbitration mechanisms, though nearly all have ultimately ended in compromise. More recent ructions in relations resulting from disagreements over Iraq and multilateral cooperation in international security more generally have clouded the very existence of the West as both an emotive and practical entity, making ideas of formal commercial integration – which would be as much a political as an economic process – that much more distant.

However, though no formal, overarching U.S–EU regime exists to define the broad terms of the commercial relationship, there is nevertheless a considerable degree of institutionalized cooperation. This institutionalization exists in the less visible but perhaps more fundamental mid-level official cooperation and deeply engrained private sector cooperation among both businesses and civil society organizations. One can think of this relatively invisible sector of deep, cooperative interaction as a colony of anti-termites in the foundation of an alternate-universe home: they are the undetected beings quietly strengthening the foundation of the house, even as the homeowners argue about how to arrange the furniture.

The European Union and Mexico

For most of the period up to the 1990s, Mexico was but a faint blip on the European trade radar screen, accounting for less than one percent of Europe's international trade. However, as the EU trade agenda began to place greater emphasis on increasing trade with less-developed countries, and as the United States moved toward a free-trade agreement with Mexico,

European perceptions began to change. The completion of NAFTA posed an immediate problem for the European Union: it weakened Europe's position in a liberalizing and potentially dynamic Mexico, Latin America's second largest market and home to nearly 100 million consumers. These fears were warranted: from a more than 9 percent share of Mexican trade in 1993, Europe saw its share drop by one-third to 6 percent in 2000. Meanwhile, the U.S. totals jumped 5 percent (to a more than 80 percent share) over the same period.[8] While these trends were clearly in place before NAFTA, the inauguration of a free trade area in North America promised to worsen the EU's terms of trade with Mexico, and thus further marginalize European exporters in that market. The EU's response was to initiate, and in 1999 to complete, a bilateral free trade area with Mexico – and thus to make Mexico the only country other than Israel to have a FTA with both the EU and the United States.

The free trade agreement, known officially as the "Economic Partnership, Political Coordination and Cooperation Agreement," or more pithily (if less modestly) as the "Global Agreement," has been referred to by Pascal Lamy as "in terms of coverage the most ambitious free trade agreement ever negotiated by the EU."[9] Specifically, the Global Agreement set hard targets for complete liberalization of trade in industrial goods (the EU by 1 January 2003; Mexico by 1 January 2007), and broad liberalization of agriculture (by 2010, 80 percent of EU imports and 42 percent of Mexican imports) and fisheries (by 2010, 100 percent of EU imports and 89 percent of Mexican imports). It also granted Mexico preferential treatment in the services sector, while further liberalizing government procurement, investment, competition, and intellectual property policies. Institutionally, it established a Joint Council, which meets at the ministerial level to uphold the Global Agreement's aims (or "pillars") of political dialogue, trade liberalization, and general cooperation, and which maintains a dispute settlement mechanism should disagreements arise.

Like the EU, which sought a free trade area with Mexico in large part to redress the deterioration of its terms of trade after the creation of NAFTA, Mexico's broad motivations for pursuing a deal with Europe are not difficult to divine. Like Canada, during the 1980s and (especially) 1990s Mexico saw its trade dependence on the United States grow to staggering levels: in 1982, Mexico sent 53 percent of its total exports north of the border; by 1999 that number had ballooned to 90 percent.[10] The Mexican government's liberalization policies over this period had increased the proportion of the Mexican economy that was dependent on international trade, and thus intensified Mexico's vulnerability to economic shocks in the United States. Thus, even though Mexico shared the U.S. economic boom of the late 1990s (and its recession in 2001), it had every reason to seek to diversify its trade relationships – and particularly to embrace Europe, a market very similar in size and purchasing power to that of the

United States. Mexico's need to reduce its dependency on its northern neighbor became more salient with the U.S. administration's post-9/11 dismissal of Mexican initiatives to deepen NAFTA through additional agreements on aid and immigration. Europe in 1982 absorbed over 20 percent of Mexican exports – a proportion that had fallen to just 3.1 percent in 1999[11] – so perhaps a free-trade deal that evened out the playing field *vis-à-vis* NAFTA would reestablish the vitality of this trade relationship, something both the EU and Mexico were keen to encourage.

The European Union and Canada

The recent trajectory of the politics of EU–Canada commercial relations has broadly followed that of EU–U.S. relations. This fact comes as little surprise: given the broad political and economic similarities (in nature, if not size) between North America's two advanced industrial countries, one need not puzzle long over the EU's inclination to harmonize its relationships with the two, even as it maintained them separately. Canada – always eager to step out of the shadow of its overweening neighbor to the south, and dependent on the EU as its second largest trading partner – has not always championed this similar-yet-distinct path, but has yet to prevail on the EU to take seriously any new approach to EU–Canadian relations.

During the 1990s, the EU established a set of commercial fora with Canada nearly identical to those it created with the United States. A 1990 joint declaration inaugurated biannual Europe–Canada summit meetings, which ultimately led to the agreements of the 1996 EU–Canada Action Plan to erect a framework for bilateral relations and the 1998 EU–Canada Trade Initiative (ECTI) to enhance bilateral cooperation on multilateral issues, as well as to the Canada–Europe Roundtable (CERT), a business-led forum similar to the TABD. The EU and Canada also negotiated more specific agreements on customs cooperation in 1997, MRAs in 1998, and competition law enforcement in 1999. In nearly every case, these agreements closely mirrored similar developments in EU negotiations with the United States.

This broad parallel to the EU–U.S. approach occurred despite Ottawa's various attempts to pursue a separate path in EU–Canadian relations. While Canada and the United States do share many structural similarities as well as common positions on several quarrels with the Europeans – notably on genetically-modified food and hormone-treated beef – the former has its own interests to look after in its ties to Europe. While commercial relations are mostly harmonious, Canada has had several ugly confrontations with Europe (and with the Spanish in particular) over fishing rights in the North Atlantic off Canada's eastern coast. On the positive side, Canada has sought to enhance its commercial relationship with the EU to diversify its foreign trade portfolio, which at present is massively dependent on the U.S. market – a staggering 86 percent of Canadian exports go to the United

States.[12] Moreover, Canada may feel even more acutely than Europeans the effects of American hegemony, sharing reservations about the intrusions of American popular culture and about U.S. positions on international issues such as landmines, arms control, and the International Criminal Court.

However, realizing Canada's lesser presence in the Europeans' field of vision – and thus that a separate EU–Canadian bilateral track is unlikely to promote distinct Canadian interests – Canada has sought to embed EU–Canadian relations in a broader EU–NAFTA context. Indeed, Canada has, like the United Kingdom, sought to play the role of facilitating middleman in a putative interregional relationship between the EU and NAFTA. The government of Jean Chretien sought repeatedly in the mid-to-late 1990s to convince European leaders of the merits of a more interregional approach. In 1998, Canada's minister of trade, Sergio Marchi, envisioned a time "when Europe looks to North America [and] sees a NAFTA community, not just three different neighborhoods."[13]

Yet Canada's entreaties have received only the most tepid of responses from both Commission and European national officials.[14] However, the British government did give support to a specific EU–NAFTA track: in a February 2001 speech to the Canadian parliament, British Prime Minister Tony Blair declared the need for a "political declaration of intent" between the EU and NAFTA. It is not clear, however, whether Blair's statement was intended to give impetus to an interregional EU–NAFTA track, to merge the EU–North American agendas in the run-up to WTO negotiations in Doha later that year, or simply to humor the Canadian government. What is clear, however, is that Britain, together with Canada, remains a vital pivot of the transatlantic relationship in all areas, most clearly in trying to manage a post-9/11 international security agenda, but also in governing transatlantic commercial relations.

The European Union and NAFTA

Describing the relationship between the EU and NAFTA is not a straightforward task, for the simple reason that this interregional track does not officially exist. However, it is possible to consider some aspects of NAFTA that would possibly shape a future interregional relationship, as well as some moves that have been made to date that have sought to create some momentum for an explicit EU–NAFTA relationship.

The EU's commercial relations with the North American countries are strong and relatively well maintained. It appears that tariffs are no longer an important long-term issue: while there are occasional difficulties arising from one side's imposition of short-term duties to safeguard a struggling domestic sector (e.g., the U.S. steel tariffs of 2002), the main hindrance to greater EU–North American commerce – and the issue addressed in agreements like the MRAs – are nontariff barriers such as subsidies and product standards. The primacy that technical issues such as NTBs now take in

EU–North American trade relations underscores how deeply integrated the two side's economies already are. The EU accounts for 35 percent of "NAFTA's" exports (excluding intra-North American trade) and 25 percent of its imports, and thus is NAFTA's most important trading partner. Together, the EU and NAFTA account for 35 percent of world exports and over 40 percent of world imports, making the transatlantic link not only central to each side's economies, but to the international economy as a whole.[15] What happens in transatlantic economic relations – whether in official trade agreements or disputes, as well as in day-to-day commercial transactions – has repercussions far beyond the arena in which it is governed. Whether and how an EU–NAFTA track were to develop would affect every other trade regime in the world, from bilateral and regional groupings to the WTO itself.

The future of EU–North American interregionalism may be broadly constrained by two internal aspects of NAFTA: its institutionalization and its asymmetry. NAFTA is highly institutionalized: it features a clear set of rules governing trade between Mexico, Canada, and the United States, and a dispute settlement mechanism for managing conflicts that might arise. It also has specific provisions to ensure the integrity of labor and environmental standards, a feature intended to limit the possible repercussions of lax Mexican enforcement in these areas. As such, if the EU were to enter negotiations with NAFTA as an entity, it would be dealing with a bloc that has a clear institutional identity and purpose – if not nearly the depth and scope of political-economic integration that exists among the countries of Europe.

However, NAFTA as established in 1995 is not analogous to the European Economic Community in 1958, nor even the European Coal and Steel Community in 1952. NAFTA is simply a free trade area, which, in the hierarchy of forms of regional institutions, is at the low end. While highly institutionalized, it is minimally "integrationist." Born of the convergence of pragmatic self-interest among its members – versus the unique context of postwar, "never again" Europe – NAFTA is unlikely to develop into an economic union or customs union in the absence of a major shift in the international political and economic climate. The main reason for this ceiling to NAFTA's growth seems clear: the overwhelmingly dominant position of the United States within NAFTA, and the fairly consistent skepticism of the U.S. Congress to U.S. participation in most types of international economic institutions.

Unlike Europe, where a fairly symmetrical distribution of power among the largest member states (and the traditional Franco–German axis) has fostered a political environment of multilateralism and consensus, the hegemony of the United States and deep, asymmetrical dependence of Canada and Mexico on the U.S. economy place the fate of NAFTA essentially in the relationship between the U.S. administration and the

Congress. While Congress in the summer of 2002 finally granted the president "trade promotion authority" (eight years after it had elapsed), its hostility to further international trade agreements after the completion of NAFTA and the Uruguay Round of the GATT slowed U.S. participation in trade negotiations at all levels. The NAFTA debate was particularly enervating: while the battle of ideas seemed clearly won by the Clinton administration in Vice-President Gore's 1993 debate with Texas billionaire Ross Perot (discerner of the "great sucking sound" of U.S. jobs going to Mexico), its vote gathering for Congressional passage was so painstaking that in his *Doonsbury* comic strip cartoonist Gary Larson portrayed Clinton as having to offer to wash Congresspersons' cars in the White House driveway to gain their votes. The wounds of that battle are still healing, and thus when Mexico's president-elect Vicente Fox declared in 2000 that NAFTA should become more like the European Union – perhaps with structural funds? – the polite silence he received from Washington was probably the best he could have hoped for. Hence Canada's lonely calls for closer EU–NAFTA relations, and Mexico's hopes for greater intra-NAFTA integration, will both go unheeded unless political conditions change dramatically in Washington.

Moreover, despite Congressional dyspepsia after digesting NAFTA and the WTO, NAFTA is probably a transitional set-up, intended more as a building block toward hemispheric free trade than an end in itself. This state of affairs seems clear from Washington's negotiating tactics, which have involved wooing countries such as Chile to become NAFTA members before the creation of a transregional FTAA, thus strengthening the NAFTA model over a more developmentalist version preferred by Brazil and some other Latin American countries. This transitional character of NAFTA means that it is unlikely to take on any greater integrationist elements among current and/or future members; negotiations among all the countries of the hemisphere toward anything but a straight free trade area – as opposed to, say, a customs union – would be far too difficult to manage within the proposed time frame (negotiations for an FTAA are supposed to be completed by 2005). In short, while the unresolved shape of NAFTA is in itself not a barrier to an interregional arrangement with the EU – after all, the EU itself is constantly evolving in both membership and structure – its transitional status as a gateway toward the greater project of a Free Trade Area of the Americas makes it likely that both North and South Americans as well as Europeans view it as a temporary arrangement. Only if negotiations for an FTAA were to break down, or if an FTAA were to fail to be ratified by the legislature of a key participant, would NAFTA be likely to take on a more permanent status and potentially make separate trans- or interregional agreements on its own.[16]

For these reasons, a related question that this book seeks to address – whether European Union interregional trade initiatives foster "counterpart coherence" within the bloc negotiating with the EU – would seem to be answered in the negative in the context of the EU–NAFTA relationship. As Alberta Sbragia has indicated, the EU and NAFTA are not "institutionally compatible entities" – the EU being an economic/monetary union, NAFTA a mere trade/investment union – and thus NAFTA does not have any executive with the external negotiating authority similar to the Commission.[17] While in some cases of interregional relations the EU literally created its counterpart region, NAFTA already exists and will likely evolve only to the extent that Washington allows; there would be no diffusion of institutional forms from the EU to NAFTA in the way that there might be among regions that aspire to EU-like structures. Even if interregional negotiations were to begin, a transatlantic free trade area would be a discussion between Brussels and Washington. As one British parliamentarian has remarked, "When politicians in Europe talk about 'transatlantic,' they really mean the United States of America. This is an extremely important point that Canadians and Mexicans need to appreciate."[18] While this situation of institutional incompatibility does not rule out progress in EU–NAFTA relations, it does imply that convergence between the two would remain limited.

But the absence of an EU–NAFTA track is not just – or even primarily – a result of NAFTA's limitations. The interests of the EU are central to this story. So the question remains: why has there been little impetus in the EU to develop an EU–NAFTA track, and what factors will shape the prospects of transatlantic interregionalism in the near future?

3   Explaining the non-regime

What follows is an assessment of four different potential sources of EU trade preferences *vis-à-vis* the countries of North America. Given the course of events to date, they represent different possible factors that explain the absence of – and whose change could potentially create an impetus for – an EU push for an interregional relationship with NAFTA.

Interest group pluralism

From the perspective of European interest groups (particularly specific industries and firms), the question regarding commercial relations with North America is clear: what do we want that we do not already have? And the question for analysts is: is what they want comprehensive enough to lead them to band together to advocate a project as big as a Transatlantic Free Trade Area – and to do so with enough vigor to overcome other political and economic obstacles to a TAFTA?

To address these questions it is essential to understand which interest groups want what and why. Some European actors – such as financial services, environmental technologies, and knowledge-based industries – are well-disposed toward free trade in general due to their relative competitiveness in international markets. Many of these same industries are particularly interested in maintaining free access to North American markets because their interests there are intrafirm. The acceleration in mergers and acquisitions (M&A) activity has created a set of multinational corporations such as DaimlerChrysler and the Virgin Group that form a truly transatlantic constituency and which would have much to lose if any sort of trade war were to break out. Many of these and other free trade-oriented firms have been active in the business-led fora of the TABD and the CERT, and were important players behind the Mutual Recognition Agreements the EU signed with the United States and Canada in 1998 to reduce testing and certification costs.[19] Indeed, the Commission is explicitly solicitous of business group advocacy: Lamy, addressing a meeting of the TABD, asked CEOs to "keep the pressure on us" for continued transatlantic liberalization.[20] If the United States continues to use "carousel" retaliation against European imports (i.e., rotating the affected products) in response to EU noncompliance with certain WTO rulings against its trade practices, a number of previously unmobilized industries might in fact increase the pressure on the EU to find new ways to address the conflicts in the transatlantic trade relationship.

Arrayed against this set of pro-free-trade groups are a number of politically influential sectors that are a great deal more skeptical about any moves toward trade liberalization with North America. Some of these sectors – such as textiles, steel, and, of course, agriculture – were mollified in the context of the EU–Mexico free trade agreement because it postponed any adjustments they would have to make until well into the future. The date for Europe's removal of trade barriers in the agricultural and fisheries areas (2010) comes well after the expected completion of the Millennium Round of WTO negotiations and the accession of new Central European members into the EU, both of which are likely to force the EU to open these sectors to greater international competition anyway. However, certain sectoral sticking points with the United States and Canada – with whom trade is generally free but for which no comprehensive formal agreement exists – would arouse more opposition within Europe. In particular, EU–Canadian sensitivities on fisheries remain raw, and attempts by the Commission to rein in the EU fleet have met stiff opposition, particularly from the Spanish.[21] Meanwhile, the United States and Canada remain opposed to EU moves to keep hormone-treated beef and other genetically modified organisms out of European markets, and it is hard to see EU farmers – and perhaps consumers as well – accepting compromise on this issue.[22] More generally, recent additions to traditional safeguards – including huge increases in farm supports in the United States and a Franco–German agreement to retain CAP supports even in the face of EU enlargement – seem to make any agreement that actually reduces supports a distant dream, at least within the EU–North American context.

Other "problem sectors" might not be quite as intractable. For instance, the EU shares a common position on textiles liberalization with the United States, Canada, and Mexico (along with Turkey, an EU aspirant), with all agreeing to work together to fight off the demands of India and other developing countries that they make concessions in WTO negotiations beyond those agreed in the Agreement on Textiles and Clothing, which is in force until 2005. Meanwhile, the row over the Bush administration's imposition in 2002 of temporary tariffs on steel imports (from which Canada and Mexico were notably exempted) died down as Washington waived restrictions on an ever-growing proportion of imports, suggesting that the safeguard action was a tactical maneuver to forestall opposition of the U.S. steel industry to the passage of trade promotion authority.[23] Still, a surge in U.S. protection in several industries sensitive in both North America and Europe is unlikely to put European producers in the mood to accept a rollback in their own protection.

Given the relative parity between European free-trade groups and their more skeptical counterparts, and the relative acceptability of the status quo to all involved, there has not been, and seems to be little prospect of, an interest group-led groundswell for a TAFTA. Yet the logic for such a free trade area does exist. Some have suggested that the Global Agreement was just a way for European firms to get better access to the U.S. market, making Mexico "a gateway rather than a destination," a "springboard into the United States."[24] However, if this were the case, why not push for a deal that cuts out the middleman? Would European firms not prefer a straight deal with the United States, or all of NAFTA, given the maze of rules of origin provisions that NAFTA set up to try to clog this gateway?

Reasons for pro-free trade business groups to push for a TAFTA exist, but either have not been envisioned as part of a broader free trade project, are not all that compelling, or have not effectively been promoted through the Commission or national governments. Thus a focus on interest group pressures is not only insufficient to explain the absence of an EU push for TAFTA (overall, it would benefit most sectors, and the sensitive ones could simply be left out of liberalization), but, given recent experience, we would simply expect sectoral groups to push for their own arrangements (e.g., MRAs) rather than build intersectoral alliances for broader free trade. Some sort of inherent "state" interests seem necessary to explain the shape of transatlantic trade relations.

EU institutional processes

To some extent, the EU's disinclination to pursue an interregional accord with North America might be better understood as a function of the continued dominance of the Council over the Commission in setting the broad direction of European trade policy.[25] While in the late 1990s the Commission appeared well-disposed toward some form of TAFTA, the voices of skeptical member states in the Council have stymied any forward movement on this front.

In the mid-1990s, the Delors Commission was riding the wave of big thinking that led to the creation of the single market, plans for a single currency, and, perhaps most ambitiously, the establishment of a common foreign and security policy (CFSP) – the last of which the Commission was eager to see fall under its own purview. Yet the only real authority the Commission maintained in external affairs was in trade negotiations (less so in actual trade policymaking). However, in an era when trade increasingly came to be seen as strategic, the Commission perhaps wanted to gain backdoor entrance into a CFSP through expanding its power of initiation in trade policy. Given the importance – and unsettled state – of transatlantic relations after the end of the cold war, the Commission broadened its horizons on liberalizing commercial relations across the Atlantic from mere technical agreements (though it never actually neglected these) to a more ambitious TAFTA. In 1998, EU trade commissioner Sir Leon Brittan pushed hard for a comprehensive transatlantic (specifically, EU–U.S.) trade agreement. However, the Council, animated by France's hostility to the idea, demurred. Though the Commission may remain interested in the TAFTA concept, it has since reverted to resting its position on technical, rather than strategic, grounds: it supports TAFTA "provided that a strong economic case can be made for a transatlantic accord."[26]

Despite the Commission's continued desire for task expansion in the foreign affairs milieu, and the advance of qualified majority voting (QMV) in the Council, intra-Council politics and norms provide a tight constraint on any Commission ambitions toward negotiating an interregional accord with NAFTA. The independent foreign policies of Britain, France, and, increasingly, Germany make the Council a powerful brake on any EU–wide foreign policy, which would require the support of each of the big member states as well as most if not all of the smaller states. Moreover, the spread of QMV is not likely to progress quickly in matters of international affairs, and the prevailing consensus norm in the Council further hinders strong policymaking even in areas where majority voting formally applies. Therefore, even as the Commission seeks greater latitude to pursue transatlantic deals, the Council seeks to tie its hands. So it was with the EU–U.S. Blair House agreement over agriculture at the climax of the Uruguay Round negotiations of GATT in 1992: though the Commission, then at the apex of its influence under Delors, managed to broker a deal, the disapproval of certain EU member states later allowed the Council to unravel the agreement.[27]

Further hampering any Commission capacity to pursue a TAFTA is its own internal institutional fragmentation in trade policy. Again, the agricultural sector provides an example. The locus of authority in EU agricultural trade is the Directorate-General of Agriculture (DG Agriculture) rather than DG Trade. As a result, European farmers – which are protected against external competition by the EU's Common Agricultural Policy, well-organized in their determination to maintain this protection, and well-connected to their regulators in DG Agriculture – are essentially able to dictate terms to the Commission on agricultural trade policy. As Cadot and Webber have shown, this fragmentation of authority within the Commission goes a long way to explain a recent, particularly corrosive transatlantic spat over trade in bananas. In this case, the strong position in DG Agriculture (and with certain member governments) of minority banana-trading interests made compromise both internally within the EU and externally with the United States extremely difficult.[28] Alternatively, in negotiations in which the EU is asymmetrically powerful and thus able to satisfy the demands of powerful domestic sectors – as with agriculture in the Global Agreement – this institutional fragmentation is less consequential. More generally, the combination of the Commission's institutional fragmentation and its reliance on close connections to the interests it regulates (a feature of national bureaucracies everywhere) would make the compromises necessary in bargaining – or even agenda-setting – with a peer counterpart such as the United States/NAFTA quite difficult. Unless negotiations on key sectors such as agriculture were either pushed well into the future or left off the agenda entirely, it is easy to see how tightly the Commission's hands are tied *vis-à-vis* a TAFTA.

This "institutionalist" view provides a plausible account of the obstacles facing the constituency of pro-TAFTA officials in the European Union, and thus the absence of a strong push toward a broad-based agreement with North America. Yet if trade with North America is indeed "strategic" for the EU and its constituent member states, we have yet to find a convincing source of the Union's strategic preferences (given the relatively narrow and technical agenda of firms and industry groups, and the internally-focused tug-of-war between the Commission and the Council). Explanations that consider Europe's place in the world may offer some clues here.

Balance of (economic) power and nesting considerations

Another approach to understanding EU trade policy toward North America focuses on how the Union derives its trade preferences from considerations of the economic "balance of power," particularly *vis-à-vis* the United States, and how the terms of this economic, and ultimately political, competition might benefit the EU relative to its American competitor.

Europeans have in recent years shown less willingness to stifle their dissatisfaction with Washington's tendency to pursue unilateral policies in various arenas of international politics. What's more, the two have been beating each other about the head and shoulders with the WTO stick on various trade-related issues. As noted above, such transatlantic rows are nothing new; yet they may have taken on a different quality since the collapse of the Soviet Union removed the common security threat that served to limit the fallout of these conflicts. Even more recent disagreements, whether over the American rejection of binding international law and agreements (e.g., the Kyoto protocol on global warming, the Anti-Ballistic Missile treaty, or the International Criminal Court) or preemptive pursuit of post-September 11 security objectives (e.g., war in Iraq), have reinforced perceptions that Europe and America increasingly stand apart on the vital matters of the day, and that, although overt security competition between the two remains unlikely, political-economic competition is ever less constrained by a clear, mutually-perceived set of shared interests.

In this view of U.S.–European relations, we would expect EU preferences in trade to derive from a desire to increase the Union's influence on the world stage *vis-à-vis* the United States. This expectation does not immediately preclude the pursuit of a trade agreement between the two sides of the Atlantic; most policymakers might be expected to understand that trade is not zero-sum, and that a trade war between the two would leave both worse off. Rather, the EU might be expected to pursue trade strategies that would engage the United States in an agreement – whether through the WTO or in a trans-/interregional deal – whose terms reflected the interests of Europe more than those of the United States, and thus provided relative gains to the former. However, it is difficult to see how the United States would agree to such an arrangement; hence we might expect the European Union to prefer a hub-and-spoke strategy toward other countries and regions that institutionalized relatively powerful EU's preferences while seeking to shut out the United States.

To some extent such a strategy seems to be evident in the European approach to the Americas. To date, the EU has strictly adhered to a bilateral approach toward each of the countries of North America, which maximizes the EU's bargaining power *vis-à-vis* each of them while excluding Washington's direct influence from any negotiations bar those between the EU and United States (except, of course, in WTO negotiations). The EU's interregional negotiations with MERCOSUR, for their part, seem to be not so much motivated by the desire to maximize bargaining power, but rather by the specter of a future FTAA. That is, deals with Latin America are not only part of a proactive strategy to maximize Europe's influence and market access, but rather a reaction to similar American initiatives in the region.[29] The EU's overt rationale for concluding a free trade agreement with Mexico in 1999 was to redress the "NAFTA effect," specifically the Europeans' worsened terms of trade with Mexico.[30] Its ongoing negotiations with MERCOSUR suggest a preemptive move against similar losses from the creation of an FTAA.

Similar positional considerations were also important in the EU's pursuit of interregional ties with an even more strategically important region, East Asia. Europeans reacted with some dismay to the coming-of-age of the

U.S.-led Asia–Pacific Economic Cooperation (APEC) forum in 1993–94, which threatened to privilege U.S. trade with this dynamic region at the expense of an emerging Eurasian relationship. The European response was to sponsor, in 1996, the creation of the Asia–Europe Meetings (ASEM), which promised to promote and institutionalize commercial ties along this relatively underdeveloped third leg of international economic relations. Notably, this relationship was conceived as one among equals – despite the relative institutional poverty among the countries of East Asia – and thus from a strategic angle served less as a part of an EU-centered hub-and-spoke strategy and more as a pragmatic response to the ascension of APEC. And, though it is hard to make precise statements about cause and effect here, it is notable that ASEM's forward momentum slowed nearly simultaneously to the deceleration of the APEC process.[31] The more general point is that, like the United States, the EU appears to be not only hedging its bets in the face of the possible breakdown of multilateral liberalization through the WTO, but also seeking to improve relative access to key developing country markets.

Perhaps paradoxically, a central assumption underpinning an analysis that focuses on the EU and United States pursuing their interests separately is the continued stability of the transatlantic relationship itself. But what if this assumption were false – what if the vitality of EU–U.S. political and economic relationship were fundamentally challenged by either internal dissention (e.g., the cumulative weight of successive trade-related disagreements, or the collapse of NATO), or if a credible external threat to western civilization were to arise? In any of these scenarios might we expect EU (and U.S.) policymakers to make a political statement by strongly reaffirming and strengthening the transatlantic link through formal commercial integration? The answer probably remains no, for the simple reason that doing so would be tantamount to the West turning its back on the rest of the world, a decision that European (and American) policymakers would have difficulty contemplating even under the most dire circumstances given its wide-ranging political implications. Politically, creating a TAFTA in reaction to global turmoil would suggest EU acquiescence in the creation of civilizational fault lines; economically, there would be the tangible costs to the European producers and consumers of de-globalizing the international economy. Even during the darkest days of the Cold War, when it actually seemed possible that the West might stand alone against a hostile world, no serious steps toward formal transatlantic economic integration were taken. Such steps seem even more distant in the post-9/11 world, despite the fact that the West as a whole is a major target of globally operating terrorist networks. While these scenarios are merely counterfactual speculations, they do suggest that there is little strategic reason for the creation of a transatlantic free trade area, whether under current conditions or in the foreseeable future.

Nesting considerations, for their part, do not seem to be a central factor in this case. For one thing, there are no EU–NAFTA rules in existence or in discussion that might need to be made consistent with WTO rules. Indeed, to the extent that the EU has pursued arrangements with these two countries – such as in the ITA or MRAs – it has done so outside the WTO domain because all these countries did not believe that sufficiently liberalizing agreements could be had within a WTO-centered approach. But while WTO-consistency remains a nonissue in EU relations with the United States and Canada, nesting did to some extent shape the provisions of the Global Agreement with Mexico (and, on the North American side, NAFTA). Still, while global rules are an essential feature of the EU economic relations with the countries of North America, nesting constraints have not been a primary factor in the absence of a formal regime between the two.

Transatlantic identities, convergent or divergent

We might also look to the realm of ideas and identities to generate explanations for European trade preferences toward North America. In particular, we might consider the fate of "the West" – and how policymakers view the fate of the West – as a useful guide to whether Europeans will look to increase or circumscribe their commercial relations with North America. Once again, this view leads us to focus on the relationship between Europe and the United States.

There has been a fair degree of disagreement among observers of transatlantic relations about the basis of the idea of the West. Some, such as Owen Harries, view the notion of the West as an expedient of the Cold War, created by American and European policymakers to strengthen popular resistance to encroaching communist powers.[32] For them, with the Cold War over, the West as an ideational construct will collapse, leading to the disintegration of NATO and increasing divergence in the interests and identities of Europeans and Americans. The divisions within the West regarding war with Iraq in 2003 – though, importantly, not specifically between the United States and a united Europe – seem to lend support to the pessimistic view. Others such as Miles Kahler think that the roots of an idea of Western civilization run deeper, given America's European ancestry and Europe's growing experience with American cultural exports even before the Second World War.[33] From a different point of view, Samuel Huntington's notion of a "clash of civilizations" also sees a strong future for the West in the face of other hostile civilizations, a thesis that, despite most analysts' derision at the time of publication, has received much more attention since September 11, 2001.[34]

Given the cultural content of trade and investment, we might expect EU preferences to reflect the relative willingness of Europeans to see a cultural convergence with the United States. On the one hand, European policymakers intent on maintaining strong cultural and political ties between Europe and the United States might promote new ways to tie the two sides of the Atlantic together. For example, Britain, which already shares strong cultural affinities with both Europe and the United States (and Canada), has been the champion of the idea of a TAFTA, which could strengthen the conviction among Europeans and Americans that they share a common cultural space.[35] Moreover, despite evidence that the 9/11 terrorist attacks have not significantly reasserted U.S. and European elites' fading sense of common cultural bonds, were Europe to suffer similar attacks, transatlantic solidarity might dig deeper roots with the full realization that the assaults were not just anti-American but fundamentally anti-Western. In this unhoped-for scenario, terrorism could serve as a catalyst for the convergence of transatlantic identities and interests through the emerging perception of a shared "other." In this context, closer economic relations as well as political and security ties becomes particularly plausible.

However, the more prominent trend within Europe at least since the inauguration of George W. Bush seemed to be to highlight cultural differences between Europe and the United States. Perhaps embodied in the forty-third U.S. president, Europeans have increasingly found common ground amongst themselves in denouncing various practices and institutions that they see as endemic to the American character, including the death penalty, missile defenses, violent crime, income inequality, "frankenfoods," and several others.[36] This growing anti-Americanism may also be connected to a greater skepticism about globalization, which many Europeans see as a primarily American-driven phenomenon that threatens their relatively generous welfare states – a social model that continues to defy the Americans' sink-or-swim approach to socioeconomic solidarity. More generally, it may be possible to characterize Europe as representing a "postmodern" society, increasingly postmaterialist and environmentalist in nature, while the United States represents a hypermodern society, materialist to its core.[37] Were these characterizations to hold sway, we might expect Europeans to prefer less than completely free trade with the United States, as it seeks to maintain its distinct cultural identity – embodied in its un-Disneyfied cultural output, un-McDonaldized diets, and uncompromised agricultural standards – by keeping the United States at arm's length. The EU's reluctance to accept free trade or investment in the entertainment industry lends support to such a view.

This question of transatlantic identities might also find its origins specifically within Europe and the dynamics of European unity. It might be possible to suggest that the more European leaders focus on deepening Europe, the less willing they will be to integrate with the United States. Successful deepening of European institutions requires the ongoing construction of a European identity, an identity that has proven quite difficult to imbue among EU citizens. Some have suggested that a convergence of European and American identities would of necessity undermine the goal of first creating the European identity.[38] As such, European leaders may find it expedient to do the opposite, to seek to unite Europe on the back of the transatlantic relationship by trumpeting European values as superior to their American counterparts.[39] Henry Kissinger, in a July 2001 interview on National Public Radio, accused European elites of doing exactly that. However, if the dynamics of European unity favor enlargement, with the inclusion of an ever more diverse group of "new" Europeans under the EU umbrella, we might expect a more propitious environment for Western cultural convergence (or at least less divergence). Indeed, the enlargement of the European Union to the east would bring within the EU countries such as Poland that have tended to demonstrate strongly pro-American views.

In addition to Europe's internal identity, we might also consider how transatlantic relations respond to the EU's ongoing development of an "international identity" – and how that international identity stands in contrast to that of the United States. [40] In an influential essay, Robert Kagan, an American political commentator, described the contrast between the two: the EU, a "weak" actor born of cooperative multilateralism, seeks a "self-contained world of laws and rules based on transnational negotiation and cooperation," while the United States believes that "international laws and rules are unreliable" and "true security and the promotion of a liberal order still depend on the possession and use of military might."[41] The Europeans' legalistic approach to international relations seems to have emerged from the EU's own internal evolution, and can be seen, for example, in Europeans' approach to the international criminal court (pooling sovereignty) and its preference for hard targets in the Kyoto protocol (analogous to the economic criteria of EMU). This approach finds a strong contrast in the longstanding American preference for flexibility and freedom of maneuver in international politics, a preference that is particularly strong in the current U.S. administration. While Kagan's argument is, by his own admission, a vast simplification, his ideas about European elites' views of international governance and their basis in Europe's unique postwar experience of integration do identify a clear and substantive point of difference with the United States, and thus suggest a further roadblock to their potential ability to see eye to eye on how to govern transatlantic commercial relations.

A realist analysis of international relations would lead us to expect an increasingly coherent EU to maintain the preferences of the strong – i.e., like the United States, for freedom of maneuver to pursue one's interests and security. However, closer attention to how the EU externalizes an approach to governance developed through the experience of multilateral interactions among its members (and perhaps networks of concertation among governments and interest groups within many member countries) may be a better guide to understanding how EU and U.S. perceptions of their interests and prescriptions for behavior in international politics may continue to diverge. And if divergence is the order of the day, then the absence of an interregional track between Europe and a U.S.-dominated North America would hardly be surprising.

4   Conclusion

The commercial relationships that the European Union has developed with the countries of North America are probably the most mutually beneficial transregional commercial ties in human history. While these links have developed separately, today they form a fairly coherent whole: EU trade with Canada, Mexico, and the United States is mostly free and unproblematic, much like trade among the NAFTA members themselves. So why don't the EU and NAFTA simply formalize this relationship in a Transatlantic Free Trade Area?

To some extent, we can explain the absence of transatlantic interregionalism from a functionalist standpoint: there is little need for a TAFTA. Specifically, there is no compelling economic rationale for a TAFTA, or for any overarching framework to codify transatlantic economic integration. Why fix what, despite some occasional sputterings, is not broken? There is also a compelling political rationale not to pursue a formal interregional relationship. Both the tangible and symbolic repercussions of any but the most "open regionalist" transatlantic free trade arrangement would be quite dire for the rest of the world, especially developing countries.

But functionalist approaches are not sufficient to help us understand the source of European trade preferences and how they are translated into interregional outcomes. The problem is that it is difficult to identify which of the four hypotheses is most convincing in its explanation for the absence of a viable EU–NAFTA track; in none of the four do the relevant factors suggest that the EU should clearly be pursuing transatlantic interregionalism. However, some do seem better than others.

Least illuminating is the interest group hypothesis. This hypothesis assumes that if a certain outcome is consistent with the preferences of a decisive set of interest groups, they will mobilize (i.e., lobby) to gain that outcome. Though the relevant incentive exists, effective mobilization has been absent, and an interest group explanation cannot effectively explain outcomes unless its assumption of mobilization holds. The main reason why pro-free trade groups have not mobilized for a TAFTA lies in the moderate size of the potential gain: the status quo is more or less acceptable for most of them, while a TAFTA might not bring a large return on their investment in mobilization. However, particularly in its relations with the United States and Canada, European officials have in the TABD and CERT sought to privilege and amplify the voices of pro-liberalization groups (i.e., to reduce their costs of mobilization), and yet these groups, despite the fact a TAFTA would clearly be in their interest, have not generated political momentum for it. But their failure to do so cannot be found in the dissent of anti-liberalization groups, which are much more concerned about the possible adjustments necessary in agreements with less developed countries. Ultimately, TAFTA would be more of a *political* project than a commercial one. In already accessible markets such as those of North America, European business groups' relatively narrow focus may allow them to advocate successfully for technical, sector-specific agreements such as the MRAs, but they do not have a sufficiently broad worldview to be the key drivers behind a political project like TAFTA. Thus even if European firms and industries mobilized more strongly for a TAFTA, it is doubtful that their advocacy alone would suffice to bring the EU to pursue it.

The European Commission, for its part, has never been known to shy away from a political project. Its interest in a TAFTA, and the Council of Ministers' disinclination to allow the Commission to pursue that interest, can indeed help us understand to some extent why the Union as a whole has not gone down the interregional path with NAFTA. Simply put, when push comes to shove the Council still gets what it wants. Given the incrementalism that generally characterizes changes in the balance of institutional power in the EU, even in the face of new members and a new constitution, this approach also provides a clear prediction that the absence of an EU–NAFTA track is likely to continue well into the future. However, in its neglect of factors external to Europe – notably the characteristics of the counterpart region – this hypothesis can only give us a partial account of the dynamics of this relationship.

Greater attention to the international power dynamics involves starts to bring into focus a big part of what is truly unique about transatlantic relations. Europe's commercial relationship with NAFTA cannot be understood outside the context of EU–U.S. relations more generally. As the two great centers of economic power in a world in which globalized market forces are increasingly redefining the rules of engagement among nations, the need to secure export markets for the vitality of European producers and for the sake of domestic prosperity has become a primary strategic goal of the EU. The United States, whether in its creation of NAFTA, APEC, or an FTAA, presents a challenge to this European goal. In this context, access to potentially lucrative markets is relative, and, as its rationale for pursuing an FTA with Mexico (among others) suggests, the EU is very much concerned with its position relative to the United States. If we were to consider this approach together with a focus on EU institutions, we might find a persuasive interpretation in the idea that the Council's aloofness from the idea of a TAFTA may derive in large part from its representation of national opinions that in some cases see the EU's main purpose to be as a counterweight to American power. Trade is a primary means by which economic power, influence, and prosperity are redistributed across nations, and by which "national" champions are created. Moreover, given the EU's glaring inability to realize a common foreign and security policy – and the increasing gap between EU and U.S. military capabilities – external commercial policy is the realistic locus of Europe's pursuit of relative material gain. Through this lens, a particularly clear picture of the limited prospects of TAFTA can be discerned.

As for the constructivist hypothesis, it is difficult to draw direct lines from questions of ideas, identities, and culture to those of trade relationships. Yet given the cultural content of trade, and the current fascination among some European and American analysts with the seeming divergence between the commonly-held values in their (two?) civilizations, this hypothesis is particularly hard to ignore in this case. Surely a shared sense of identity is not a sufficient condition for the creation of an interregional commercial relationship, nor is its absence sufficient to destroy interregionalism's prospects. Yet the presence of an EU struggling to define both its internal identity and its external identity, and the omnipresence of an American superpower that insists on going its own way in international affairs, clearly provide a powerful incentive for the EU to define itself in contrast to the bullying hegemon – and a powerful disincentive to tie itself more closely to it. While such a proposition is difficult to substantiate, and may be highly contingent on the parties and personalities in power in Washington and European capitals at any given time, it cannot be ignored in the current transatlantic political climate.

Stepping back from these hypotheses, a key question for whether the EU will press for an interregional relationship with NAFTA as opposed to separate bilateral tracks with the United States, Mexico, and Canada depends on whether the EU sees a major overlap in what it wants *vis-à-vis* each of the three NAFTA countries and a prospective FTAA. Certainly the EU's interest in Mexico – gaining access to protected sectors and redressing the eroded terms of trade for the EU resulting from NAFTA – is closer to the EU's interest in the rest of Latin America (and indeed the rest of the developing world) than it is to the need to maintain access and reduce technical barriers to trade with the United States and Canada. Because the EU has already established itself in Latin America through deals with Mexico and MERCOSUR, the only apparent reasons to deal with NAFTA as a regional entity would be if (1) the EU could get a better deal from the United States if Mexico and Canada were involved, or (2) if the FTAA process were to falter and intra-NAFTA integration were to move forward (perhaps in the absence of progress in multilateral talks). The first scenario is unlikely because Washington would almost certainly seek to avoid having its bargaining freedom circumscribed by the involvement of Canada and Mexico. The second scenario is perhaps more plausible, though one imagines that the United States would do whatever necessary to avoid the simultaneous collapse of both WTO and FTAA negotiations, and would sooner accelerate its pursuit of bilateral trade deals than retreat 'inward' into NAFTA.

Ultimately, any inquiry of EU–U.S. trade relations must recognize that transatlantic trade relations are already so deep, and the web of U.S.–European commercial, social, cultural, and political relationships so dense, that if there were any inherent need for an overarching framework for transregional trade and economic relations, one would already exist. Therefore, these existing conditions suggest that the impetus for a change in the status of these relations would have to be powerful, sustained, and unambiguous. Of all the EU's relationships with other regions, that with North America is probably the one in which the region-to-region status quo is such that there is little to be gained from establishing a formal inter-regional arrangement. The EU as a whole does quite well out of the current state of affairs – mostly unproblematic access to the U.S. and Canadian markets, and a free trade area with Mexico – and the rest of the world is not excluded from any preferential arrangement among the world's largest and most prosperous markets.

Given the economically rational basis of the status quo, a TAFTA could really be possible only if a transformative event realigned preferences in such a way as to create a new political rationale for an interregional agreement. Absent such an event, there seems little impetus for the creation of a TAFTA – whether from interest groups, EU institutions, power politics, or cultural/identity considerations. Some of these factors are better than others for explaining the past and predicting the future of any formal insti-tutionalization of the EU–NAFTA commercial relationship. And given that 9/11 was not sufficiently transformative to create this new political ration-ale for a TAFTA, it is probably best for European and North American officials to hope that no truly transformative event does occur. Ultimately, the absence of formal interregionalism is not an indicator of the ill-health of transatlantic relations – but its future presence would likely be a reflection of a more parlous state for world politics and/or the international economy as a whole.

Notes

1. I would like to thank Justin Kolbeck, Matthew Odette, Daniel Xu, and Devon Rackle for their energetic and insightful research assistance.
2. Kahler 1996.
3. European Commission 2003.
4. European Commission 2003.
5. Blinken 2001.
6. Lamy 2000.
7. Blackwill and Archick 1998.
8. European Commission 2000.
9. European Commission 2000.
10. Gower 2000.

11. Gower 2000.
12. "Canada seeks deal with EU," *The Gazette*, 17 April 2001.
13. Council of Europe 2000.
14. In some circles in the United Kingdom, however, the welcome idea of closer ties with a North American community has converged with anti-EU sentiments to generate a different angle on Canadian ideas of closer partnership. A warm reception has been given to a few powerful North American voices (notably Conrad Black, the Canadian-born owner of the London *Daily Telegraph*, and former U.S. senator Phil Gramm) calling for the United Kingdom to leave the European Union and join NAFTA. While this heterodox view has never made it into the mainstream of political discourse in the United Kingdom, Lamy felt it necessary in a mid-2000 speech to acknowledge and then to criticize this viewpoint.
15. DTI 2001.
16. One open question here is, of course, whether NAFTA would itself "disappear" as a separate entity within an FTAA, or whether it would continue to exist as a nested arrangement under the FTAA. This question will likely remain open until FTAA negotiations progress further.
17. Sbragia 2001.
18. Council of Europe 2000, pp. 17–18.
19. Council of Europe 2000, p. 6.
20. Lamy 1999a.
21. "Thrashing around," *The Economist*, 1 June 2002.
22. The *New York Times* identified U.S.–EU disagreements on this issue as based in fundamental philosophical differences regarding the "precautionary principle" – i.e., whether GMOs must be scientifically proven "innocent" before they may be imported or proven "guilty" before their import could be banned. The United States takes the latter position, the EU the former. *The New York Times*, 25 May 2003.
23. "Dangerous activities," *The Economist*, 11 May 2002. As of November 2003, however, this conflict returned after the WTO upheld a ruling in favor of the EU, and the EU threatened retaliation against politically sensitive American products.
24. Gower 2000, pp. 3–4.
25. According to Meunier 2000, "trade policy remains one of the last bastions of sole Council legislative power."
26. Council of Europe 2000, p. 3.
27. Meunier 2000, pp. 82–83.
28. Cadot and Webber 2002.
29. See Faust's chapter in this volume for more on the EU–MERCOSUR relationship.
30. In a document reporting the conclusion of negotiations with Mexico, the Commission repeatedly couches the benefits of the agreement in terms of its value as a response to NAFTA. See European Commission 2000.
31. Of course, other arguments can be made to explain the lack of recent progress in APEC and ASEM, notably the disruption of the 1998 Asian economic crisis and the restarting of multilateral trade negotiations after 1999. See Gilson's chapter in this volume for a comprehensive discussion of ASEM. Regarding APEC, see Aggarwal and Morrison 1998.
32. Harries 1993.
33. Kahler 1996.
34. Huntington 1996.

35. This viewpoint runs in the tradition of Deutsch's (1957) "transactionalism," in which repeated interactions among peoples generate a greater sense of shared identity.
36. Kagan (2002), for one, has claimed that a U.S.–European divergence is *not* a function of the temporary effects of ideological differences among ruling parties or specific leaders.
37. On postmaterialism, see Inglehart 1988.
38. Waever 1998.
39. Pascal Lamy remarked that the best way to get a rousing ovation in the European Parliament these days is to denounce the United States. The *Economist*, 7 July 2001.
40. Manners (2002, pp. 240–1) has located the source of "normative power Europe's" international identity in three factors: (1) the historical context of the postwar need to overcome nationalism; (2) the "hybrid polity" of supranational and intergovernmental institutions that "transcends Westphalian norms"; and (3) Europe's "political-legal constitution," which enshrines the norms of democracy, human rights, and social justice.
41. Kagan 2002.

References

Aggarwal, Vinod K. and Charles E. Morrison, eds. (1998). *Asia–Pacific Crossroads: Regime Creation and the Future of APEC*. New York: St. Martin's Press.

Blackwill, Robert D. and Kristin Archick (1998). "U.S.–European economic relations and world trade." Paper presented at a meeting of the Independent Task Force on the Future of Transatlantic Relations, sponsored by the Council on Foreign Relations, Washington, DC (April 15).

Blinken, Anthony (2001). "The false crisis in transatlantic relations." *Foreign Affairs* May/June, pp. 35–48.

Burghardt, Guenter (2001). "Prospects for EU–U.S. trade relations." Speech to Sanford Institute of Public Policy, Duke University. Durham, NC (15 February).

Cadot, Olivier and Douglas Webber (2002). "Banana splits: policy process, particularistic interests, political capture, and money in transatlantic trade politics." *Business and Politics* 4, 1: 5–40.

Council of Europe (2000). "Prospects for a new transatlantic trade relationship." Report of the Committee on Economic Affairs and Development to the Parliamentary Assembly (6 June).

Department of Trade and Industry, United Kingdom (DTI) (2001). "World trade and international trade rules: North America." www.dti.gov.uk/worldtrade/namerica.htm.

Deutsch, K. et al. (1957). *Political Community and the North Atlantic Area*. Princeton, NJ: Princeton University Press.

European Commission (2003). "EU–US bilateral economic relations." www.europa.eu.int/comm/external_relations/us/sum06_03/eco.pdf.

European Commission (DG Trade) (2003). Communication from the Commission to the Council and the European Parliament accompanying the final text of the draft decisions by the EC–Mexico Joint Council. Brussels (18 January).

Gower, Matthew (2000). "Titans of trade: signing free-trade deals with heavyweights like North America and the European Union has placed Mexico on the world stage." American Chamber of Commerce of Mexico (1 October).

Harries, Owen (1993). "The collapse of 'the West.'" *Foreign Affairs* (September/October): 41–53.

Huntington, Samuel (1996). *The Clash of Civilizations and the Remaking of World Order*. New York: Simon and Schuster.

Inglehart, Ronald (1988). "The Renaissance of political culture." *American Political Science Review* 82, 4: 1120–1130.

Kagan, Robert (2002). "Power and weakness." *Policy Review* 113.

Kahler, Miles (1996). "Revision and prevision: historical interpretation and the future of the transatlantic relationship." In *Europe and America: A Return to History*, by Miles Kahler and Werner Link. New York: Council on Foreign Relations.

Lamy, Pascal (2000). Speech to Confederation of British Industry. London (6 July).

Lamy, Pascal (1999b). "U.S.–EU relations – bilateral and multilateral issues." Speech to European–American Business Council. Washington, DC (14 October).

Lamy, Pascal (1999a). Speech to Transatlantic Business Dialogue. Brussels (23 May).

Manners, Ian (2002). "Normative power Europe: a contradiction in terms?" *Journal of Common Market Studies* 40, 2: 235–258.

Meunier, Sophie (2000). "What single voice? European institutions and EU–U.S. trade negotiations." *International Organization* 54, 1: 103–35.

Sbragia, Alberta (2001). "European Union and NAFTA." In *European Union and New Regionalism: Regional Actors and Global Governance in a Post-Hegemonic Era*, edited by Mario Telò. Aldershot: Ashgate.

Wæver, Ole (1998). "Integration as security: constructing a Europe at peace." In *Atlantic Security*, edited by Charles A. Kupchan. New York: Council on Foreign Relations.

8
Explaining Trends in EU Interregionalism

Vinod K. Aggarwal and Edward A. Fogarty

1 Introduction

It is standard fare in political science or political economy to characterize the nature of political and economic systems in the aftermath of some critical juncture – such as the "postwar era," the "post-Cold War era," "post-September 11," and the like. Analyses that highlight these critical junctures all face the same questions: do we know yet whether this juncture was in fact critical? Even if it was, has enough time passed for us to undertake a valid assessment of the shape of the world in its aftermath? Skeptics of hasty assessments may recall Zhou En-Lai's famous response to Henry Kissinger's question about the meaning of the French Revolution nearly two hundred years on – "It is too soon to tell."

In pursuing an analysis of a new form of trade and commercial relationships that takes as its starting point the continued debility of the multilateral institutions and processes of trade cooperation, we are surely tempting the fate of those who attempt to slice a loaf of bread that is only half-baked. And surely the GATT/WTO regime has proved durable, surviving many past threats to its primacy in international commercial cooperation, whether from protectionism or regionalism. Yet although we take the failure of WTO talks in Seattle in 1999 (and subsequent lack of progress in the Doha Round) as our critical juncture, we are not assuming that interregionalism, or regionalism, or bilateralism, or any other type of –ism, will replace multilateralism. Rather, we ask whether, in a world in which the WTO still operates but perhaps ceases to evolve in a meaningful way, interregionalism will emerge as a viable alternative form of institutionalized economic integration. We hope that, by this point, the reader will agree with us that at least an initial assessment of post-Seattle interregionalism has been justified, and that there is much to be learned from the experience of EU-centered interregionalism to date.

At the outset of this volume, we introduced a number of variables and hypotheses that we considered to be the most likely potential explanations for the rise of interregionalism in European Union trade policy. But essential precursors to these possible explanations are the initial necessary conditions. Specifically, the pursuit of interregionalism implies at least three conditions: (1) continuing integration of the world economy; (2) continuing uncertainty surrounding the multilateral WTO process; and (3) continuing support among at least some constituencies for the institutionalization of stable, rule-bound international commercial relationships. While, as noted above, we take the first two of these conditions as given, it is the third that we have sought to illuminate in this book. We have framed the conceptual evolution of interregionalism as a possible synthesis of market-driven globalism and politically-driven regionalism. Our focus has been on exploring the dynamics of the interplay of market and political actors to understand whether interregionalism represents an equilibrium policy outcome that might supplement or even supplant multilateralism in organizing and governing the international political economy.

We have concentrated on European-connected arrangements for a number of interrelated reasons. First and foremost, the European focus is practical: there are several cases of EU-centered interregionalism, which allows us to compare a number of contending hypotheses regarding EU motivations and interregional outcomes across enough cases to allow an initial assessment of the most important sets of variables driving interregional outcomes. Second, at an empirical level, an EU focus also puts at the center of the analysis the "necessary" cases of interregionalism. Because Europe is by far the most active and successful region in pursuing both internal and external innovations in institution-building and governance, we would face a great deal of skepticism about both the conceptual and real-world viability of interregionalism if we were to fail to find a stable basis of support for interregionalism in EU trade policy and outcomes. Third, this point partially motivates our analysis of both EU trade preferences and EU-counterpart regime outcomes: we wish to understand whether there is an achievable equilibrium among trade policy inputs and regime outputs that would support interregionalism. It is also one reason why we have given considerable attention to the notion of counterpart coherence: if interregionalism is to be more than a particular option for EU commercial policy, there must at least be the possibility that other regional blocs will pursue similar arrangements among themselves.

Before comparing our initial expectations with case findings to see whether there is a clear and consistent basis for an interregional trade policy, we first review the basis of comparison and the actual findings of the various cases.

Each of the authors in this book focuses on the EU and a counterpart region to determine which factors have had the greatest effect on interregional processes and outcomes over time for that particular case. They highlight three regime qualities in particular: its strength, its nature, and its delineation of Europe's commercial treatment of the counterpart region. (See section 3 for an elaboration of each of these three regime elements.)

The factors that the authors consider as possible explanations for their observed interregional regime outcomes fall into two broad categories: EU motivations and counterpart characteristics. Of the two, EU motivations are more directly comparable across cases, as the same sets of public and private sector actors as well as general systemic and ideational inclinations exist – but are likely to vary in their influence – across cases.

Briefly, the authors consider four general approaches to explain European motivations regarding international commercial policy in general and interregionalism in particular. First is a pluralist interest group hypothesis: EU policy is a function of the mobilization of and competition among relevant interest groups through lobbying at the national and supranational levels. In this view, those interests best able to impose their pure individual preferences – or the compromise preferences of an aggregated grouping on EU trade policy, whether through superior resources, strategies, political connections, and the like – will see these preferences reflected in EU trade policy toward other regions. Second, a bureaucratic politics hypothesis suggests that a struggle among the EU's supranational and intergovernmental institutions will determine EU international commercial policy. Each institution has a primary interest in task expansion or retention, and so will work within the EU's existing distribution of institutional powers to push commercial policies that favor its own bureaucratic interest. Our third approach is actually two separate potential explanations focusing on international systemic factors. The first derives from a standard realist approach to international relations: the EU as a unit responds to the structure of the international system in formulating its international economic policies, pushing those policies that promote the EU's collective economic security as well as its global structural power (via the use of relational power) in ties with individual countries and regions. The second derives from the neoliberal institutionalist tradition, focusing on states' interest in nesting subglobal commercial agreements within the overarching global WTO framework. The fourth approach highlights social constructivist concepts of ideas and identity. From this vantage point, EU external commercial policies are determined by the overarching need to construct "Europe" by defining its internal and external identity through relations with non-Europeans.

Counterpart characteristics, while amenable to placement in very general categories, are somewhat less directly comparable, given the political, economic, and socio-cultural diversity both across and within counterpart regions. These broad categories of counterpart characteristics include the other region's preferences, power, and coherence. Counterpart preferences can to some extent be analysed through applying the hypotheses of European motivations to the other region. Given the generally low level of institutional- ized cooperation within counterpart regions, however, it is something of a stretch to apply approaches that assume a well-defined set of aggregated regional preferences. Thus the authors focus on the preferences of individual countries and actors within the region – particularly those expected to have the greatest influence on region-wide views. Notions of counterpart power are similarly fraught with complication when aggregated to a regional level. Therefore, the authors similarly disaggregate these regions to focus on the power of individual countries in the counterpart, with an eye to how this power improves the bargaining position of the country and region as a whole – and how it affects the EU's motivations.

Finally, the authors consider the initial coherence of the counterpart region in terms of the extent to which the region is self-defined, the scope of intraregional commerce, the extent to which existing political-economic manifestations of the region reflect current understandings of the "poten- tial" region, and the degree of institutionalization of any existing regional regime. While we consider these counterpart characteristics as inputs into interregional regime outcomes – for they surely cannot be ignored – we are particularly interested in noting whether and how the experience of nego- tiating and establishing interregional commercial agreements with the EU encourages counterpart regions to coalesce both economically and polit- ically, and perhaps to adopt organizational forms of regional governance similar to those of the EU over time.

In the introduction, we outlined some initial expectations regarding the relationships among our outcomes of interest (regime strength, nature, and EU commercial treatment of the counterpart) and sets of variables high- lighted in each of the hypotheses regarding EU motivations. To recapitu- late, these expectations were as follows:

- *Interest group hypothesis*. We expected the variables relevant to this hypothesis to be very important for the strength of the regime, least important for the nature, and important for commercial treatment type.
- *Bureaucratic politics hypothesis*. We expected these variables to be some- what important for the strength of the regime, important for the nature, and least important for the commercial treatment type.
- *Systemic hypotheses: balancing and nesting*. We expected power and secur- ity considerations to be most important for strength of the regime, somewhat important for the nature, and most important for commercial treatment type. We expected nesting considerations to be important for the strength of the regime, very important for the nature of the regime, and very important for commercial treatment.
- *Constructivist hypothesis*. We expected this to be least important for the strength of the regime, most important for the nature, and somewhat important for the commercial treatment type.

The questions now remain: what happened in the individual cases of EU interregionalism, and what does comparison of these cases tell us about our initial expectations?

2 Cases

Before comparing and interpreting these cases as a whole, we first recapitulate each author's main findings and summarize them in terms of our variables of interest. The cases are presented in order of their interregional "purity."

EU–Southern Cone

The EU–MERCOSUR relationship is, as Jörg Faust asserts, the closest approximation of "pure interregionalism" among our cases. It is the only instance in which two relatively coherent, self-defined, and highly-institutionalized regional blocs have been negotiating a commercial agreement on a one-to-one basis. EU–MERCOSUR interregionalism is still a process rather than a full-fledged regime, but the existence of a proto-regime in EMIFCA, the institution under whose aegis negotiations continue, provides a basis on which to analyse this case.

While a final EU–MERCOSUR agreement has yet to emerge, the general outlines of the regime are beginning to come into focus. The two sides are moving toward a strong regime, both in terms of institutionalization and rule bindingness. Though EMIFCA currently lacks a secretariat, it has spawned a number of relevant committees, subcommittees, and working groups empowered to work out both political and technical details of an agreement. The rules expected to emerge from this process will be binding, with a dispute-settlement mechanism to mediate conflicts over application of these rules.

The nature of the EU–MERCOSUR regime will be broad and developmental. While the initial stages of interregional cooperation in the early 1990s encompassed mostly political rather than commercial matters, the two sides have since negotiated on a wide range of issues, including trade (across nearly all sectors, as required by WTO rules), investment, aid, and property rights. There is a developmental focus to these negotiations, but beyond a modest amount of aid, the main thrust of the EU's "developmental" initiatives have been institutional: the EU has made a concerted effort to help MERCOSUR to strengthen its own intraregional governance capacity, hoping to help these South American nations to help themselves.

The EU's trade treatment of MERCOSUR within the EMIFCA framework has reflected the pure interregional aspect of the process. Specifically, the EU has refused to deal individually with Brazil, Argentina, Uruguay, and Paraguay, explicitly stating that it will only deal with them as a group – a stance that has given a considerable fillip to MERCOSUR nations' efforts to improve their collective coherence for the sake of negotiations. Corresponding to this one-to-one approach, the EU has proposed highly uniform terms for all MERCOSUR nations within the boundaries of the proposed agreement.

Faust argues that the overall quality of the EMIFCA process – if not the specific strength, nature, or trade treatment of the emerging regime therein – can best be explained by a variety of factors. He finds the primary causes of the relatively slow pace of development of the EU–MERCOSUR regime in the dynamics among European interest groups and institutions. The familiar split among globally competitive business groups (particularly in service sectors), which are keen on gaining access to MERCOSUR – and especially Brazilian – markets, and relatively uncompetitive or protected sectors such as textiles and (mainly) agriculture, which are loath to face direct competition from their South American counterparts, has yielded something of a stalemate among these interest groups. While the EU and MERCOSUR did establish a business forum in an attempt to encourage participation of free-trade oriented groups, this forum has had only a modest impact on the course of negotiations. There has been a similar, familiar split between the relatively gung-ho, liberalizing Commission and a more skeptical Council (where protectionist interests have somewhat more sway through national governments), with the Council dragging its feet in providing the Commission with the necessary approval to begin negotiations (in 1999, almost four years after EMIFCA was established) and continuing to keep the Commission on a short leash thereafter.

While both the interest group and institutional stalemates help to explain the slow progress toward an interregional agreement, Faust finds the international environment to be the primary reason why there has been any progress at all. Within the EU–MERCOSUR context, Faust finds the EU's global systemic interests and its more political-institutional goals to be in line. The EU's general interest in a deal with the countries of South America can largely be understood in terms of the EU's need generally to balance against U.S. global economic influence and specifically to keep itself from being shut out of the high-potential Latin American economies by U.S. regional overtures – first with NAFTA and now perhaps with a Free Trade Area of the Americas (FTAA). Moreover, with respect to nesting considerations, the strength of the regime, particularly provisions on dispute settlement, is driven by the EU's interest in tying the creation of an interregional regime to the successful completion of the Doha Round of the WTO (where similar rules would presumably then be in force on a multilateral basis).

Existing WTO rules, for their part, have shaped the proposed FTA's product coverage by pushing both sides to agree to a particular array that reaches the required 90 percent level of coverage.

Although EU concerns about both its position in the international political economy and the competitive position of European firms may account for the existence of European initiatives toward South America, they do not necessarily explain the nature of these initiatives. And with respect to commercial treatment, as noted above, the EU has made explicit its desire to foster the consolidation of the MERCOSUR bloc, pursuing an Inter-Institutional Agreement with MERCOSUR to coordinate bloc-to-bloc relations before any discussions of commercial agreements or liberalization began. Whether this European approach has been specifically to promote its own form of political-economic regional organization as a model to be copied first by MERCOSUR and perhaps later by others is not yet clear, but it is at least suggestive that this encouragement of a counterpart's regional organization may indeed be among Europe's primary motivations in any interregional context.

EU–East Asia

As Julie Gilson suggests in her chapter, the EU relationship with the countries of East Asia within the Asia–Europe Meeting (ASEM) is an example of hybrid interregionalism that has shown occasional signs of becoming "purer." As Gilson attests, Asia–Europe ties represent a strategically important part of the international political economy as the third, relatively atrophied leg of the "wobbly triangle" (compared to the more robust U.S.–EU and U.S.–East Asia legs). While the EU and the ASEAN Plus Three (APT) group have outlined a fairly comprehensive set of issues on which to pursue cooperation, this seems to be the only truly ambitious element of this regime. While there are a number of working groups and committees associated with ASEM over the range of its relevant issue areas, these groups are staffed at a relatively low level and, more generally, ASEM lacks a permanent secretariat and the policy guidelines associated with ASEM are nonbinding – in Gilson's words, they have not comprised significant "deliverables" for the EU (or the APT). Thus ASEM is quite weak, both in terms of its institutionalization and its rule bindingness.

The regime nature is relatively comprehensive-developmentalist. As noted above, ASEM has a broad issue scope; and, while explicitly a relationship among equals, ASEM emphasizes aiding Asian development, especially the facilitation of European investment in East Asian countries. However, this developmental emphasis is not even across or even within countries: the Europeans emphasize aid and investment in different proportions in different countries, and are more skeptical regarding trade preferences with some poor countries (notably China) than others.

ASEM is similarly mixed in terms of the EU's commercial treatment of its East Asian counterpart: there are elements of both pure interregionalism (EU–ASEAN) and bilateralism (EU and non-ASEAN countries), and the EU's uniformity of treatment of East Asian countries varies across issue areas.

Gilson attributes the modest evolution of EU–East Asian interregionalism to the diversity of factors shaping its direction. She finds interest-group activity to be a compelling explanation for the initiation and early progress of ASEM, with the input of business groups essential to the establishment of institutionalized mechanisms such as the AEPF to promote trade and investment ties. Alternatively, these groups' (and particularly European businesses') disappointment with the lack of progress on these fronts and subsequent disengagement from the ASEM process has been central to ASEM's deceleration.

Interestingly, she finds that there was a lack of bureaucratic contention regarding ASEM, largely because member governments did not seem to take the process sufficiently seriously to warrant any real challenge to the Commission's central facilitating role in the Council. This suggests not only that Commission interest in task-expansion in general did not lead to a strong push toward a strong regime with East Asia more specifically, but that an absence of bureaucratic contention simply reflected the lack of salience of the issue of interregionalism with East Asia within the EU more generally.

Gilson suggests further that international systemic concerns surely served as an underlying rationale for ASEM, both for the Europeans – who sought to counter the U.S.-led APEC – and more generally to solidify the third side of the EU–U.S.–East Asian triangle. However, while it is likely that EU concerns about specific emerging East Asian powers such as China led it to seek to treat China differently from other developing East Asian nations in terms of trade, the generally dominant position of the EU in this process – more a function of its political coherence than its total economic capacity – was not sufficient to establish a strong regime on European terms. Nesting concerns seem to be muted, as ASEM was initiated with post-1995 WTO consistency in mind – and because little progress has been made on trade provisions that might actually raise the specter of consistency with global rules.

Finally, ASEM can to some extent be understood, particularly in terms of its nature, as being shaped by the European Union to replicate its own organizational form, adopting a broad political, economic, and social agenda similar to that of the EU within a Eurasian context. However, it is not clear that this encouragement of regionalist mimicry was a primary motivation of European policymakers (whether for integrationist goals with East Asia or within Europe itself), despite the fact that, as Gilson suggests, the promotion of ASEM and "ASEM Asia" is a helpful element in the development of the European identity. It is thus unclear whether the weakness of ASEM is related to a lack of commitment on the part of high-ranking European officials to associate the development of ASEM with that of Europe itself.

EU–Southern Mediterranean

The EuroMed Partnership (EMP), originally set up by the European Union to encourage political, economic, and social stability of the southern littoral states of the Mediterranean, has, according to Beverly Crawford, fallen far short of the hopes of both sides at its creation in 1995. The EMP is perhaps the weakest of the interregional regimes among these cases: not only are EMP guidelines completely nonbinding, but it also lacks the formal bodies such as a secretariat, parliamentary assembly, and dispute settlement mechanisms that give some other such regimes some institutional personality. Indeed, the Commission acts as the only coordinating institution, as the highly fractious grouping of Mediterranean non-EU member countries (MNMCs) lacks any sort of counterpart coordination institution.

With respect to its nature, rather more like other comparable EU arrangements, the EMP has both a comprehensive issue scope and a strongly developmental tilt. While the EU has committed to creating a free trade area around the Mediterranean by 2010, its goals in this and other included issues are primarily political: Europeans hope greater economic freedom can generate pressure for greater political freedoms in Middle Eastern and North African countries, while balancing a clear pro-democratic agenda with a push for mutual respect both between Europe and these mostly Muslim countries and among the southern littoral countries themselves. The EU has also offered significant amounts of aid to these countries on a bilateral basis, in part to help them prepare and adjust to the promised free trade area.

The EU's commercial treatment of the MNMCs has been mostly non-uniform in terms of treatment and bilateral in terms of trade types. The uniformity of treatment that exists has been initiated not by the EU but by those countries (including soon-to-be members and hopefuls such as Malta, Cyprus, and Turkey) that have followed the Copenhagen criteria for EU aspirants; for the rest, the terms of trade have been a function not only of EU evaluation of their reforms but also the most relevant issues at stake with any particular country (e.g., migration, trade profile in goods or services, etc.).

Crawford finds that different likely explanations exist for different elements of the EMP. She believes that balance of power concerns best help us understand the genesis of the regime: the EU promoted the EMP to simultaneously counter U.S. influence in the region, shape trans-Mediterranean relations via its dominant relational power, and contain political Islam. However, other explanations better explain why the EU chose an interregional regime to manage this relationship as well as the specific elements of the regime. The EU's self-image as a Kantian "normative power" and subsequent policies following that model, as well as the ambitions of the Commission to use the EMP to expand its own policy remit, are the key factors shaping the comprehensive and developmental nature of the regime.

The regime's weakness and bilateral-leaning commercial treatment prevail for other reasons. Interest groups' over-time decline in support for and interest in the EuroMed framework – related to the lack of progress of domestic economic liberalization in MNMCs – have been both cause and consequence of the gulf in European and MNMC attitudes toward strong, liberal-leaning rules and institutions. Meanwhile, the reality of the asymmetric dependence in this relationship has undermined the EU's inclination to pursue a liberal interregional arrangement in terms of two "equal" regions, which has hampered the creation of a strong, mutually binding regime in which the EU treats the MNMCs in a uniform, interregional manner. Moreover, the structural power of the United States inevitably shapes the context in which the EU pursues its own policies toward the MNMCs, with Washington's somewhat erratic involvement in the Middle East in particular hindering the creation of a stable European approach.

EU–Africa, Caribbean, and the Pacific (ACP)

As John Ravenhill notes in his chapter, Europe's relationship with the countries of Africa, the Caribbean, and the Pacific Islands represents its first, and perhaps most unwieldy, attempt at establishing an institutionalized interregional relationship. Born in the wake of decolonization, Europe reconstituted its commercial relationships with these ex-colonies in the Yaoundé and Lomé conventions, which managed to build a strong, developmental regime between Europe and these generally small, poor countries. The strength of the Lomé regime derived primarily from its high degree of institutionalization, as it featured five separate joint EU–ACP institutions to manage relations on an interregional basis; yet while Lomé certainly featured a clearly-defined set of rules for ACP access to European markets (and vice versa), these rules were only moderately binding. That is, though Lomé provisions were "contractual" in nature, the Europeans ignored them when they found it necessary to do so, particularly in Lomé's waning years.

Lomé was both highly comprehensive and highly developmentalist in nature, covering a wide range of issues from trade, investment, and aid to more socio-political matters such as social, cultural, and individual rights. The economic side of these arrangements was heavily preferential – despite some inconsistencies with the multilateral trade regime – setting up a number of mechanisms through which ACP countries became Europe's "preferred partners." These provisions and institutions applied generally throughout the EU–ACP relationship with a high degree of uniformity, though the Europeans did provide special treatment within Lomé to the poorest of the ACP countries.

The EU's commercial treatment of the ACP countries was somewhat more mixed in its interregional-bilateral basis: although there existed a unified secretariat to coordinate ACP positions and thus create a purely interregional relationship, in fact individual European countries tended to favor dealing more directly with their traditional clients, thus undermining a true region-to-region track.

Ravenhill suggests that explaining the evolution of the EU–ACP inter-regional relationship is complicated by the fact that different factors prevailed at different times. He argues that systemic security considerations – and in particular matters of economic security for Europeans such as the stability of the supply of raw materials – were a primary consideration in the early development of the regime, and that the Lomé process began to lose steam – and the regime began to weaken – as these security concerns began to abate in the 1980s and 1990s. Meanwhile, the difficulty of maintaining a strong regime that was proving ever more difficult to nest within the WTO – and with a set of partners that was decreasingly important in Europe's international commercial relations – ultimately undermined the Lomé regime and led the EU to align its trade treatment of the ACP more closely with those types allowed within the WTO's Article 24.

Economic interests were very important in shaping both the nature and the strength of the Lomé regime. The terms of Lomé's preferential (i.e., developmental) access to European markets was defined in large part by the interests that did not accept an arrangement not tilted in their favor, most notably European farmers, or by those that benefited from preferential access, notably European banana and sugar traders. This latter group's concern in the late 1990s that its global interests could be hurt by maintaining the Lomé arrangements in the face of WTO condemnation caused their ardor for Lomé to cool, and provided perhaps the final nail in the coffin of the existing regime. Meanwhile, whereas NGO activists' initial support for Lomé's developmental provisions provided a much-needed fillip to the regime, their later qualification of support added another blow from societal interests to the tottering regime.

Bureaucratic politics in this case were largely an internal affair within the Commission. The Development Directorate in the Commission had as its main responsibility maintaining the relationship with the ACP countries, and as a result defended this regime ferociously against other encroaching directorates (e.g., the External Relations and Agricultural Directorates). However, as disillusionment with Lomé within the Development Directorate grew, and as the more global Trade Directorate's purview expanded with the negotiation and completion of the Uruguay Round of GATT as well as the growing solidification of a single European trade policy, the bureaucratic impetus supporting Lomé evaporated.

Ravenhill suggests that notions of regional identity played little role in promoting a "European" approach to ACP countries, though there were national/postcolonial identities that initially shaped the French and British approach to their former colonies in the Lomé process. While the prevalence of the NIEO in the international discourse certainly did play a role in defining the nature and perhaps the strength of the Lomé regime, this idea was more a function of a Third World identity (and thus ACP countries' approach to Lomé) than a European one, and over time seems to have done little to strengthen a sense of regionalism in either Europe or among subgroupings of ACP countries. Overall, then, each of these factors seemed to work in concert, first to promote the Lomé process and later to undermine it, largely driven by the decreasing economic importance of ACP countries and the loosening of post-colonial bonds.

EU–Eastern Europe

One of the more distinctive cases of EU interregionalism is the post-Cold War Western European engagement of the postcommunist countries of Central and Eastern Europe. As Cédric Dupont and Hilde Engelen show, this overall case is in fact three separate sub-cases: the EU has pursued separate engagement strategies each with the Visegrad group in Central Europe, the Baltic states, and the former republics of the Soviet Union. Moreover, in each case these "transient subregions" engaged the EU not as permanent entities in themselves, but rather, at least in the first two subcases, as temporary groupings searching for the best route to formal integration into the European Union.

The Central European countries – Poland, the Czech Republic, Slovakia, and Hungary (and Slovenia) – initially sought to enhance their chances of early accession into the EU through the creation of integration mechanisms of their own, the Visegrad group and the Central Europe Free Trade Area (CEFTA). However, these nations' attempt to promote a region-to-region approach gave way to an EU-directed bilateral approach based on Europe Agreements (EAs) – a highly-institutionalized, broad-scoped, developmental set of agreements that set out the terms of EU assistance to these countries and the necessary reforms they needed to undertake to gain EU membership. Dupont and Engelen attribute this general shift from incipient interregionalism toward bilateralism primarily to interest group pressure among those producers concerned about competition from lower-cost competitors to the east and EU concerns about allaying Russian fears about a wholesale Western takeover of its former client states, as well as the only moderate success of Central European countries in promoting their own interim collective integration.

EU relations with the Baltic states followed a similar trajectory from initial interregionalism to bilateralism. Like the Central Europeans, the Baltic states generated their own progress toward sub-regional cooperation, a process that was supported by the EU. By the mid to late 1990s, however, both sides moved toward a preference for a bilateral approach, and the EU ended up signing EAs with each of the three along similar lines as those with the Central European countries. With this set of countries, Dupont and Engelen argue, international security concerns were even more dominant, given that the Baltic states were formerly part of the Soviet Union proper and still were home to large ethnic Russian minorities, and EU leaders sought to avoid a negative Russian reaction to the Baltics' inclusion in Western security organizations.

In each of these two sub-cases, while Dupont and Engelen identify particular factors that helped shape the overall transition from interregional to bilateral thinking, the strength, nature, and counterpart treatment in each of the relevant countries were ultimately shaped by the EU blueprint for prospective members. In this sense, these two groups of countries are different from all other cases and sub-cases because they consisted of countries that were destined to become EU members, and thus were subject to a dominant influence that was clearly lacking elsewhere.

With the more formally organized group of former Soviet republics, the Commonwealth of Independent States (CIS) – countries whose futures were less directed toward gaining EU membership – the Union maintained a stronger tendency toward interregionalism. The EU set up an evolving set of arrangements with the CIS, first involving technical assistance and aid and later evolving into broader cooperation that institutionalized dialogue on a wide range of economic, social, and political issues. However, these arrangements have been conducted largely on a bilateral basis, as the unclear status of the CIS remains a barrier (among others) to a more formal interregional relationship.

Dupont and Engelen are chary of assigning explanations to the specific elements of an interregional process between the EU and the CIS that may only be in its very beginning stages. However, it seems clear that international security concerns (how to institutionalize relations with a former superpower adversary) and identity concerns (who belongs in "Europe") may be particularly relevant to this process as it evolves.

EU–North America

The defining feature of the EU–North American relationship among these cases is the absence of any interregional regime process between these two pillars of the international economy. As Edward Fogarty suggests, however, this fact is primarily a result of the success of the EU's economic relations with the countries of North America: with commercial relations on the whole unproblematic and well-managed through both multilateral trade and economic institutions and mid- and low-level official cooperation and consultation, there has been little obvious need for an overarching interregional regime with NAFTA as a whole. The EU has pursued some bilateral agreements each with the United States, Canada, and Mexico – the first two as the basis of broader international agreements (particularly on sectoral issues), and with Mexico as a response to the diversionary effects of NAFTA – but there has been little impetus from any side for pursuing a comprehensive interregional track between Europe and North America.

This negative case requires an explanation for the lack of support, particularly in the EU but also in North America, for an interregional accord.

While none of the general hypotheses suggests that the necessary conditions are in place for an EU–North America interregional regime, Fogarty concludes that some explanations for the interregional gap are better than others. Specifically, he finds the interest group approach wanting, as any interregional regime would represent more a political-strategic than an economic project (particularly between the Europeans and the United States), and thus narrowly-focused business groups would not be particularly relevant to explaining the presence or absence of such a broad political project. That said, the influence of interest groups has been quite relevant throughout the period in ensuring that occasional political spats do not upset the EU's bilateral commercial relations with each of the three North American countries.

The Council's refusal to allow the Commission to pursue such a political project may be a factor in the absence of a TAFTA. The Commission showed interest in pursuing a binding, well-institutionalized agreement with North America as a whole, with Canada as such an arrangement's most vocal North American supporter. However, the Council's demurral never allowed the idea to get off the ground.

The nature of the relationship between the EU and the United States is a major element defining the organization and dynamics of the international economy. The EU, which acts as a unit much more in economic affairs than in the political-security realm, inevitably uses the United States as the meter of its competitive position in the international economy, and vice versa. As such, the overall relationship between these two – as well as the strength, nature, and commercial treatment in a hypothetical transatlantic agreement – is inevitably tied to the "geoeconomic" position of each *vis-à-vis* the rest of the world. The primary goals of each – and the focus of international commercial policymaking energy – are in solidifying access to other important markets and ensuring they are not disadvantaged in their access to these markets relative to the other. This "structural economic power" competition is constrained by WTO rules – the same rules that derive largely from transatlantic negotiation, and thus make the idea of a separate transatlantic trade agreement redundant. As long as both transatlantic commercial ties and the overall multilateral trade regime remain stable – two crucial conditions – each side views its remaining interests in terms of its position in emerging markets, and will not dwell on whether or not there is some formal arrangement across the Atlantic. The EU's FTA with Mexico emerged largely for this reason: threatened by the "NAFTA effect," the EU had a strong incentive to pursue a relatively strong agreement with Mexico that had a distinctively different nature from the less comprehensive but still well-institutionalized relations with the United States and Canada.

This inclination against the formalization of transatlantic economic ties likely grows apace with the chorus of voices within Europe pressing the establishment of the EU's international identity in juxtaposition to the United States. Certain Europeans might be more than willing to see an erosion of relations across the Atlantic if such a development were the price for greater European unity and the emergence of the EU as a credible counterweight to the United States in international politics. While it is not at all clear that this is a viable method of achieving a palpable "Europeanness," it does suggest that, regardless of other considerations, a strong interregional regime between the EU and North America would be extremely unlikely until the EU strengthened its political and institutional identity in contexts absent the United States.

Thus the fate of commercial relations between the EU and the United States (and North America more generally) may be largely a function of the combined economic-security and political-identity interests of the EU. Absent a major shock to the organization of the international political economy and a sudden favorable resolution of Europe's perpetual identity crisis, little movement toward a transatlantic agreement should be expected.

3   Comparing interregional regime evolution

Table 8.1 lays out the evolution for each of the six cases of EU-centered interregionalism on our three outcomes of interest – regime strength, regime nature, and EU commercial treatment of the counterpart.

This table provides a before-and-after picture of interregional evolution, with the "before" columns (which appeared in our introduction) representing the first instance of significant EU cross-regional initiatives, and the "after" columns representing the current status of these elements of the regime. The table presents a fairly complex picture, so we consider the evolution of each of the three regime elements in turn, before moving on to evaluate our contending hypotheses across these cases.

Regime strength

Regime strength is a function of two factors: its institutionalization, (i.e., the presence/absence of permanent forums such as a secretariat, dispute-settlement mechanism, parliamentary assembly, working groups, and the like) and the scope of enforceable rules that constrain actors' behavior.

Some implications about rule bindingness and regime institutionalization can be drawn from this cross-case, over-time comparison. First, interregional regimes' rule bindingness tends to be low, except in the very notable exception of the case of Eastern Europe (i.e., countries that will accede to the EU and be directly bound by its internal rules). The EU has generally been unwilling to commit itself to be bound by strong rules in its commercial relations with other regions, preferring to retain a high degree of flexibility to operate against the spirit of the agreements when necessary.

Table 8.1 EU interregional relationships (evolution)

Relationship (T = 1 year)	Regime strength (T = 1)	Regime strength (2003)	Regime nature (T = 1)	Regime nature (2003)	EU commercial treatment (T = 1)	EU commercial treatment (2003)
EU–Southern Cone (1995)	Medium-weak	Medium	Medium-narrow, quasi-developmental	Comprehensive, quasi-developmental	Uniform, interregional	Uniform, interregional
EU–East Asia (1996)	Medium-weak	Medium-weak	Comprehensive, quasi-developmental	Quasi-comprehensive, quasi-developmental	Nonuniform, interregional + bilaterals	Nonuniform, interregional + bilaterals
EU–Southern Mediterranean (1995)	Weak	Weak	Comprehensive, developmental	Comprehensive developmental	Nonuniform, bilaterals	Nonuniform, bilaterals
EU–ACP (1975)	Medium-strong	Medium	Comprehensive, very developmental	Comprehensive, developmental	Mostly uniform, interregional	Quasi-uniform, subdivided interregional
EU–Eastern Europe(1990) CEEC/Baltics	Medium-strong	Strong	Comprehensive, developmental	Comprehensive, developmental	Nonuniform, interregional + bilaterals	Mostly uniform, bilaterals
USSR/CIS	Weak	Medium	Narrow, developmental	Comprehensive, developmental	Uniform	Nonuniform, bilaterals
EU–North America (1990)	US/Canada: medium Mexico: weak	US/C: medium Mexico: medium	US/Canada: narrow, nondevelopmental Mexico: comprehensive, developmental	US/Canada: narrow, nondevelopmental Mexico: comprehensive, developmental	Nonuniform, bilaterals	Nonuniform, bilaterals

Indeed, even in the Eastern Europe case the rules do not affect the EU – whose members already abide by these rules – but only those countries seeking to join it. That said, however, there has been some increase over time in the reciprocal bindingness of rules connecting the EU with countries from Latin America (both MERCOSUR and Mexico) as progress toward free trade agreements has emerged with these countries. In the other cases, rule bindingness remains at a low level – and in EU relations with ACP countries, has decreased. What this suggests is that there may be some general condition that tends to keep rule bindingness low, but that specific conditions may send its evolution in different directions in different cases.

Second, the EU's interregional regimes have tended to become more institutionalized over time (again, with the exception of the relationship with the ACP countries). It is perhaps not surprising that regimes have become institutionalized rather than binding: it is far less costly to establish working committees, forums, and the like to discuss mutual interests and concerns than it is to commit oneself to rules that impose real costs and circumscribe freedom of action. A dividing line regarding institutionalization involves the presence of two key institutions, a secretariat – which provides a regime with an organizational identity and bureaucratic face – and a dispute settlement mechanism – which generally exists in connection with binding rules. These two types of institutions tend to exist only in "serious" regimes (e.g., Lomé) and are absent in less serious ones (e.g., ASEM) – though as the experience of APEC shows, having a secretariat does not a strong regime make. While secretariats and dispute settlement mechanisms are still far from universal across our cases, they have become more prevalent, particularly in EU relations with Latin America.

However, secretariats and dispute settlement mechanisms are not the only indicators of significant institutionalization. The EU relationships with the United States and Canada, for instance, are considerably institutionalized (and binding) – not necessarily at the highest levels of government involvement, but rather through deep cooperation at middle and lower levels of their bureaucracies on matters like standards and law enforcement. This suggests that institutionalization as an element of regime strength is relevant more for increasing official and private interregional cooperation that starts from a low or moderate level, and less so when this type of cooperation already exists.

Regime nature

Regime nature as we have defined it is a function of two factors: issue scope (i.e., the degree of inclusion of trade, investment, and other socio-political issues within the terms of an agreement) and development focus (i.e., the degree of prevalence of developmentalist provisions and language).

The obvious commonality among the cases with regard to regime nature is that, with the exception of EU relations with the United States and

Canada, they tend toward a comprehensive issue scope and a developmental emphasis. Similar to the relationship between rule bindingness and institutionalization, having a broad issue scope seems to come "cheaper" than a development emphasis. Indeed, a broad issue scope is perhaps the most universal element of EU interregional regimes: the EU is quite consistent across time and space in promoting democratic institutions, human rights, and a robust civil society alongside its commercial objectives in its relations with other regions. Even in its more narrowly defined "regimes" with the United States and Canada, the narrow issue scope in this specific context only applies because there are other, more specialized regimes managing political and security cooperation. Especially compared to the United States, the EU has made a point of pursuing a broad range of issues in all its relationships.

The developmental aspect of interregional regimes has become more complicated over time for the EU. When it established Lomé in 1975, the multilateral trade regime (GATT) was relatively pliant with regard to preferential treatment of a certain set of trade partners; after the establishment of the WTO, however, nesting has become somewhat more difficult. The devolution of Lomé is a case in point. As such, while the EU has not abandoned the idea of developmental provisions in its interregional relationships, they have had to take new forms. These provisions have varied by case: for example, in ASEM they have focused on FDI, with MERCOSUR they have focused on institution-building, and with the Southern Mediterranean countries they have focused on aid. Meanwhile, developmental provisions in relations with countries of Eastern Europe have been somewhat less problematic, as these countries are in line to become members of the EU (a regional grouping whose internal developmental provisions generally fall outside the scope of WTO rules).

EU commercial treatment of the counterpart

EU commercial treatment of counterpart involves two factors: the degree of uniformity of EU treatment of specific countries in the counterpart region (i.e., one set of terms for all countries in the counterpart region would be perfectly uniform, while a separate set of terms for all countries would be perfectly nonuniform) and the EU's negotiations/agreement type with the counterpart (i.e., whether the EU pursues region-to region (pure interregional) approach, a region-to-country approach (bilateral), or something in between).

In EU commercial treatment of counterpart regions, with the exception of Eastern Europe (where the shifting requirements of EU accession determine commercial treatment type), there seems to be a certain logic connecting interregionalism and uniformity of treatment, bilateralism and nonuniformity of treatment, and a mixed approach to each – though it may be that the prevailing logic depends on the pairing. For instance, while uniformity/interregionalism may derive from an EU inclination to reduce bargaining costs (e.g., EU–ACP) or promote regional integration elsewhere (e.g., EU–MERCOSUR), bilateralism/nonuniformity may be a result of an EU desire to increase bargaining leverage (e.g., EU–North America) or an inability to coax any coherence within the counterpart region (e.g., EU–Southern Mediterranean). However, each of these individual logics is likely embedded in a broader explanation such as those outlined in our broader hypotheses.

What is also notable is that while EU commercial treatment of the counterpart varies by case it does not, again with the exception of Eastern Europe, seem to vary across time. Once the EU has gone down a particular path of commercial treatment with a counterpart region, it seems to remain on that path. Even in EU relations with ACP countries, Lomé appears to be giving way to a subdivided set of interregional relationships with the constituent African, Caribbean, and Pacific pieces of the former regime. This suggests that the logic that determines EU commercial treatment of various counterpart regions tends to be stable over time.

4   Evaluating hypotheses of interregional regime evolution

When we outlined a set of four approaches and allied hypotheses in the introduction, we did so not with the expectation that any one hypothesis, and the set of variables it focuses on, could either fully describe or fully explain interregional regime outcomes. Although it may not be descriptively satisfying to have a single explanation based on one or two variables, our approach to this point has been to assess the contributions of the different deductive approaches we have identified. In this section we discuss whether interregionalism could be a stable equilibrium approach to international economic organization from the relatively simple deductive logic of the given hypotheses, and then make some brief suggestions of how future research could pursue more complex reasoning based on more multicausal explanations.

Interest group hypothesis

The cases suggest a number of tentative conclusions regarding this hypothesis. The over-time element of interest group involvement – and particularly that of business groups – is important. A consistent feature across cases is that business group enthusiasm for, and participation in, interregional regimes start high and then wane over time. The trajectory of European business support seems to be similar to that of EU interest overall in these regimes. This suggests that business support, and perhaps the lack of a countervailing coalition, is strongly associated with the establishment of strong regimes, particularly in the development of binding regime rules but also in the viability of regime institutions.

The role of interest groups is greater than we originally expected in the nature of regimes. Certain interest groups can benefit handsomely from developmental provisions of regimes (e.g., banana and sugar interests in Lomé), and civil society organizations (e.g., environmental, human rights, and development groups, etc.) can be effective in shaping the range of issues involved.

Their role in shaping commercial treatment of the counterpart, however, is somewhat less clear. There is no doubt that highly influential, highly protected industries such as agriculture have been successful in shaping the EU's commercial treatment of counterparts, and that variation in uniformity of treatment within (and across) counterpart regions reflects in significant part the nature of the interest coalitions that mobilize to shape the relevant commercial policies. But interest groups seem to have little influence over the particular trade types – interregional, bilateral, or a mix of the two. A lack of interest group influence on this front of course does not undermine the hypothesis as a whole, but it does suggest that to explain this element of an interregional regime we need to look elsewhere.

Two key factors in this hypothesis are preference intensity and mobilization. Those actors whose preferences are intense – most notably, protectionist-oriented sectors such as agriculture or textiles – are most likely to overcome collective action problems and mobilize effectively to shape regime characteristics. The creation of interregional institutions to reduce collective action costs among business groups in particular seems to be a general feature of EU interregional regimes, but these have not necessarily made mobilization more effective. If interregional regime benefits for some interest groups remain diffuse (and moderate) and the costs remain concentrated (and high), these latter groups will continue to mobilize relatively effectively against liberalizing interregional regimes just as they do against global agreements.

Overall, there is little specific evidence *against* a pluralist hypothesis: strong interest group support is correlated with the rise of interregional regimes in our cases, and the decline of this balance of positive support is correlated with their failure to move forward. However, this is more relevant for regime strength than nature or commercial treatment.

Bureaucratic politics hypothesis

The cases tend to confirm two oft-noted truths regarding the institutional state of affairs within the European Union. First, the Council remains firmly in control of the strategic agenda, and this is likely to remain true after the adoption of the new constitution. Any future European foreign minister will report to the Council, not the Commission, limiting the role of the Commission to implementing rather than shaping the EU's relations with other countries. Second, the Commission is institutionally more pro-free trade and pro-interregionalism than the Council, but is hampered in promoting this agenda within the EU due largely to its own internal divisions (e.g., a "strategic" External Relations DG versus a liberalizing Trade DG, versus a protectionist Agriculture DG, versus an "altruistic" Development DG). External Relations and Trade DGs seem to be gaining the upper hand over time, suggesting that, while internal ructions may continue, the Commission is likely to become more unified in its support of liberalizing international regimes in the future.

Bureaucratic politics – and especially the level of intra-Commission debate – seems to be a stronger determinant of regime nature than we had anticipated. Having comprehensive regimes (which are the norm) is consistent with the need to keep all DGs happy, while the tendency for these regimes to become somewhat less preferential and more consistent with free-trade thinking and WTO strictures fits with the notion of the relative rise of the External Relations and Trade DGs.

However, as expected, bureaucratic politics seems less important to regime strength and counterpart treatment. In a couple of cases the EC has acted as a *de facto* secretariat for an interregional regime, a situation that may suit the Commission well enough – and might actually hinder the creation of viable, truly interregional institutions. Meanwhile, while as expected the Council eclipses the Commission with regard to commercial treatment, this is less a reflection of inter-bureaucratic competition than broader strategic concerns. However, we tended to underemphasize the degree to which the Commission prefers to bargain with collectivities (i.e., to prefer pure interregionalism to multi-bilaterals in commercial treatment of the counterpart), especially when the counterpart region involves a large number of countries. But this factor is more a function of bargaining preferences than policy preferences – though it is still notable as a motivation for an interregional approach.

Systemic hypotheses: balancing and nesting[1]

The cases show that an analytical distinction between structural power and relational power is essential.[2] The EU is a paradigmatic example of an actor that has far less structural power in the international political-economic system than relational power in specific interregional relationships. A focus on the latter would suggest a direct relationship between the EU's relational power in an interregional regime and its willingness to pursue such a regime, for the simple reason that it would be better placed to define the relevant elements of the regime. The cases generally support this prediction, particularly with respect to its commercial treatment of counterparts (especially trade treatment, but also uniformity) and overt support for counterpart coherence in cases where this coherence is unthreatening (e.g., EU–MERCOSUR vs. EU–North America).

With reference to structural power, however, the EU appears a far more reactive interregionalist. The extent to which EU initiatives mirror those of the United States is one way to evaluate the EU's concern with structural power. There is clear evidence that the EU is motivated by structural power concerns, as it in many cases pursues arrangements in response to U.S. initiatives: ASEM after APEC, EMIFCA after FTAA; and EU–Mexico after NAFTA. Notably, ASEM bogged down after APEC did so; the EU–MERCOSUR process slowed down after FTAA did so; and the EU–Mexico FTA was successfully completed after NAFTA came into effect. The only way to demonstrate that structural power concerns are not relevant would be if the United States pursued regimes and EU failed to respond; we have not seen this.

Meanwhile, the EU has been surprisingly inattentive to nesting considerations, despite consistent rhetorical support for the need to ensure WTO consistency. The major exception to this general lack of concern has been the case of Lomé. In this situation, the EU chose to abandon this highly-institutionalized, broad-based arrangement, seeking to replace it with WTO-friendly arrangements with the African, Caribbean, and Pacific countries as its conflicts over bananas with the United States heated up (driven in part by the stronger dispute settlement mechanism after the mid-1990s). More cynically, in the case of Lomé, nesting considerations may also have provided a ready excuse for the EU to abandon an agreement that was providing rapidly declining returns. With the other cases, however, the EU's interregional arrangements (EMIFCA, EMP, and ASEM) got off the ground after the creation of the WTO in 1995, but WTO-compliance does not appear to be an important issue because these regimes are so weak. From this perspective, then, interregionalism can be seen as posing *less* of a threat to the global regime than we might have expected.

Constructivist hypothesis

In general, this hypothesis is hard to evaluate. Most cases find some support for the idea that the EU is seeking to shape its external identity in interregional regimes, particularly in its explicit support for the coalescence of counterpart regions – most notably with MERCOSUR but also in East Asia and the Southern Mediterranean. However, it is difficult to tell whether these activities are motivated primarily by promotion of EU organizational forms or whether they are serving less metaphysical interests such as those identified in the other hypotheses.

As we expected, identity concerns seem more important in regime nature than in either strength or counterpart treatment. The comprehensive and developmental or quasi-developmental nature of most of these interregional regimes is consistent with the notion that the EU seeks to replicate its own internal developments (e.g., shared social and political goals, structural funds) in its relations with counterparts. The EU has not sought to hide the fact that these elements of the nature of its interregional regimes provide a contrast to the more commercially-minded transregionalism of the United States.

However, there is also some evidence that ideas and identity have influenced some elements of interregional regime strength and commercial treatment. The EU has been quite consistent in its support of interregional institutions that treat the two sides as equals, a move that promotes the pure fiction of institutional (or material) equality of the counterpart to the EU and that, in conferring a certain status on the counterpart, replicates and reinforces the EU model. This motivation may help explain the far higher institutionalization of these regimes relative to their rule bindingness. Cooperative forums must exist before their participants can enact mutually acceptable rules; the Treaty of Rome, for instance, was not built in a day.

Meanwhile, similar motivations may help explain the pursuit of interregional trade types when economic and political differences among counterparts might have suggested a more differential approach – perhaps most notably with respect to the countries of the Southern Mediterranean. Still, in most cases these types of considerations were likely secondary in the minds of EU policymakers and in shaping outcomes more generally.

There is little to suggest that EU policymakers have sought to use interregionalism to promote an internal European identity. However, while there is little positive-case evidence for this, the main negative case – EU–North America – is an exception. Anti-Americanism is an increasingly popular position across much of Europe, perhaps more so among publics than more pragmatic leaders, and if nothing else is certainly consistent with the EU's skeptical position toward any sort of formal regime with the United States (or NAFTA). Whether anti-Americanism is seen as a useful and legitimate means to promote either or both Europe's internal and external identity remains unclear, but it could provide a boost to EU interregionalism as a general strategy.

As we suggested above, while evaluating hypotheses that focus on a narrow set of explanatory factors helps us to understand whether there is a dominant logic to interregionalism, we may be able to gain more real-world verisimilitude from combining them. Given the basic approaches, several combinations could obviously be developed that bring together two, three or more hypotheses. Here, we simply provide an illustrative discussion to indicate the directions that one might undertake in attempting to systematically combine hypotheses in future research to provide richer explanations of interregional outcomes.

One combination links interest group politics with bureaucratic politics. This approach addresses the key question of how interest groups overcome collective action problems in effective mobilization, and how bureaucracies pursue actual policy goals – rather than merely seeking control over processes.[3] As identified above, a pure pluralist approach tends to assume that mobilization will occur if the incentives are right. But from a combined perspective, we get a more agency-centered explanation for successful mobilization: state actors – particularly the Commission, but also the national governments and the Council – facilitate the mobilization of interest groups by courting them, funding them, and giving them privileged access to policymaking process, which will then tend to increase the authority of the institution that makes itself the center of activity for these groups. Reciprocally, these institutions do not necessarily have inherent interests regarding commercial policy, so the makeup of whatever coalitions they embrace provides a clearer sense over what actual policy debates are at the core of inter-bureaucratic contestation. An example of this with respect to interregionalism is the case when various DGs in the Commission sought to protect the Lomé regime. They did so because they were jealous of their own prerogatives within this regime, but only as long as they were able to maintain a critical mass of support among relevant interest groups (banana importers, development NGOs, etc.).

A bureaucratic politics approach linked to a realist view provides a contrast to both a pure systemic power-based argument that sees a unified state interest driven by a country's relative capabilities in the system and an internally driven, "all politics is local politics" combination we have seen of interest groups and bureaucratic politics. This perspective focuses on how bureaucracies get their substantive interests from external pressures – and explores how policymakers located in specific domestic institutional environments respond to the challenges and opportunities in the international system. The preferences and implementation of interregional strategies are shaped by the contrasting responses of the Commission and the Council to the question of how to use the EU's relational power in specific interregional relationships to promote the EU's overall structural power (particularly *vis-à-vis* the United States). The advantage of this approach is that a straight realist focus *a la* Kenneth Waltz implies an *undifferentiated* response by the EU "state."[4] By bringing the Council–Commission tensions into the mix, one could explain why they often clash in their policy responses. Thus, although both the Council and Commission have reasons to support an interregional approach for power reasons, the Commission clearly has a vested interest in negotiations since it is at the center of the process, while the Council tries to hold the Commission back.

A combination of realism and constructivism also takes us beyond the systemically driven imperatives of the international system. Akin to the work of Stephen Krasner in his book *Defending the National Interest*,[5] in this view systemic imperatives are underspecified: one cannot derive clear preferences about trade policy choices and the specific choice of interregionalism versus some other mode of interaction by simply looking at relative systemic capabilities. For Krasner, U.S. policy is ideologically determined and led by state policymakers' perception of U.S. interests. In our case, this approach focuses on the EU's struggle to define its place in the world, specifically against the United States. As a military pygmy, the EU has only two real sources of power: its economic power and its normative power. Cognizant of this constraint, EU policymakers may use commercial policy in a grander sense to change the rules of the game internationally by promoting the legitimacy of its commercial-democratic model as a counterpoint to the U.S. commercial-military model. The combination would argue that interregionalism plays to the EU's strengths: it applies the EU's commercial strength and appeal as a trading partner to fulfill its desire to promote the EU's own values and institutional forms abroad.[6] At the same time, the focus on realism may oversell the extent of EU–US competition, which at this point is still at a fairly shallow level, as opposed to a milder competition of ideas in the international system about appropriate modes for organizing the international trading system.

Another possible combination is that of the bureaucratic politics and constructivist hypotheses. This resembles a sociological institutionalist approach, highlighting the interplay between EU bureaucracies and the normative-institutional environments both within and outside Europe.[7] The focus, as in a realist-constructivist combination, is on how EU commercial policy promotes institutional change in the international political economy; the difference here is that outcomes are more closely identified with perceptions of the *appropriateness* of institutional change. Here, the Council–Commission struggle is to define the appropriate locus of governance in an unstable EU institutional field caught between state and supranational units, and their competition and its possible resolution (e.g., in EU treaties) are revisited and reproduced on the global stage. The relevant question for EU interregionalism, then, would be how ongoing Council–Commission competition affects and is affected by the organization of the international political economy through EU cooperation with other actors. Within the EU, the Council is exemplar of cooperative interstate multilateralism, an approach that is institutionally consistent with the prevailing state-to-state multilateralism of the WTO in the international trade regime. However, if the Commission grows in stature within the EU, its supranational form and identity could alter the institutional dynamics of the international political-economic system by promoting supranational regionalism throughout the world – an institutional development that, if generally realized, would then reinforce the Commission-led model within Europe.[8] From this angle, the prevalence and purity of interregionalism would ultimately be a function of the Commission's struggle to create a field of international economic relations that privileges the supranational regional unit over the state unit in multilateral cooperation.

Lastly, we present a triple combination of bureaucratic politics, interest groups, and nesting. This approach raises a fundamental question about our initial starting point: the view that multilateralism is under fire and that the EU (and other actors such as the United States and Japan, among others) are pursuing bilateral, regional, and interregional alternatives. This combination helps us delve into the basis of EU support for multilateralism and the likelihood of erosion in this commitment. This approach can be seen as a further refinement of the pluralist/bureaucratic politics combination above. In this instance, the EU trade policymaking process is constrained by the EU's external legal requirements under the WTO. Put differently, the Commission is buffeted by competing forces. For example, on the one hand, it is under pressure from the banana and sugar lobbies to support the Lomé preferential approach. On the other hand, it is constrained by its longstanding commitment to the GATT/WTO. As we have seen from John Ravenhill's discussion, one must, of course, be careful in fully attributing the EU's abandonment of Lomé simply to nesting considerations. One could also view the high costs of Lomé and the concerns of other interest groups who have a vested interest in liberalization through the WTO process as driving this change in policy, rather than an institutional commitment to multilateralism *per se*.

5   Evaluating counterpart coherence

One of the key concepts that we have considered in connection with interregional regimes is counterpart coherence. To some extent this concept only makes sense within a study of EU-centered regimes, given that we measure coherence largely in relative terms to that of the EU itself. But we have also considered these cases with other criteria for the coherence of regional blocs and its evolution, as shown in Table 8.2.

As noted in the introduction to this volume, these criteria are fourfold. The first is binary: was the region self-defined, or was it created specifically for the purpose of engaging with the EU? (This is a one-off measure that is not subject to over-time evolution.) The second criterion measures intraregional economic integration: what percentage of the trade of countries within the region is with others in the region as opposed to the rest of the world? The third criterion – what percentage of the "potential region" is represented in any existing bloc – is much more difficult to assess objectively, even for an advanced grouping such as the EU. On this measure, we simply draw upon the authors' determinations regarding the relevant counterpart region in their case. The percentage shown is derived by dividing the number of countries that are formal members of a regional bloc by the total number of countries that are perceived to exist within that region. The final element of counterpart coherence is the strength of any regional regime, measured in the same terms as interregional regime strength.

These criteria provide rough indicators of four distinct aspects of regional evolution: the self-generated will to create a regional bloc; the level of economic integration that shapes incentives to create or strengthen a regional bloc; the presence of cultural, political, and/or geographic cohesion that

Table 8.2 Evolution of counterpart coherence

Relationship (T = 1 year)	Region self-defined? (Y/N/ambiguous)	Distribution of trade (% within region) (T = 1)	Distribution of trade (T = 2)	% of potential region (T = 1)	% of potential region (2003)	Region regime strength (T = 1)	Region regime strength (2003)
European Union (1990)	Y	64%	61.4% (2001)	50%	71% (2004)	Strong	Strong
Southern Cone (1995)	Y	MERCOSUR: 18.7%	MERCOSUR: 18%	80%	80%	Medium-strong	Medium
East Asia (1996)	N/ambiguous	Intra-ASEAN: 22.5% Intra-APT: 42%	Intra-ASEAN: 23.2% Intra-APT: 41%	67%	87%	Weak	Weak
Southern Mediterranean (1995)	N	N/A	N/A	90%	90%	Weak	Weak
ACP (1975)							
Africa	N	Sub-Sah: 5.9%	Sub-Sah: 10.2%	90%	100%	Weak	Weak
Caribbean	N	5.9%	9.3%	90%	98%	Medium	Medium-strong
Pacific	N	3.6%	2.3%	90%	100%	Medium	Medium
ACP	N					Weak	Weak

Table 8.2 Evolution of counterpart coherence – Continued

Relationship (T = 1 year)	Region self-defined? (Y/N/ambiguous)	Distribution of trade (% within region) (T = 1)	Distribution of trade (T = 2)	% of potential region (T = 1)	% of potential region (2003)	Region regime strength (T = 1)	Region regime strength (2003)
Eastern Europe (1995)							
Visegrad	Y	X: 14.5%, M: 11.2%	X: 12.3%, M: 9.9%	57%	100%	Weak	Weak
Baltics	Y/ambiguous		X: 13.5%, M: 6.5%	100%		Medium	Medium
CIS	Y	X: 28%, M: 42.6%	X: 21.1%, I: 37%	100%	100%	Medium-strong	Medium-strong
North America (1990)	Y	38.6%	46.2%	67%	100%	CUSFTA: medium-strong US/Canada-Mexico: low	NAFTA: medium-strong

Sources:
MERCOSUR: CEPAL (Comisión Ecomómica para América Latina y el Caribe): Panorama de la Inserción Internacional de América Latina y el Caribe, Santiago de Chile, March 2003, p. 159; WTO Trade Statistics (http://www.wto.org/english/res_e/statis_e/its2001_e/appendix/a04.xls; accessed December 2003).
East Asia: Ng, Francis and Alexander Yeats (2003). "Major trends in East Asia." World Bank Policy Research Working Paper 3084 (June); WTO Trade Statistics (http://www.wto.org/english/res_e/statis_e/its2001_e/appendix/a04.xls; accessed December 2003).
ACP: IMF Direction of Trade Statistics (accessed June 2003). Distribution of trade figures at T = 1 are from 1980.
Eastern Europe:
North America: WTO Trade Statistics (wto.org/English/res_e/statis_e/statis_e.htm; accessed June 2003).

Notes:
X = exports, I = imports

shapes ideas about regional identity and thus bloc membership; and finally the degree to which countries have acted on these "regionalizing" forces to formally institutionalize regional cooperation.

What do we find? First, very broadly speaking, trade within these regions has grown relative to their overall trade with the rest of the world. This evolution in trade distribution is most likely a reflection of a more general trend toward regionalization that occurred in the 1990s. Sub-Saharan Africa, the Caribbean, North America, and East Asia all saw growth in regional commercial integration. The exceptions to this broad trend include regions coping with very specific conditions: Eastern European countries saw a natural gravitation of their trade relations westward after several decades of Soviet-enforced economic isolation; and intra-MERCOSUR trade suffered in the late 1990s and early 2000s from successive financial shocks to the Brazilian and Argentine economies. This overall trend toward intraregional trade growth has occurred independently of participation in interregional regimes with the EU, but generally increased the incentives for countries in these counterparts to cooperate on a regional level in any region-to-region engagement with the European Union.

Second, the percentage of countries participating in counterpart regional regimes that "belong" in those regimes – whether for cultural, political, or geographic reasons – has also tended to grow over time. For instance, in East Asia, the expansion of ASEAN to include the full complement of Southeast Asian nations (with the addition of Vietnam, Cambodia, Laos, and Myanmar), has made the APT into a more fully "East Asian" grouping – though problematic cases such as North Korea and Taiwan are still excluded. Similarly, North America became "whole" when Mexico joined the United States and Canada in NAFTA, while Chile's continued standoffishness toward MERCOSUR kept this grouping from becoming fully representative of the Southern Cone.

At a general, global level, ever fewer countries are not members of at least one regional cooperative arrangement – a trend that is in no small part connected to the success of the European model of integration. But whether the EU has been a direct catalyst of counterpart regions' coalescence is much more difficult to discern. On the one hand, the very concepts of "Eastern Europe," "Southern Mediterranean," and "East Asia" exist as they do today to a large extent because of these regions' relationship to Western Europe – Eastern Europe for political-historical and geographical reasons, and the Southern Mediterranean and East Asia (or at least the APT) because the EU explicitly decided to engage these groupings as such.[9] On the other hand, the EU has withheld formal engagement in interregional forums from countries that "belong" in some counterpart regions such as Myanmar in ASEM or Cuba in its relationship with Caribbean nations. It seems likely, then, that the evolution of counterpart regions' membership will remain primarily a function of intraregional dynamics, as the effect of the EU here may remain ambiguous.

It is with the third criterion – regional regime strength – that counterpart engagement with the EU may be most important. Like interregional regimes, each of these counterpart regimes is typically stronger in terms of institutionalization than rule bindingness, which is consistent with the idea that regional regimes require some sort of institutional identity if they are to engage with external actors as a unit. This idea is most clearly visible with MERCOSUR, which began its interregional regime process with the EU immediately after it upgraded its own regional bloc to a customs union. Meanwhile, though there is probably no direct cause–effect relationship, the establishment of ASEM occurred at the very beginning of a wave of institution building in what had previously, with the exception of ASEAN, been a very institution-poor region, perhaps paving the way for other East Asian cooperation mechanisms such as the ASEAN Regional Forum and the as-yet hypothetical Asian Monetary Fund. These countries' and regions' participation in interregional processes with the EU have generally encouraged and required region-wide thinking and representation – even if the interregional institutions, like regional institutions, are less powerful than they are abundant. That is, the EU can encourage counterpart coherence without having to commit to binding rules simply by encouraging a proliferation of interregional institutions.

To some extent, however, the evolution of counterpart regions' regime strength as interregional regime processes proceed is only part of the effect of EU interregionalism. While focusing on regional evolution over the course of an EU-led process suggests that ongoing interregional negotiations are the catalyst for increased counterpart institutionalization, much of the impetus for this institutionalization may occur before any such interregional process begins. This effect may be somewhat like the requirements of prospective EU members: they are told explicitly what reforms they must undertake first to be worthy of treatment as a future member and later to actually accede to the Union. The parallel is that counterpart regions may find that interregional processes can only be begun if counterparts commit to some degree of intraregional cooperation, and can only proceed satisfactorily if this cooperation evolves satisfactorily. Thus the EU begins its interregional process with MERCOSUR once the latter takes a large institutional step (by establishing a customs union), and proceeds in negotiations as MERCOSUR matures (by enduring major financial shocks). Alternatively, similar processes with the Southern Mediterranean and East Asia slow to different degrees because these regions make relatively little progress in enhancing their intraregional institutional identity. The point here is that the EU's influence on counterpart institutionalization through interregional processes may follow a path of initial leaps that are either consolidated or not, with the trajectory of interregional processes following that of the counterpart's intraregional institutionalization. While this idea is speculative, it suggests that the relationship between interregionalism and counterpart coherence is indeed one worth watching closely in the coming years.

6 Further research

Our objective in this volume has been to examine the new trend toward forms of interregionalism in the global economy. Ironically, the strengthening of the GATT and greater institutionalization of the multiproduct, multilateral trade regime through the WTO has been accompanied by a rise in bilateralism, regional agreements, sectoral accords, and interregionalism. Of these "alternatives to the WTO," the broadest efforts are interregional and transregional. The United States has pursued transregional agreements in minilateral forums such as APEC and the FTAA as well as in bilateral agreements with countries in East Asia and the Middle East, but has shown little interest in a more "pure" interregional approach alongside its NAFTA partners. The EU, on the other hand, has been particularly active in the interregional game, and is far ahead of any other grouping in pursuing region-to-region links. The prominence of the EU in this approach should hardly be surprising, given that the EU itself is the most institutionalized and influential regional bloc.

So is there a unified logic to interregionalism as a general approach to international commercial relationships, and does the experience of the EU, as the "necessary case" of interregionalism, suggest that this approach has a future? These two questions – which form the core of our study – are interrelated and, unfortunately, still difficult to answer unambiguously. The answer to the first is probably "no." The variation across our cases suggests that there are a number of reasons to pursue interregionalism, but that they depend significantly on the context. Interest groups, bureaucracies, power, nesting, and identity all matter to some extent and in some circumstances. Probably the most compelling individual factors are those of interest groups worried about the possible ramifications of instability in the WTO-centered trade regime and of actors' concerns about both relative power in trade negotiations and their overall place in the international economy. But no single variable or set of variables can adequately capture the complexities and subtleties involved in defining and executing trade policies and agreements, so we have identified several possible combinations of our original hypotheses that might offer a richer, more nuanced assessment of interregionalism. The different multicausal approaches would be suited to different aspects of interregionalism as policy and outcome: a policy networks approach would focus on inputs to the trade policymaking process; a bureaucratic-realist or constructivist-realist combination would explore 'state'-level motivations for pursuing interregionalism; and a sociological institutionalist approach would explore how the practice of interregionalism affects the organization of international political-economic cooperation more generally through the possible proliferation of new supranational governance units.

The absence of a unified, unitary logic for interregionalism hardly means that this approach is doomed either conceptually or practically. Even the clearest, most deductively-derived approaches to both policy and analysis are based on a dominant logic rather than a single logic. The presence of evidence for each of the four logics we evaluated – as well as for more multicausal logics – suggests that while it may be difficult to predict specific interregional regime outcomes, interregionalism as a general approach to commercial policy has the type of broad-based grounding that informs all viable policy choices. It seems that interregionalism is here to stay.

This conclusion is borne out by the EU experience. EU-centered interregional regimes have advanced to varying degrees, and for varying reasons. But, except for the special cases of Eastern Europe and North America, the EU has over the last decade or so shown a consistent commitment to organizing its relations with its commercial partners on an interregional basis. This commitment has faltered somewhat in some cases, and moved forward strongly in others. The EU asserts its continued commitment to the multilateral trade regime, but, like the United States, shows no sign of foregoing other options – regardless of the ups and downs of the WTO-centered system.

This brings us back to our biggest "what if": what if the multilateral trade system falters? What if it does not? In the latter scenario – the more hopeful one, from our point of view – interregionalism will likely remain a secondary approach to commercial relations. It is not obvious that most regional blocs around the world will have enough incentive to upgrade their own coherence to the point where they can and will pursue interregionalism on their own. The EU, as we have suggested, will likely continue to pursue interregionalism with at least a moderate degree of zeal, driven less by market efficiency imperatives than a desire to promote its political-institutional influence around the world. However, if the Doha Round of WTO negotiations were to fail, the appeal of an interregional approach – as well as for transregional and bilateral approaches – would grow for all.

Indeed, perhaps due to a lingering skepticism about the Doha Round, the general trend toward interregional and transregional arrangements has accelerated in recent years. As many regional arrangements around the world become more coherent and develop a more unified stance in their external commercial policy, understanding the driving forces behind interregionalism is likely to become a crucial theoretical and policy concern. EU interregionalism may well prove to be only the movie trailer for the full-blown action that we are about to see.

Notes

1. The general international context – i.e., events that have transformed international politics and the global economy such as globalization, the end of the Cold War, the creation of the WTO, the Asian financial crisis, the Seattle WTO ministerial, and 9/11 – is essential to understanding the evolution of interregional regimes. These events are empirical rather than theoretical explanations of actors' behavior; they are critical junctures that affect the structure of the system, and thus the likely behavior of the EU and other actors therein. But the general international context is not a set of factors that belongs exclusively to "systemic" hypotheses, because it affects the behavior/interests of the actors given primacy in all of our hypotheses. Therefore, we focus here specifically on the structure of the international system in terms of power relations and on EU concerns about nesting its trading arrangements within the GATT/WTO.
2. We thank Julie Gilson for her elaboration on this distinction within her chapter, which clarified our thinking on this matter. On the difference between structural and relational power, see Strange 1987.
3. This pluralist-bureaucratic politics combination resembles the existing literature on policy networks – noted in the appendix to the introduction – though here notably with a focus on the EU's external policies rather than internal ones. On EU policy networks see Peterson 1995, and Stone Sweet and Sandholtz 1997.
4. Waltz 1979.
5. Krasner 1978.
6. This line of thinking also bears some resemblance to Joseph Nye's elucidation of the concept of "soft power" in U.S. international influence, with soft or normative power serving as an alternative rather than a complement to military power. See Nye 1990.
7. On sociological institutionalism, see Powell and DiMaggio 1991. Our constructivist hypothesis as initially defined had a sociological institutionalist flavor to it in its identification of institutional isomorphism. This combination with the bureaucratic politics approach, however, invokes the Commission–Council struggle for influence more explicitly as a mechanism for change in the institutional field of international trade relations.
8. For studies that consider more functional approaches to the spread of supranational and/or regional units in the international economy, see Cerny 1995 and Ohmae 1995.
9. This is not to say that these regional identifications would not exist without relation to Western Europe, but rather simply that engagement with the EU/Western Europe has been a major influence on the evolution of these regional identifications over the last decade or so.

References

Cerny, Philip G. (1995). "Globalization and the changing logic of collective action." *International Organization* 49, 4: 595–625.

Krasner, Stephen (1978). *Defending the National Interest: Raw Materials Investments and U.S. Foreign Policy*. Princeton: Princeton University Press.

Nye, Joseph (1990). *Bound to Lead: The Changing Nature of American Power*. New York: Basic Books.

Ohmae, K. (1995). *The End of the Nation State: The Rise of Regional Economies*. New York: Free Press.

Peterson, John (1995). "Policy networks and European Union policymaking: a reply to Kassim." *West European Politics* 18, 2 (April): 389–407.

Powell, Walter W. and Paul J. DiMaggio, eds. (1991). *The New Institutionalism in Organizational Analysis*. Chicago: University of Chicago Press.

Stone Sweet, Alec and Wayne Sandholtz (1997). "European integration and supranational governance." *Journal of European Public Policy* 4, 3 (September): 297–317.

Strange, Susan (1987). "The persistent myth of lost hegemony." *International Organization* 41, 4: 551–574.

Waltz, Kenneth (1979). *Theory of International Politics*. Reading, MA: Addison-Wesley.

Index